A Process-Based Approach to Psychotherapy

A Process-Based Approach to Psychotherapy

Principles for Practice

CLARISSA W. ONG
ERIC B. LEE

OXFORD
UNIVERSITY PRESS

OXFORD
UNIVERSITY PRESS

Oxford University Press is a department of the University of Oxford. It furthers the University's objective of excellence in research, scholarship, and education by publishing worldwide. Oxford is a registered trade mark of Oxford University Press in the UK and in certain other countries.

Published in the United States of America by Oxford University Press
198 Madison Avenue, New York, NY 10016, United States of America.

CIP data is on file at the Library of Congress

ISBN 9780197696378

DOI: 10.1093/oso/9780197696378.001.0001

Printed by Integrated Books International, United States of America

The manufacturer's authorized representative in the EU for product safety is Oxford University Press España S.A., Parque Empresarial San Fernando de Henares, Avenida de Castilla, 2 – 28830 Madrid (www.oup.es/en or product.safety@oup.com). OUP Espaãa S.A. also acts as importer into Spain of products made by the manufacturer.

MIX
Paper
FSC FSC® C183721

The manufacturer's authorised representative in the EU for product safety is Oxford University Press España S.A. of El Parque Empresarial San Fernando de Henares, Avenida de Castilla, 2 – 28830 Madrid (www.oup.es/en or product.safety@oup.com). OUP España S.A. also acts as importer into Spain of products made by the manufacturer.

This book is dedicated to our students, from whom we continue to learn every day.

Contents

List of Figures

List of Tables

Acknowledgments

Clarissa

Thank you to Stefan Hofmann, Joe Ciarrochi, and Steve Hayes, for teaching me so much about process-based thinking and without whom this book probably wouldn't exist. Your big ideas about the future of clinical psychology are both intimidating and inspiring; I do my best to orient to the latter.

Thank you to Joe for your insightful feedback and suggestions on Chapter 5, Zach for your practical comments on Appendix G, and Raegan for your idea about including dashed arrows in networks. Thank you to Michaela for recommending *Brief Dynamic Therapy* as a PBT-consistent resource for psychodynamic therapy.

Thank you to my lab buddy for life, Eric, for taking this PBT book journey with me. I am so grateful that you still put up with me after all these years. There's no one I'd rather spend a week with in Carbondale brainstorming PBT ideas—and being snuck up on by sneaky cats—than you.

Thank you to Mike Twohig and Mike Levin (aka "the Mikes") for your continued guidance and willingness to mentor me, even after I've left the Utah nest. I'm always amazed that you make time for me when there are so many better things you could be doing in the mountains. And especially to Mike Twohig, for teaching me that there's more to life than work and more to me than I could have ever presumed. Also, thank you for bringing Jonas and Sepp into my life. My life is richer for it.

Finally, thank you to Brad for listening to me talk about psychology enough to know the difference between ACT and CBT, and Stefan and Steve. Your boundless generosity makes me want to be a more positive force in the world.

Eric

To Clarissa: My blmf (best lab mate forever). Thank you for letting me ask dumb questions and always being up for another project. You inspire me to be a better scientist and therapist.

To my many mentors past and present; two in particular: Chad Wetterneck, for seeing something in me and believing. Mike Twohig, for giving me the space and opportunity to spread my wings.

To my students: For keeping me humble, inspiring me to do better, and reminding me that the rat is always right.

To Harper and Grace: My favorite little stinkers in the whole world. You are perfect.

To Beck: My best friend. Thank you for being you, for your love, your friendship, and the ways you make this life beautiful. Nothing I've accomplished would have happened without your support.

1
The Big Picture

The aim of this book is to teach you about *process-based therapy* or PBT well enough that you can use it with your clients and that you'll know what questions to ask to learn more about it. In other words, it is designed to be an initial step in your PBT journey. Although this book is for anyone who wants to learn more about PBT, it will be most informative if you have some basic clinical skills to work with. For example, graduate trainees who have done 1–2 semesters of clinical training will likely find the content more accessible than someone who has never seen a client before.

In the following chapters, we will orient you to PBT as a framework and set of guiding principles, such that you'll understand how to use a process-based approach in varied situations. We will not prescribe formal instructions you must follow for treatment to "count" as PBT, because to practice PBT, you first need to understand *how* it works. Knowing what PBT "should" look like is inadequate, because it looks different every time, depending on your clients, yourself, and context. This first chapter covers how to think about PBT, before we define it.

A Brief History

PBT is all about context, so let's consider the context in which PBT developed. The first academic article on PBT was published in 2017, titled *The Third Wave of Cognitive Behavioral Therapy and the Rise of Process-Based Care* by Steven Hayes and Stefan Hofmann (2017). In their article, Hayes and Hofmann (2017) described a need for a paradigm shift in clinical psychology: from protocols for syndromes to evidence-based procedures linked to evidence-based change processes; from psychopathology to psychological prosperity; from siloed schools of thought to coherence across therapeutic approaches. As such, PBT was developed in response to perceived gaps in the state of evidence-based psychological treatment, including (1) problems defined by categorical diagnoses; (2) treatment packages mapped

A Process-Based Approach to Psychotherapy. Clarissa W. Ong and Eric B. Lee, Oxford University Press.
 DOI: 10.1093/oso/9780197696378.003.0001

to diagnoses (which are highly heterogeneous; e.g., Allsopp et al., 2019; Borgogna et al., 2023); (3) reliance on nomothetic (group-level) research, which cannot be assumed to generalize to particular people (Molenaar, 2004); and (4) plateauing of the efficacy of evidence-based treatments over time (Bhattacharya et al., 2022; Cristea et al., 2017).

Accordingly, PBT takes a bottom-up approach to case conceptualization that starts with clients in their specific context (rather than a diagnostic manual) and uses treatment components or *kernels* to target specific problems clients are struggling with (rather than a protocol for a diagnosis). Think more along the lines of "difficulty taking the perspective of loved ones" and less "narcissistic personality disorder." In addition, PBT positions clients' goals as the arbiter of treatment success, not just symptom severity, recognizing that a life without distress is not necessarily a life well-lived.

With respect to research, PBT relies on methods that account for differences between and within individuals, only generalizing patterns across individuals when doing so is reasonable (Gates & Molenaar, 2012). This way, the unique vagaries of particular people are acknowledged and retained, instead of being washed away as "random error," as randomized controlled trials typically do (Hayes et al., 2022). The hope from doing all this—and more, as you will learn from this book—is to have a flexible and inclusive therapy that meets the diverse needs of our clients and ultimately breaks through the treatment efficacy plateau.

A Metaphor for PBT: Chess

A Clear Goal

One way to think of PBT is like playing chess. The goal is clear from the outset. In chess, you must take the king to win the match. In PBT, the goal is typically some combination of improving clients' well-being, meeting their treatment goals, reducing symptoms, and/or alleviating suffering. Even if therapists disagree on the means—for example, by exploring attachment patterns (most prominently related to John Bowlby's research on attachment theory) vs. changing thought content (per cognitive restructuring in cognitive behavioral therapy [CBT])—we can usually agree that we want our clients to live healthier and more fulfilling lives. Establishing this goal is important because a game without a goal cannot make sense. It would be akin to moving pieces around aimlessly on a board ad infinitum.

Staying focused on the goal is key to PBT. Sometimes, as therapists, we may find ourselves chasing our clients' "problem of the week" (e.g., car broke down, argued with co-worker, was sick for several days), only realizing after some time that we're going around in circles. Alternatively, we may become so overly concerned about protecting our therapist ego and wanting to be "right" that we stubbornly stick to our treatment plan in the face of contradictory evidence. Or we may be tempted by distractions—salacious gossip that piques our interest but is irrelevant to our clients' goals, like a queen bait in chess—and lose sight of the objective of the game.

In PBT, we need to look past "little things" that only feel big in the moment and consider the game holistically, in context, and over time. For example, losing a queen may limit your range of subsequent moves but you can still win without it. Even winning with a single pawn left is a victory. Similarly, if your client has difficulty grasping a particular emotion regulation skill (e.g., opposite action from dialectical behavior therapy [DBT]), that may limit their options for effective coping, but they may still be able to achieve their goals if they learn other means of managing strong emotions.

Rules of the Game

There are basic rules to how the game works. In chess, pieces can only be moved in certain directions. These rules provide structure. To properly participate, we have to know and follow these rules. Otherwise, we would not be playing chess, we would be play-acting chess. Similarly, there are fundamental unassailable rules in therapy, such as those outlined in the American Psychological Association's (APA) Ethics Code: beneficence and nonmaleficence (do no harm), fidelity and responsibility, integrity, justice, and respect for people's rights and dignity (APA, 2017). These rules transcend any one player's style; they are simply the price of admission to providing therapy. If you don't follow these rules, you are not providing therapy.

Yet, knowing these rules only takes us far enough to participate on the most rudimentary level: we know enough not to break the rules. But the rules tell us nothing about tactics or strategies for winning. We probably cannot appreciate or enjoy the game if all we know is how to move the differently shaped pieces.

Tactics and Strategies

To appreciate the wondrous complexity of PBT, in addition to knowing the rules, we need skill, in the form of *tactics* and *strategies*. Tactics are short-term sequences of moves intended to achieve a specific, measurable objective, such as using a self-compassion exercise to decrease the power of self-critical thoughts. Tactics can be deployed and evaluated relatively quickly, given their shorter timescale; you could ask your client at the next session how much their self-critical thoughts impacted their functioning after doing the self-compassion exercise.

In contrast, strategies are longer-term ideas and plans about how therapy is going and how you will get your clients from where they are to where they want to be (i.e., a treatment plan). Therapeutic strategies may contain multiple components, be non-linear, or even seem counter-intuitive at times, but they are always in service of the game objective. For example, a treatment plan could entail teaching distress tolerance skills from DBT to help a client first decrease instances of feeling "out of control" and then following that with acceptance-based practices so the client learns that they don't always need to be in control of their emotions to live a meaningful life.

Strategies tend to evolve over time, as you adapt your treatment plan based on input from your clients over the course of treatment. Returning to the example of the client who experiences their emotions as "out of control," if we notice resistance to acceptance-based methods, we might pivot to psychoeducation about what we mean by acceptance or use more structured emotion regulation skills, like opposite action or check the facts from DBT. Alternatively, we might learn that the client has a strongly held core belief that "being out of control is bad," so we could shift to targeting thoughts using kernels like cognitive defusion from acceptance and commitment therapy (ACT). Strategies need to be responsive to your clients' moves.

Admittedly, depending on the client, the same tactics and strategies may work again and again. This may be the client who has never received evidence-based treatment and is struggling with a fairly localized problem, such as a fear of spiders. This client would also be free of cultural and contextual stressors like systemic oppression, abusive relationships, and financial insecurity. In cases like these, tried-and-tested treatment protocols for diagnoses without many adjustments may work well. Thankfully, we have a plethora of evidence-based protocol options, including exposure-based treatments for specific phobias (Wolitzky-Taylor et al., 2008), behavioral activation for depression (Cuijpers et al., 2007), exposure and response prevention for obsessive-compulsive disorder (Reid et al., 2021), CBT for generalized anxiety disorder (Cuijpers et al., 2014), DBT for borderline personality disorder (Kliem et al., 2010), ACT for chronic pain (Veehof et al., 2016), and so on. For these clients, therapists can probably straightforwardly implement a treatment protocol and call it a day.

However, the therapist who plays in a rote manner can only ever play against one type of opponent—which is fine if they only ever need to play against that kind of opponent. However, most therapists face a diverse pool of clients, whose circumstances and choices behoove therapists to use a range of tactics and strategies to support their clients in reaching their treatment goals. Even two clients facing the same problem may need different approaches based on their backgrounds—the client whose self-criticism stems from decades of parental criticism may benefit more from introspective self-compassion work, whereas another client whose self-criticism is tied to a situational stressor may benefit from a solution-focused approach. Conversely, within the same match with the same opponent, we likely still have to shift our strategy multiple times, depending on what's going on in our clients' lives. The client who becomes pregnant or starts a new job will likely have different needs from the same client before these events occurred.

Responding to Unpredictability

Humans are rarely guileless opponents. Clients bring with them a history shaped by infinite known and unknown parameters. That history manifests in their automatic and purposeful responses to the world around them and continuously interacts with their current environment, creating new experiences as their brain churns through incessant stimuli, spitting out all sorts of output from moment to moment. Because of the unique constellation of variables that makes up each person's lived experience, clients are only predictable to a certain extent. We may have a "best guess" as to how clients will respond to the moves we make, but our imperfect knowledge means there is always a chance we are wrong, no matter how many matches we have played or how many opponents we have faced.

That is why we need flexible strategies for "winning." We cannot realistically expect our clients to be predictable and readily enlightened by our regular rotation of metaphors. (Indeed, clients are not problems for us to solve or opponents for us to outsmart—the most glaring incongruence of our chess analogy.) The skill of PBT is not memorizing and executing a sophisticated plan; it's effectively responding to what our clients throw at us midsession, much like how a chess master constantly recalibrates their strategies to counter their opponent's unexpected moves.

In fact, given the vast range of possibilities and boundless human complexity, the goal is not merely to get better at predicting client behavior—though that certainly helps—it's also about learning to respond to unpredictability. Part of this depends on having an arsenal of therapeutic tools at the ready (i.e., a strong clinical foundation) and knowing how to use those tools creatively. That way, when faced with a novel situation, you're able to fashion an effective response in the moment, like using your shoe to open a wine bottle in a pinch. For a clinical example, let's say you're feeling stuck with a client who has difficulty being physically alone. You've tried all the usual methods, and they're not seeing any changes. Using your knowledge of values, you could send them on a solo values treasure hunt and ask them to take photos of five things associated with five different values.[1] Through this exercise, your client has the opportunity to independently interact and connect with the world around them, while clarifying what's important to them as a person. It's still values, just in a new form.

Understanding the game beyond elementary rules and adapting to your clients' moves while anchoring yourself in their treatment goals encapsulates the spirit of PBT. But just as one does not become a Grand Master overnight—or even over months—learning to deliver effective therapy skillfully requires practice, reflection, and feedback. Learning tactics or evidence-based protocols can be helpful for increasing your range of plays early on, by showing you examples of how a match can go, but it will eventually hit a ceiling. Once you get to the point where the same moves you have been using are no longer working for your clients, it may be worth diving into the possibilities afforded by a process-based approach to therapy.

Goals of This Book

A core feature of PBT is its focus on function: what purpose does a behavior serve? What are the effects of a specific response? How does this action impact your clients' well-being? All responses are judged by their function.

[1] Thank you to the inimitable Dr. Wes Bullock for sharing this therapy idea.

We would like to do the same for this book, so we first need to clarify what purpose this book is intended to serve.

Broadly speaking, we wrote this book to teach the rules of PBT and help you develop an understanding of the approach so you can play and enjoy the game. This book heavily focuses on the foundational principles of PBT, so you have guidance on what to do in a variety of situations. In other words, we are teaching you how to respond to your opponent's moves, not specific moves to make or tactics to deploy. We do not teach evidence-based intervention strategies, because there are already many well-written books and manuals dedicated to that (see Chapter 9 for a few recommendations). In some ways, delivering treatment components is the easier part. Knowing which components to deliver to which clients at what point in treatment is the challenge we hope to tackle by teaching you how to think about your clients' presenting problem and develop a strong case conceptualization and flexible treatment plan.

As a matter of pragmatism, we do not go deeply into the evolution science theory underlying PBT. There are several journal articles and another PBT book that do this already (also listed in Chapter 9). While having an appreciation for the evolution science roots of PBT will likely help you graduate from an intermediate to advanced PBT therapist, we wrote this book for people newer to a process-based approach. At this stage, we believe that learning the rules and general principles and then putting them into practice is the most useful way to make progress. In fact, there will be points in the book where we opt for accessibility over precision, explaining things more simply rather than enumerating the nuances associated with each consideration. Again, all we want is for you to play chess and know enough to think independently about how to play the game, so we are striving for clinical utility over technical accuracy.

The Authors

We would like to acknowledge the influence of our professional background and theoretical orientation on our approach to the learning, training, and practice of PBT. We are partial to contextual behavioral science and Skinnerian behaviorism, having received our graduate training in a lab researching acceptance and commitment therapy. As such, we are more familiar with cognitive behavioral interventions, and our examples tend to skew in that direction, though we attempted to provide a range of examples as much as our knowledge permitted. We are also based in the U.S., which means we are most familiar with presentations and structural problems in this country. Thus, many of our clinical examples are U.S.-centric. We describe some of our personal biases below.

Clarissa: I acknowledge my privilege in having access to academic and financial resources due to my position as a faculty member in a university. As such, I may overlook struggles associated with limited access to such resources. In addition, I operate primarily in an academic setting and am disconnected from the struggles of full-time clinicians doing the hard work of meeting clients where they're at every day. I recognize that my positionality has influenced the content and examples presented in this book, which will inevitably fall short of being inclusive of all human experiences. Nonetheless, I am committed to considering clients' unique contexts and taking their perspectives to the extent I am able to, understanding that I will never fully "get" someone else's struggle due to my different lived experiences.

Eric: I am an academic and practicing psychologist with largely majoritized identities. As I seek to write a book that resonates with a diverse audience, I recognize that my identities and position have afforded me opportunities and advantages that are not universally accessible. These factors undoubtably influence my perspective on clinical work, supervision, research, and the field of psychology at large.

Chapter Summary

- Process-based therapy (PBT) is an *approach* to treatment and is guided by principles, rather than formal techniques or procedures.
- Think of PBT like chess, where memorizing strategies and tactics—like evidence-based treatment components—are helpful, but knowing how to deploy them flexibly is more important.
- The goal of this book is to teach you the basic rules of PBT so you can begin trying it out for yourself.

2

What Is Process-Based Therapy?

To start, the term "process-based therapy" is a misnomer. The term "therapy" implies a set of techniques organized around a theory of human behavior, like cognitive behavioral *therapy*, dialectical behavior *therapy*, prolonged exposure *therapy*, or acceptance and commitment *therapy*. In contrast, PBT is a *model* or *approach* to doing therapy, without endorsing any specific theoretical orientation or techniques. In fact, the only "new" thing here is the framework or way of understanding our clients' experiences and existing interventions.

Imagine for a moment a large kitchen, maybe like those seen on cooking reality shows. Every conceivable kitchen tool and appliance is there. The shelves and fridges are stocked with an impressive assortment of every kind of ingredient you'd need to make even the most obscure dish. Now imagine you are a novice chef, placed in this enormous kitchen, and instructed to "cook something delicious." Thankfully, you've taken a few cooking classes from a chef who taught you Italian techniques, so you know—and have practiced—a killer cacio e pepe recipe. You immediately set off on recreating that dish using the ingredients and techniques you're familiar with. The dish turns out great and is considered a success. Hooray!

Now imagine you are asked to make pad thai. You've never made pad thai before. In fact, you've never really cooked much *other than* cacio e pepe. Perhaps you scramble to pull a recipe out of a book on the shelf and muddle through the instructions to create the dish. Ultimately, it's edible but not much more. Next is an order for French onion soup, then Peking duck, then a cheeseburger, then mishkaki, then lamb vindaloo, and on and on. For each new order, you reach for a different book and work your way through the recipe. Over time, you become a better chef. You learn new skills and techniques and are able to cook dozens of dishes. However, with each new request, you must find and learn a new specific recipe for that dish. You long to be like those master chefs who are able to craft amazing meals on the fly that perfectly match what their customers want, all without ever using a recipe.

A Process-Based Approach to Psychotherapy. Clarissa W. Ong and Eric B. Lee, Oxford University Press.
 DOI: 10.1093/oso/9780197696378.003.0002

OK, back to the real world. Perhaps you see where this story is going. We often see beginner therapists in a similar position to this novice chef. They see their first client, do their best to boil the client's concerns down into a diagnosis or two, then pull the appropriate treatment manual off the shelf and follow the steps, session-by-session. We grant that so long as these treatment manuals comprise evidence-based techniques, there are far worse ways to do therapy. In fact, these beginner therapists would likely create acceptable dishes that largely satisfy the needs of their clients. However, we believe there's a better way.

Instead, imagine a cookbook that doesn't give you specific recipes but instead teaches you how to use ingredients, how to identify and combine them effectively, and how to create your own recipes. (Samin Nosrat did this in her cookbook, *Salt, Fat, Acid, Heat.*) That's PBT. It's about understanding the foundational elements of therapy—the "ingredients"—and how they can be combined in different ways to suit your clients' needs. PBT encourages therapists to move beyond the confines of recipe protocols and instead develop a deeper understanding of therapeutic ingredients. It acknowledges that therapists come from diverse backgrounds and traditions, much like chefs with different culinary training (e.g., French vs. Chinese cuisine). However, the emphasis is on foundational principles of therapy, such that therapists are encouraged to blend techniques and ideas from various approaches, tailored to each client's unique needs.

Taking a process-based approach means that therapy is attuned to the complex and ever-evolving interweaving network of symptoms, experiences, and behaviors in clients, allowing for more precise intervention planning. If this approach to therapy is appealing to you—if you aren't looking for another cookbook—read on. We will eventually get into the nitty-gritty details of PBT and how you can develop your culinary skills, but for now, let us clarify some of the basics of PBT, a foundation we can build on.

"But wait," we can almost hear you saying, "I don't even know what a *process* is. Is this relevant to the therapy I do?" We hear you, and frankly, it's a concept that can be tricky to fully grasp with words, a bit like explaining to someone who has never used a knife before how to dice an onion. Put simplistically, process refers to the *how* and *why* over the *what.* To be more specific, "process" in the context of PBT refers to the dynamic and fluid aspects of psychological experiences rather than static symptoms or diagnostic categories. By dynamic and fluid, we mean that processes may change or evolve in a non-linear fashion and are unlikely to follow simple A → B → C causal paths. Rather, processes are generally part of complex networks of experiences that involve multiple causal pathways and feedback loops: more like A → B → A → C → B.

As an example of a complex interplay of experiences, let's say you're feeling stressed and decide to distract yourself in an attempt to relax. Maybe you find a show you really like and get so into the episode that you forget about the stress. Then, one of the characters talks about work and your mind goes back to the tasks you've been procrastinating. Now you feel guilty for avoiding those tasks in the first place. You go to check your email to procrastinate more "productively" and see that a deadline has been postponed, so you feel relieved and return to happily watching your show. There are several symptoms to examine here: stress, procrastination, and guilt. But using a process-based angle, we might also ask *how* work contributes to stress (e.g., thoughts about inability to complete tasks) or *how* stress leads to avoidance (e.g., difficulty tolerating distress). It's unyielding attention to these elastic underlying processes that differentiates PBT from diagnosis-focused protocols.

That said, we'll offer a bit of advice: if you're still unsure what we mean by process, that's OK. Don't let that stop you. The goal of this book is to be useful to you and your work as a therapist, not to nail down the most technically accurate definition of every word and concept. There are plenty of other books and articles that delve into the nerdy details if you want that too. Keep going, and we assure you that it will click as you apply the concepts to your clinical work—just like dicing makes more sense once you've held a knife and practiced roughly chopping some vegetables. We'll start with what PBT is and what it is not, as well as reasons we believe PBT—and this book—is worth your time.

Basic Assumptions and Features of PBT

Processes Over Symptoms

In PBT, the focus is not just on the content of a client's experience (such as specific thoughts or feelings) but also on how these experiences unfold over time and influence other aspects of their life. This approach, akin to prioritizing function over form, involves a de-emphasis of rigid diagnostic categories. Instead of labeling and treating specific disorders, PBT seeks to understand the role of symptoms in particular people's lives. This includes patterns of thinking, feeling, and behaving, and how these patterns interact with each other and the environments in which they occur. Indeed, another way to think about process is as a *clinically relevant pattern of responding.* For example, rather than concentrating solely on anxiety and its severity, a process-based approach might explore how clients relate to their anxiety, how various cognitive, emotional, and behavioral components interact with anxiety, and the contexts in which anxiety arises. In other words, as part of assessment, the therapist would seek to understand the dynamic processes that maintain or exacerbate the problem (e.g., externally defined self-concept), rather than stop at identifying and categorizing the symptoms or problem (e.g., social anxiety disorder). This is why we say that "process" in PBT is about understanding the *how* and *why* of psychological experiences, not just the *what.*

Principles Over Techniques

PBT is a model of conceptualization and treatment that transcends specific therapeutic interventions or techniques. The approach emphasizes overarching principles used to target the specific needs of clients in their given context. (Read Chapter 3 to learn more about PBT principles.) Like how a chef might develop a unique recipe for a special event using their knowledge of cooking principles, big picture, PBT principles guide therapists in their decision making without prescribing a specific protocol or intervention. In contrast, step-by-step treatment protocols tend to emphasize procedure and technique over contextual factors (e.g., cultural identities, family of origin), which are difficult to account for in a static manual.

That said, treatment manuals have their merits and uses, especially for newer therapists. They can be a great way to develop your skills, gain confidence as a clinician, and learn new therapeutic techniques. Coming to PBT after learning from more structured manuals will likely be helpful so long as you are willing to lean into the discomfort that may come from putting the cookbook down and practicing principle-based recipes. We believe that doing so will foster a more flexible approach to therapy more tailored to the needs of your clients.

PBT principles also apply to the specific treatment techniques used in therapy, which are sometimes doled out to clients without consideration for what is being targeted or when a technique might best be used. For example, using a cognitive restructuring exercise with your clients does not automatically impart cognitive restructuring skills to them. Depending on how the exercise is presented, completing a cognitive restructuring worksheet with a client could help them become more attentive or aware of their thoughts, identify core beliefs that motivate behavior, replace unwanted thoughts, recognize thinking traps, evaluate the accuracy of their thoughts, and so on. As such, specific techniques are a means to the end of client learning, and myopic concern about the means without awareness of the end goal can muddy the therapeutic waters. This is where we believe PBT shines. It helps to organize and structure the *how* and *why* of treatment.

Pragmatism Over Ontology

PBT adopts a pragmatic approach focused on achieving tangible changes in clients' lives. The primary aim is to meet clients' goals, reduce suffering, and enhance well-being and purpose. While other approaches to therapy share similar goals—most therapists want what is best for their clients—they can get bogged down with concerns that get in the way of meeting these goals. For example, an approach overly concerned with ontology (e.g., which mental structures are real or whether a diagnosis actually exists within a client) might lead to implicit goals of "finding the truth" or "identifying the root cause of a problem" that ultimately do little to serve our clients. In contrast, a pragmatic stance ensures that therapy is grounded in real-world applicability, addressing the needs and aspirations of clients in a concrete, meaningful way. A pragmatic stance emphasizes what works to achieve these goals and deemphasizes knowledge and understanding simply for their own sake.

Theory Over Chaos

Despite—or maybe because of—its welcoming stance toward all orientations, PBT needs to be anchored in a coherent set of theories and principles to be useful. These theories and principles are intentionally allowed to be broad and comprehensive such that any evidence-based approach is likely to fit within the model, but whichever ones are chosen must be theoretically coherent with each other. That is, the ideas entailed in selected theories must have a cogent story for what causes, maintains, and changes behavior.

Then, all that is required to "buy in" to the PBT approach is an agreement that evolutionary principles can map onto and help conceptualize the complex systems our clients' lives are made up of. Much like how chefs with different training backgrounds and culinary expertise can still agree on the fundamental effects of adding salt or acid to a dish, most therapists can agree that cognition and emotion are two core dimensions of behavior and that the principles of variation, selection, and retention apply to adaptation and learning.

Once we agree on this elemental understanding of human behavior, therapists can readily integrate their own theoretical perspectives into the framework of PBT, which we believe will enhance depth of conceptualization while remaining grounded in the therapist's theoretical foundation. By demanding theoretical grounding, PBT provides a structured yet flexible way of organizing and conceptualizing human behavior and psychological processes, without getting lost in the chaos of infinite possible theoretical timelines. Kind of like once you understand how gravity works, you're free to pursue whatever innovations that honor gravitational force.

Empiricism Over Eclecticism

PBT is deeply rooted in empiricism. The PBT model demands a reliable evidence base, in addition to coherent theory. This commitment to empiricism ensures that PBT remains relevant, effective, and up to date with the latest psychological research, rather than a free-for-all therapeutic marketplace. It underscores the importance of rooting therapeutic interventions in sound methodologies and continuously evaluating their efficacy. Without this empirical bar, the flexibility of PBT could easily become corrupted by pseudoscientific interventions. In therapy as well, the approach to conceptualizing and treating clients is empirical. Therapists are encouraged to make specific, testable hypotheses related to their clients and to modify their approach as new data come in. Thus, PBT is empirically driven both outside and inside the therapy room.

Personalization Over "One Size Fits All"

We know our clients are unique. Their experiences, backgrounds, concerns, goals, and psychological processes are distinct, given the innumerable variables along countless scales that can vary among people. One of the core tenets of PBT is personalized care, which means delivering therapy designed for specific clients—in light of their experiences and circumstances—rather than serving the same dish to whoever walks through the door. This is why principles matter over techniques: making an excellent cacio e pepe is fine if all your customers only want cacio e pepe, but to meet the diverse needs of the people you are dedicated to serving, you'll need to be able to manipulate basic therapeutic ingredients creatively and flexibly.

What PBT Is Not

Above, we listed several features of PBT that make it what it is. At the same time, given that PBT is another "therapy" (remember, this is a misnomer) in a clinical world brimming with therapies, we thought it might be prudent to briefly describe what it is not.

PBT Is Not a Therapy

Unlike therapeutic approaches such as CBT or DBT, PBT doesn't offer a set protocol to follow. PBT does not prescribe the use of specific interventions or techniques, like interoceptive exposures or guided imagery. It does not define the appropriate length of or number of sessions. It doesn't demand the use of any particular language or terms when conceptualizing experiences with clients. All that is up to the therapist and their clients.

However, it does provide a meta-therapeutic framework, a lens through which various therapies are viewed and understood. Thus, although PBT is not a therapy in itself, it is a particular way of thinking about psychological assessment and treatment, grounded in evolution science. A PBT perspective also values the therapist's clinical judgment and clients' individuality, recognizing that different strategies may be needed for different people, even if they present with similar issues. In a sense, PBT is a structured vessel. Therapists can choose what to fill it with, but within the confines of PBT principles. We believe that the PBT model can expand current approaches to therapy by providing a higher-order structure and perspective and help therapists better use the tools they already have.

PBT Is Not Eclectic

At least, PBT is not unconditionally eclectic. PBT is *procedurally* eclectic in the sense that any technique or intervention that is evidence-based and fits within a theoretically informed case conceptualization is fair game—it doesn't matter whether it comes from cognitive, behavioral, psychodynamic, person-centered, emotion-focused, or any other evidence-based treatment. What does matter is that techniques are used to target the specific needs of your clients in their given context.

However, PBT is not *theoretically* eclectic, meaning that while you can bring your own theoretical orientation, which provides concepts and language that inform your case conceptualization, you cannot then haphazardly merge this theory or worldview with others, such that they become incoherent. For example, someone working from a psychodynamic orientation might conceptualize worry as the manifestation of unconscious conflicts and unmet needs stemming from childhood. This would inform how they conceptualize and work with their clients. However, if they were to try to integrate cognitive theory (e.g., cognitive distortions and modification) into their conceptualization it would result in a mess of concepts and explanations that do not tell the same story. Attempting to blend theory like this is bound to lead to confused therapists and clients and ambiguous conceptualizations and treatment plans.

This is not to say that a psychodynamic therapist can't use interventions from cognitive theory, in fact, a PBT approach would welcome and encourage this procedural eclecticism. For example, they might choose to use a thought restructuring exercise to target cognitive inflexibility using the broader evolutionary science framework of PBT; however, they would ground the exercise in psychodynamic language and theory (e.g., exploring different meanings of the worry) and integrate it into their conceptualization in a theoretically sound way.

PBT Does Not Reinvent the Wheel

We often get the feedback that PBT "isn't different from existing therapies." Our response is, "that's kind of the point." *Kind of.* It doesn't change the content of existing therapies—that's correct—but it changes how we think about and use existing therapies. The aspiration of PBT is not to reinvent the wheel, but to *redesign* or *reorganize* the wheel, so that you can understand and use the wheel you already have more effectively and intentionally. Therapists with existing skills and experience will find that PBT doesn't render their tools obsolete; instead, it challenges them to think more deeply about how and why they use these tools.

The PBT approach aims to integrate and leverage the best parts of all wheels, wheels that have been refined over time and through significant effort by various manufacturers. The result is a master blueprint for wheel design: a set of guidelines that inform how to design a wheel to suit your purposes, based on knowledge from all the wheels that have come before you. Translated to the therapy context, this means formulating treatment processes and components into a coherent and useful framework for everyone to use, built upon knowledge accumulated over decades of clinical research and practice. So, keep your wheel, but maybe consider giving it an upgrade.

The Extended Evolutionary Meta-Model (EEMM)

In PBT, the extended evolutionary meta-model or EEMM (rhymes with team) is a visual framework for organizing clinically relevant information. The EEMM is a three-dimensional grid, comprising psychological dimensions (first 6 rows), other levels (bottom 2 rows), evolutionary principles of change (columns), and context (*z*-axis; see Figure 2.1).

The EEMM summarizes key concepts in PBT: (1) holistic consideration of particular people in context (hence the various dimensions and levels); (2) an evolution science–informed approach to treatment (represented by the columns variation, selection, and retention); and (3) recognition that responses can be adaptive or maladaptive depending on context (*z*-axis). In fact, the *z*-axis in the original EEMM published in Hayes et al. (2019) contained the terms *Maladaptive* and *Adaptive* instead of *Context*. The current version better captures the idea that the same response can be either maladaptive or adaptive depending on context, and context is really what matters.

The notion that the EEMM is meant to distill fundamental PBT ideas may seem ironic, given that it can be quite an overwhelming figure to take in. Thus, we have found it helpful to think about the EEMM in four parts:

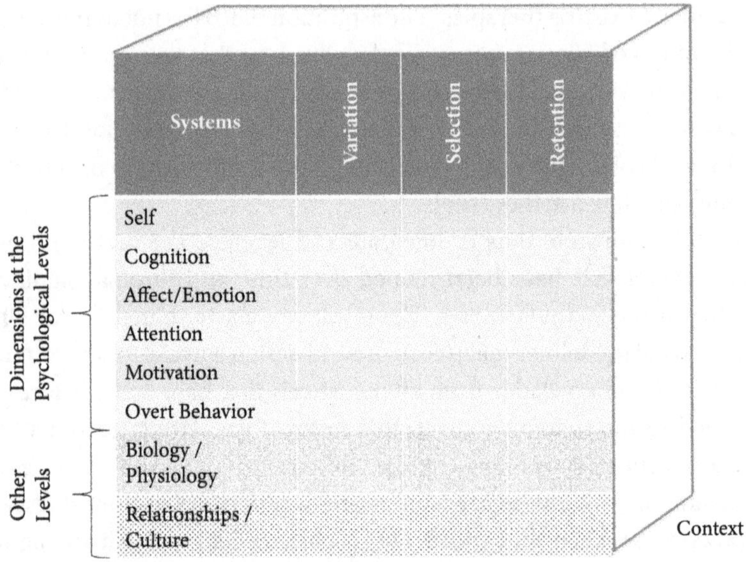

Figure 2.1 Extended evolutionary meta-model. Copyright 2024 by Steven C. Hayes & Stefan G. Hofmann. Used by permission.

Source: Ciarrochi, J., Hernández, C., Hill, D., Ong, C., Gloster, A. T., Levin, M. E., Yap, K., Fraser, M. I., Sahdra, B. K., Hofmann, S. G., & Hayes, S. C. (2024). Process-based therapy: A common ground for understanding and utilizing therapeutic practices. *Journal of Psychotherapy Integration*, *34*(3), 265–290. https://doi.org/10.1037/int0000348

(1) dimensions, (2) levels, (3) principles of change, and (4) context. Each part serves a function and is useful at different points in treatment. For example, dimensions may be pertinent when conceptualizing your clients' problems, levels for considering how their environment impacts their experience of their problems, principles of change for probing how your client is stuck, and context for nurturing flexibility in various situations.

Dimensions

The six dimensions listed in the leftmost column of the EEMM span the spectrum of psychological functioning. That is, we can think of psychological functioning as organized along self, cognition, affect/emotion, attention, motivation, and overt behavior. The EEMM uses the term *overt* behavior rather than behavior because some people (including us) consider self-conceptualizing, thinking, feeling, attending, and motivating to be behaviors too, except they are unobservable.

- *Self* refers to how people see and treat themselves, their sense of self, or how they respond to their self-concept or sense of self. Perspective taking, which entails shifting the vantage point of the self, also belongs to this dimension.
- *Cognition* refers to what people think or how they respond to thoughts.
- *Affect/Emotion* refers to what people feel or how they respond to feelings and emotions.
- *Attention* refers to what people pay attention to or how they modulate attention.
- *Motivation* refers to the reasons or consequences that drive behaviors or inaction.
- *Overt behavior* refers to observable actions and inactions.

Together, these dimensions can be used as a checklist to remind therapists to consider *all* aspects of psychological functioning and well-being. Think of the dimensions like various parts of a closet. Going over each dimension would be like checking to make sure we have on underwear, a top, bottoms, socks, shoes, and accessories before leaving home.

If you tend to emphasize certain dimensions when working with clients, going through the EEMM dimension checklist may lead to a more well-rounded treatment plan. For instance, if you typically focus on behaviors and cognitions in your treatment plan, considering your clients' ability to regulate attention or exploring their motivations for change may indicate other clinically relevant aspects to address in treatment. Perhaps clarifying their values will catalyze change.

Levels

Levels indicate the scale on which you are considering particular people. In theory, the scale could range from the cellular level to international geopolitics and include everything in between. But for the sake of utility, the EEMM considers three broad levels.

Technically, the six dimensions comprise the first level: psychological or individual. As in, the six dimensions of psychological functioning largely occur *within* individuals, and because most therapies are individual-focused or teach intrapersonal skills, consideration of the individual level is usually a given.

- *Psychological* refers to what is within people's direct control or that occur on an individual level (i.e., responses can proceed without relying on external factors).
- *Biology/Physiology* refers to physical health and biological, physiological, hormonal, or neurological functioning. Variables that influence physical health, such as exercise, diet, sleep, and medication go here. So do those that reflect bodily changes, like hot flashes during menopause or mood swings related to a pregnancy. Note: we use *Biology/Physiology* and *Biophysiology* interchangeably in this book.

We have found it helpful to break Relationships/Culture down into two categories, to give sufficient emphasis to systemic factors beyond individuals' control that can significantly impact functioning (e.g., systemic racism, economic inflation)—captured under Culture below—in addition to their social environment. Moreover, clients may more easily intervene on interpersonal problems (e.g., through family therapy) than sociocultural problems.

- *Relationships* refer to social relationships and how people interact with and within them, including the relationship between the therapist and client.
- *Culture* refers to broader societal norms and structures that are outside of most people's direct control.

By definition, the psychological level is easiest to address in individual therapy, given that we are working directly with the client, whereas we can't dictate how our client's boss or parents should treat them. As therapists, we are also not responsible for impacting functioning at every level. For example, a personal trainer may have more direct influence on the biophysiological level, whereas grassroots organizers and politicians may be better poised to change societal problems.

Nonetheless, understanding how Biology/Physiology, Relationships, and Culture influence your clients' lived experience is crucial for case conceptualization, even if you cannot directly intervene on them, because these levels comprise your clients' *context*. Similar to Bronfenbrenner's ecological systems with the microsystem, mesosystem, exosystem, macrosystem, and chronosystem (Bronfenbrenner, 1977), the EEMM levels ask therapists to consider how clients' nested environments interact with each other and with clients to shape their clinical presentation.

Imagine you had a client who was struggling with managing their anger. It would be helpful to know if the anger was related to a history of reinforcement of angry responses (e.g., people only listened when they expressed anger) or current events that have increased their experience of oppression and powerlessness (e.g., restriction of access to abortions), as that would likely inform your treatment plan. In the former situation, we may validate that while anger was an adaptive means of responding previously it may no longer be useful in their current environment and identify other methods of communication to get needs met. Whereas, in the latter case, acknowledging the client's cultural context, we may instead invite them to explore how the anger is impacting them, acknowledge its roots, and explore ways to leverage anger for empowerment (e.g., channeling angry purpose into values-based activism).

Principles of Change

The evolutionary principles of variation, selection, and retention broadly refer to trying things different from what one typically does (variation), seeing what works based on personal goals and needs (selection), and continuing to do what works (retention).

- *Variation* refers to trying out new responses or new reasons for responding (i.e., doing the same things but for different reasons).
- *Selection* refers to identifying responses that improve well-being or meet goals or needs.
- *Retention* refers to integrating helpful responses into one's repertoire or converting one-off actions into consistent habits.

Collectively, these principles of change parallel the process of buying new clothes. We usually try on different options (variation) before determining which ones we like enough to buy (selection). Once we buy them, we include them in our outfit rotation (retention). If any one of these pieces breaks down, we are unlikely to be successful with clothes purchasing. For instance, if we keep wearing the same clothes—problem of poor variation—they may wear out or we might be unprepared for new situations, especially as sartorial trends change. If we try on different options, but then randomly buy one without considering our needs—poor selection—we may also end up with a dud. If we find the perfect shirt but forget to take it out of its shopping bag—poor retention—it can't do anything for us. Every single component matters.

As a clinical example, consider Prue who struggles with restrictive eating, fatigue, and irritability.

- **Variation**: Part of treatment may entail having Prue vary her eating patterns (e.g., adding protein-rich snacks to her diet). Targeting variation assumes two things: (1) that Prue is stuck in the same pattern of responding either in form (eating the same meals every day) or function (trying to lose weight) and (2) that pattern is not working for her—this is usually why people seek therapy in the first place. Clients want change, even if they don't know what change should look like. With variation, we are referring to variation in function, not just form. For example, we would want Prue to vary not just her eating habits and exercise, but also her focus on losing weight at the cost of her health. In other words, we might vary the *reason* behind her behavior, in addition to the behavior itself. If Prue changed her diet but remained steadfast in her desire to lose weight, we might not consider treatment helpful.
- **Selection**: Once Prue has added snacks to her diet and is more connected with being strong (let's say this is her new goal) rather than being skinny, we would then observe how the snacks are affecting her well-being. We must be able to discern if the new pattern of responding has brought Prue closer to her goals or improved her well-being in some way (e.g., more energy, better mood), so that we'll know if it should be selected for retention. After all, trying on hundreds of outfits is moot if we don't know what we're looking for.
- **Retention**: Once it's clear what behaviors are working for Prue and her goals, we can turn our attention to retaining those behaviors. This may entail developing a behavioral plan, goal setting, or setting up a reward system for positive reinforcement. For instance, Prue might start a snack tracker and give herself 10 minutes of TV time for each planned snack she consumes.

One advantage of these principles is they provide diagnostic information that facilitates treatment planning. Clients may struggle with any of the evolutionary steps: variation (difficulty initiating changes in the first place); selection (not knowing what is working for them, maybe because they don't know what they want in life); and retention (difficulty continuing to use adaptive behaviors). Pinpointing where your clients are having trouble can be helpful for more precisely targeting what to work on in treatment. For instance, if your client is struggling with retention, teaching new skills may be less helpful than reinforcing the skills your client has already learned. We have found this zoomed-out perspective especially helpful when we are feeling stuck with clients.

Context

Context (z-axis, bottom right of Figure 2.1) refers to matching responses to environmental demands. Returning to the clothes metaphor, this means choosing outfits based on the occasion, like wearing flip-flops to the beach but not on a steep hike or a thick coat during winter but not summer. What works amazingly in one context may be useless in another. For instance, adding snacks might initially boost Prue's energy, but if she starts weight training to build strength, she may need to incorporate heavier meals into her diet to support her increased physical activity. Similarly, if Prue got injured, then responses focused on rehabilitation and recovery will probably be more adaptive than weightlifting.

All strategies are adaptive in a given context. Just as we have astronaut costumes for Halloween and neon face paint for raves, every behavior has a context in which it is the most reasonable option, even behaviors that seem obviously maladaptive to us. The problem is usually that people do the same thing even outside the context in which it was adaptive, like a child who wears their astronaut costume everywhere or the client who uses their assertive skills even in situations where conciliatory action and compromise are needed.

Using the EEMM

In our experience, the EEMM is most useful in two ways: (1) as a checklist to ensure that we review crucial relevant elements in our case formulation and treatment planning, and (2) as a means of organizing how we think about our clients and treatment. To meet these objectives, we ask ourselves the following questions:

1. Did I cover all the dimensions?
2. Did I consider each level of analysis and how it impacts my clients?
3. In which dimensions is new responding or new reasons for doing things needed?
4. In which dimensions is knowing how to identify what is working needed?
5. In which dimensions is maintaining useful responses needed?
6. In which dimensions is matching responses to context needed?

For a particular client, our possible responses to these questions are presented in Table 2.1.

You may have noticed that our responses are not exhaustive—they are not intended to be. We see the EEMM as a useful *starting point* that gives our case formulation and treatment plan some shape to begin with, but that shape will continue to evolve as we gather more data and spend more time thinking about the case.

At this juncture—likely post-intake—our objective is to identity a few viable treatment targets that capture major aspects of clients' struggles and will lead to positive change if intervened upon. We are less concerned about "correctly" categorizing processes; in fact, we caution against reifying the EEMM and using it like a diagnostic manual. In PBT, we only care about dimensions and levels to the extent that they allow us to design a precise treatment plan with the potential to improve our clients' functioning.

For example, we might spend some time determining whether striving to please others is a problem in variation or selection. It could be that the client rigidly seeks approval from others without caring about other purposes in life (motivational variation problem) or that they believe attaining external approval will have a positive impact on their life despite their experience telling them otherwise (motivational selection problem). Perhaps it is both. In Table 2.1, by treating striving to please others as a variation problem, we are simply noting that the client will likely benefit from connecting with new forms of motivation—and that is sufficient for now. We will discuss treatment planning and adjusting treatment in later chapters. If you ever notice yourself getting caught up in being technically accurate rather than clinically pragmatic, practice taking a step back, acknowledge that this is an easy trap to fall into, and reorient to the purpose of treatment.

Table 2.1 Case formulation using the EEMM framework.

	Variation	Selection	Retention	Context
Affect/Emotion	Relies only on short-term emotion regulation strategies	Uses emotion regulation strategies that satisfy others' needs		
Cognition	Gets stuck in ruminative spirals			
Attention	Shows attentional bias toward threat			Hypervigilant even with loved ones
Self	Sees self as "undeserving of love"		Occasionally uses self-compassion but does not practice it when stressed	
Motivation	Strives to please others			
Overt Behavior			Starts but does not maintain helpful habits	
Biology/Physiology	Takes 1–2 hours to fall asleep every night			
Relationships		Partner reinforces client for prioritizing partner's needs		
Culture		Pressure from gay community to appear "perfect" and "fun"		

Rationale for Using PBT

Delivering therapy is daunting. Humans are remarkably complex organisms with infinite variables affecting their lives. Contemplating everything, from genetics and heritable factors to environment, family, culture, and so on, it seems hubristic to even consider that we could precisely influence or even understand our clients. And then there are all the therapeutic modalities, theories, techniques, and schools of thought to consider. Where does one even begin? It can be overwhelming. We too have felt the weight of the expectations placed on us as therapists. While certainly not a panacea, we propose that adopting a PBT approach has numerous benefits that counteract some of these formidable realities.

Integration of Multiple Techniques

In the dynamic world of therapy, most practitioners find themselves drawing from a diverse array of techniques spanning multiple orientations. PBT steps in as a unifying framework, offering a way to cohesively tie these disparate techniques together. By relying on broader evolutionary theory, techniques from different schools of thought can be conceptualized as targeting processes relevant to any theoretical orientation, as long as you are operating from a theoretically coherent framework (e.g., EEMM). PBT recognizes that therapists often benefit from pulling techniques from various treatment packages and provides structure to this approach.

Using the EEMM as an example and thinking about principles of change, let's consider a client who is struggling with *varying* their cognitive responding with respect to thoughts about their future. They believe their "future is hopeless" and "there's nothing [they] can do about it" and consistently respond by coming up with reasons for why these thoughts might be true, such as listing ways they have "failed" in life. There are various cognitive techniques to select from, and we are not bound to any particular orientation. In fact, divergent orientations might be more suited to providing the client with a broad range of new responding to choose from. For example, the therapist could teach cognitive defusion from ACT and cognitive restructuring from CBT. On the surface, these techniques seem contradictory. Defusion is about noticing thoughts as they are, without taking them seriously, whereas cognitive restructuring is about conscientiously evaluating the accuracy of thought content. But in the framework of cognitive variation, these skills are seen through the lens of different options that can be matched to different contexts. For instance, when the client is in the middle of an important task, defusion could be helpful for letting thoughts go without allowing them to interfere with current goals. Whereas, if the client has time to properly evaluate the thought and examine evidence for it, cognitive restructuring may be more appropriate. In this way, PBT allows for moving beyond therapeutic camps (e.g., ACT vs. CBT) to take an expansive approach in the service of evolutionary principles of change.

Lingua Franca

Historically, when two parties who did not share a common language came together to trade, a lingua franca, or bridge language, was developed to facilitate communication and trading. The current therapy landscape shares similar difficulties, with many different therapies using terms unique to their orientation, even though the constructs those terms represent may be shared with other approaches. A strength of PBT is its ability to offer a common language that transcends therapeutic orientations, built on a foundation of evolutionary science that nearly all therapists can understand and appreciate—in the form of the EEMM.

For instance, techniques targeting cognitive flexibility—the ability to vary cognitive responses in adaptive ways—live under different names across various therapies—cognitive defusion in ACT, cognitive restructuring in CBT, and schema work in schema therapy. PBT helps in harmonizing these concepts, such as by highlighting that these differently named techniques share the goal of increasing clients' range of responses to certain difficult thoughts, whether it be via holding thoughts more lightly or challenging them directly. Naming the intended function of various procedures clarifies understanding and communication of therapeutic approaches, regardless of the specific orientation a therapist may be trained in.

Parsimonious Organizing Framework

PBT simplifies the multifaceted landscape of psychotherapies by focusing on core psychological dimensions, levels of analysis, and principles of change rather than an overwhelming array of techniques and theories. This streamlined approach enables therapists to better understand and target the fundamental mechanisms driving their clients' problems. By identifying key processes along EEMM dimensions and levels, PBT allows for a more focused and efficient approach to therapy, reducing redundancy and enhancing clarity in treatment planning. For example, when working with clients who do not fit neatly into a single diagnostic category—that is to say, most clients—we can find ourselves lost at sea with list of symptoms and problems that seem a mile long. We can fall into the trap of trying to categorize and find a treatment protocol for each of these problems, leading to overwrought treatment plans that overwhelm our clients, and us too.

PBT is also designed to address problematic patterns or processes underlying multiple problems, by considering function over form. It is less concerned with individual symptoms decontextualized from our clients' lives. Rather, PBT looks for processes—clinically relevant patterns of responding—that may be relevant to multiple intertwining symptoms or problems, such that targeting these processes can potentially impact a wide range of problems simultaneously. For example, a PBT-informed case formulation may identify fear of failure as a treatment target instead of the downstream symptoms it is associated with like low mood, procrastination, worries about the future, and social anxiety.

Personalization and Cultural Considerations

When used well, a PBT approach allows for exceptional versatility with regard to the types of clients we work with and their problems. While testing and validating interventions in diverse populations are unquestionably valuable, it is unrealistic to expect to find a treatment protocol developed to perfectly match all our clients' identities and lived experiences. One of PBT's strengths is the inherent consideration of cultural and personal contexts built into case conceptualization and treatment planning, by using a bottom-up approach to understanding clients' struggles and explicit representation of biophysiological and sociocultural factors in the EEMM.

Chapter Summary

- PBT is not a new therapy; it is an approach or framework for therapy, allowing therapists from any theoretical orientation to use the approach.

- PBT encourages therapists to focus on processes underlying symptoms rather than diagnoses. Processes describe the dynamic patterns of human responding that shape how clients interact with the world.
- PBT seeks to provide a common language wherein approaches and constructs from different schools of thought can be integrated in a unifying framework.
- The extended evolutionary meta-model (EEMM) provides a visual framework for PBT and can be used to organize elements in case conceptualization and treatment planning.
- Dimensions describe areas of psychological functioning, including *Self*, *Cognition*, *Affect/Emotion*, *Attention*, *Motivation*, and *Overt Behavior*.
- Levels reflect the scale on which you are situating particular people in context. The EEMM includes three levels: *Psychological*, *Biology/Physiology*, and *Relationships/Culture*.
- Principles of change describe different ways clients could be stuck: variation, selection, and retention.
- Context underscores the need to match responses to environmental demands.

3
The Five Principles of PBT

Humans adore rules. Rules provide an organizing force in an entropic world; they give us a sense of predictability, stability, and safety in an unpredictable, ever-changing, and sometimes dangerous landscape. Broadly speaking, there are two kinds of rules: *descriptive* and *functional*. Descriptive rules prescribe specific actions that need to be followed exactly, such as, "say please and thank you." Whereas functional rules—what we will call *principles*—describe the intended effect of the rule or a class of behaviors, such as, "treat others as you would like to be treated." Thus, the difference is that principles don't tell you exactly what to do.

Descriptive rules are helpful when we lack contextual knowledge to figure out how to apply a functional rule. For instance, if I'm meeting someone new, I may not know how they would like to be treated, so I may be better off following a descriptive rule like, "ask the other person questions about themselves." Similarly, a starting therapist might need to be instructed to "ask open-ended questions," rather than to "create an inviting space for clients," if they are not yet equipped with the clinical knowledge and skills to follow the functional rule.

However, descriptive rules can get unwieldly rapidly. We could instruct a therapist, "If you have an adolescent client who says 'I don't know' to open-ended questions, then use closed questions. But if your client gets distressed when you ask too many questions, create more pauses. But if your client is being avoidant, then address the avoidance." Essentially, because descriptive rules prescribe a specific behavior irrespective of context, a comprehensive set of descriptive rules would need to match each rule to a (literally) infinite number of situations.

Although functional rules do not tell us what to do, because they set the intention of prescribed actions, they can be applied to a wider range of situations than descriptive rules. Using the previous therapeutic example, if we are working with a client who has difficulty responding to questions—perhaps due to cultural programming, transference, or a history of trauma—then "creating an inviting space" may take the form of sitting in

A Process-Based Approach to Psychotherapy. Clarissa W. Ong and Eric B. Lee, Oxford University Press.
 DOI: 10.1093/oso/9780197696378.003.0003

silence. Alternatively, depending on the client and therapeutic relationship, "creating an inviting space" may entail self-disclosure. However, a therapist who is not attuned to such contextual variables would have difficulty deducing the principle-consistent response. As such, effective application of principles requires contextual awareness.

Core PBT Principles

We have distilled what we see as the five core principles of PBT. Similar to other functional rules, they must be applied with respect to context, which includes client identities, the therapeutic relationship, clinician skills, treatment setting, and so on. If we tried to describe every possible scenario and provide a rule for each one, this chapter would go on forever. And it wouldn't be helpful at all.

You are not a robot who needs to be programmed to follow orders. Rather, we want to illuminate the intention and forethought that defines the PBT approach. Like in chess, effective moves made by chance are useful in the moment but difficult to replicate in other matches. Understanding the reasoning behind moves—why they worked and why they didn't—allows you to adjust your strategies no matter what configuration of the chessboard you're facing.

You may notice that none of these principles are revolutionary, and you're likely already doing behaviors consistent with some of them. If you are, that's wonderful. As a next step, we invite you to consider your rationale for following these principles and what following these principles does for your clients. If these principles are new to you, that's wonderful too. It means you'll find some of this chapter instructive, and we encourage you to try out these principles with your clients.

The Process Principle: Think Process

One of the more prominent features of PBT is its focus on process (refer to Chapter 2 for a definition of "process") over symptoms and diagnoses. This means that when developing a case conceptualization, PBT therapists are always asking, "what is *maintaining* this symptom or what is the *underlying pattern* here?" PBT facilitates this approach using a visual representation of case formulations in the form of networks (see Figure 3.1 for an example; more on this in Chapter 5).

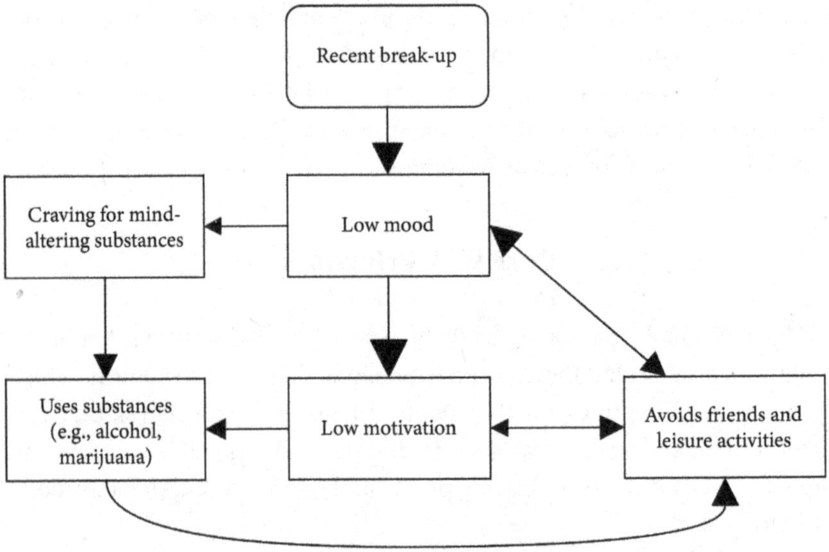

Figure 3.1 Network perspective of presenting problem.

As you can see in the network diagram (Figure 3.1), aspects of clients' presentations, including symptoms, are never considered in isolation and are instead depicted relative to interconnected variables. That is, we're interested in how different aspects of clients' problems relate to each other. We do not presume that a latent disorder is causing the various symptoms (as in Figure 3.2; e.g., "Rowan experiences anhedonia *because* he has depression"). Rather, we are concerned with how the various symptoms, experiences, and contextual factors interact and affect clients. In most network and PBT literature, each box containing a variable is called a *node* and each arrow is called an *edge*. We will use the terms *node* and *arrow* throughout the book.

When interpreting a network, our focus is on the arrows and the nodes they're connected to rather than the nodes per se. For example, in Figure 3.2, we care more about the relationship of [low mood] → [craving for substance] → [uses substances], rather than each of these problems as discrete symptoms to be reduced. Notice how the focus on relationships directly influences treatment planning. Based on the hypothesized relationship indicating that craving and substance use are a *consequence* of low mood, we may target low mood over substance use directly. Whereas, without noting this directionality, we may have opted to focus on treating the substance use. Overall, a network should visually answer the question of why your clients are doing the things they are doing. That is, it should make sense of and

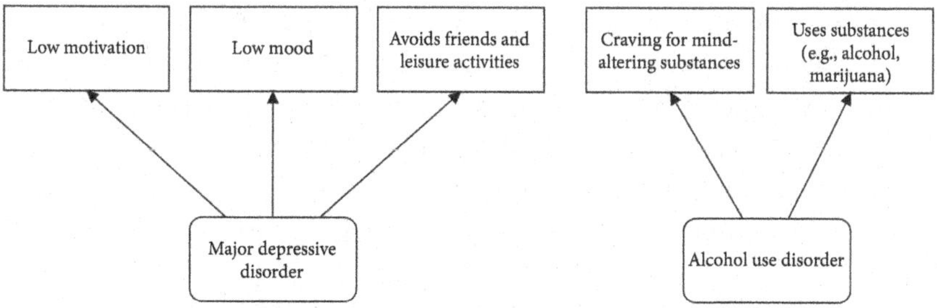

Figure 3.2 Latent disorder perspective of presenting problem.

provide context for their struggles. Chapter 5 provides a detailed guide for creating a network, including how to select nodes and identify arrows.

The other implication of a process-based focus is that treatment naturally becomes more precise. When we are targeting [avoids friends and leisure activities] rather than major depressive disorder, we are more likely to use a treatment component, like pleasant activity scheduling, than a diffuse treatment package, like CBT.

The EEMM Principle: Consider the Full Picture

For a network to be helpful, it needs to consider the range of dimensions of functioning and levels in which processes and problems could be occurring (see Chapter 2). When deciding what goes in clients' networks, we recommend going over each dimension and level as if they were aisles in a grocery store. Do you need anything from the Affect/Emotions aisle? Did you miss something from the Self aisle? Using the EEMM as a checklist ensures that we don't miss any important aspect of clients' environment that may be impacting their functioning. For instance, do you ask every client about their diet and sleep (Biology/Physiology)? Or about what gives their life purpose (Motivation)? Or even about which cultural identities are most important to them (Culture)? Not every dimension or level will be central to your clients, and determining what to keep vs. leave out is a key topic of Chapter 5.

We are also concerned about nodes that cannot be changed or are difficult to change through therapy, so long as they are part of the full picture. As such, we want to consider past experiences that continue to affect clients (e.g., childhood upbringing, learning history, traumatic events), biological factors (e.g., genetics, family mental health history), and less modifiable current factors (e.g., how much they like their job, income stability, major life events). Understanding the role these variables play in clients' presentations may clarify which approach to take in treatment, even if they are not directly targeted by the treatment. For instance, if a client is experiencing significant distress related to housing insecurity, we might want to integrate problem-solving skills into therapy, such as connecting them with a rental assistance program, instead of solely teaching skills to manage distress.

Similarly, when thinking about initiating and sustaining change in treatment, the principles of change—variation, selection, and retention—can help you grasp the nuances of what type of change needs to occur. Do your clients need to try new responses (variation)? Do they need to clarify their criteria for what counts as working (selection)? Do they need to improve their ability to use successful responses across time and contexts (retention)? Context also comes in when considering if clients need to be more intentional about when to use certain responses. Using the EEMM in its entirety reminds you to conceptualize change more holistically and be sensitive to the specific kinds of change your clients need.

The Personalization Principle: Make It Personal

PBT addresses particular people, not diagnoses, and entails treating your clients as beautifully complex humans. Just as you see yourself as more than a "therapist" or "student" or "parent" or "partner," your client too is more than "depressed" or "dysregulated" or "struggling." So when you are discussing a client through a PBT lens, you might describe him as a newly stay-at-home dad who is experiencing low mood and social withdrawal related to his transition away from working, rather than as someone who has major depressive disorder (MDD). After all, there are over a hundred ways people have been found to meet the diagnostic criteria for MDD across cultures (Park et al., 2017; Zimmerman et al., 2015), so the label of "MDD" could literally mean over a hundred different things.

In every aspect of treatment, be sure to consider unique client variables, such as their strengths, access to resources, identities, motivation, perspectives on therapy, worldview, and conceptualization of their own problems, because infusing these factors into therapy will meaningfully influence what you choose to do. For instance, if a client believes that talking about their problems will make them go away, it may be wise to provide psychoeducation on how learning psychological coping skills can also make life easier, in addition to providing validation and supportive counseling.

Relatedly, we need to tailor our assessment and treatment plan to our clients' unique needs and desired outcomes, rather than sticking to a one-size-fits-all approach. One-size-fits-all refers to not only using the same treatment for the same diagnosis—which, admittedly, many therapists don't necessarily do—but making generalized assumptions, such as using the same standardized measures that ask about the same symptoms, working toward the same goal of symptom reduction, and treating self-described "anxiety" as the same thing no matter the actual symptoms or concerns.

In a way, the Personalization Principle is about *asking* instead of *assuming*. Ask your clients what problems and outcomes they think would be helpful to track, what their goals are, and what they mean when they say "anxious" or "depressed." One of us had a client who complained of significant and persistent "anxiety," however, when we asked more about the "anxiety," it became clear that the client was using the word to refer to—what we might term—uncontrollable worry. Thus, a simple term like "anxiety" can have significant implications for how we conceptualize a client's problems and provide treatment appropriate for their needs, depending on how it's being used.

In addition, personalization means making assessment and treatment relevant and useful to your clients. For example, if you are tracking depression scores over time, but your client cares about connecting with their family and friends, the decrease in depression scores may not be the most important marker of progress. This does not mean eschewing all standardized measures simply because they were not designed specifically for your clients, because the items on a standardized scale could still be relevant and useful to them. However, that is determined by asking your clients first, rather than assuming. For instance, for a client whose symptoms map onto the PTSD Checklist for DSM-5 (PCL-5) and whose goal is to decrease PTSD symptom severity—that is, a decrease in PCL-5 scores would fairly assess treatment response—then administering the PCL-5 might be justified. Conversely, the Process-Based Assessment Tool (PBAT; Ciarrochi et al., 2022), a measure developed from the PBT framework, is designed to be used in a piecemeal fashion, wherein therapists and clients identify specific items that are relevant to the client and use a subset of its 18 items. In the case of the PBAT, the items are "standardized" in that everyone draws from the same pool of items, but the exact subset can vary tremendously and even be non-overlapping for different clients.

Moreover, there are multiple ways to track progress besides standardized measures. Creativity and attention to detail are helpful when devising new ways to assess progress. Clients could come up with their own metric of progress, such as the number of times they practice the trumpet, or the amount of time spent crocheting per week. Therapists could use their own observations of how clients relate to their thoughts in therapy. For example, a client may have begun therapy saying, "I'm a bad person and I deserve to be alone," and shifted toward reporting, "It's so difficult for me to let go of my core belief that I'm a bad person." In this transition, the client is showing that they recognize "I'm a bad person" as a thought to which they are strongly attached as opposed to a statement of reality. How our clients respond to treatment can be subtle, and picking up on these soft undulations can make you a more sensitive barometer of progress.

Finally, because PBT is about your clients, it is necessarily collaborative and takes the stance that your clients are active participants in the therapeutic process—to the extent that they choose to be. In general, it is difficult to consider treatment personalized if the only person making decisions is the clinician, without input from clients. As such, it is common in PBT to share case conceptualizations and clinical hypotheses with your clients, ask for feedback on treatment planning, or even empower your clients to develop their own treatment plan following appropriate psychoeducation. A caveat to this transparency is that clinicians still need to consider what is clinically useful. Sometimes a high level of transparency without preamble can feel overwhelming or contravene cultural expectations about the role of the clinician, undermining rapport or progress.

The Workability Principle: Stay on Target

This principle answers the question, "What's the point of therapy?" To paraphrase the Cheshire Cat from *Alice's Adventures in Wonderland*, if you don't know where you're headed, then it doesn't matter where you go. In fact, you may notice that sometimes when you're feeling stuck with clients, it's often helpful to return to treatment goals. Therefore, embedded in the Workability Principle is, foremost, to clarify what you and your clients are working toward. The long-term maintenance of your clients' goals will be the raison d'être of your therapy sessions. On an outcome level, you could be working toward increasing well-being or decreasing negative interactions with a partner. In terms of a network, you would be working toward destabilizing the original network—by eliminating or weakening nodes or arrows—and replacing it with a healthier stable one.

Importantly, staying on target does not tell you *how* to do so. Like hiking, the goal is to get to the top of the mountain. How you do it depends on the conditions (see EEMM Principle on context) and the people you're hiking with (see Personalization Principle). If someone has knee problems, you might need to take multiple switchbacks and lots of breaks. If everyone in the group is an experienced hiker outfitted with aggressive hiking boots, then you can take the most direct route to the top—that's fine too. The point is to stay focused on why you came to the mountain and be flexible in how you get to the summit. So, perhaps, after exhausting yourselves out on the steepest inclines, you decide that taking switchbacks might not be such a bad idea. As much as adaptability is key to workability, following overarching guiding principles that apply in most contexts—such as the ones outlined in this chapter—can be helpful too, such as making sure you have enough water and staying on marked trails.

Another way to think about workability is *treatment utility*, such that every step you make is evaluated in terms of its effect on meeting your clients' goals within a reasonable timeframe. For instance, we would not say that resting is ineffective on a long hike, because it will ultimately bring you closer to summiting the peak, even though you are not ascending the mountain at that moment. To assess progress, you need to check in regularly with your clients. After all, they are the ones whose hike you are on. Ask them what they think about the network conceptualization and treatment plan. Ask them how sessions have been going or what they've learned so far in treatment. Hiking with our clients is a special experience because we do not know if the peak we're seeing is the same one they're seeing, so only our clients can tell us if we're on track.

The Empiricism Principle: Follow the Data

The final principle has to do with epistemology, or how we know what we know. In PBT, we know what we know based on data, evidence, or direct observation. In other words, empiricism. It's important to make this foundation explicit because it informs how you deliver PBT. That is, even if you follow the first four principles—thinking in terms of process, considering the full picture, matching assessment and treatment to particular people, and focusing on clients' goals—if you don't use evidence-based treatment components or generate falsifiable hypotheses to test against empirical data, you're missing the mark.

PBT relies on the large body of cumulative evidence in clinical psychology that tells us which treatments tend to work better than others. Not because these treatments work for everyone, because we know they don't (e.g., Hofmann et al., 2012), but because starting from a place of some evidence is likely more useful than starting from a place of zero evidence. This is where the Personalization Principle is especially relevant. We start with what seems to work on average, then match specific techniques to clients depending on what they need. Hence, PBT is not a free-for-all approach to therapy; it's constrained by what the data support.

Hypothesis generation entails seeing if your intervention is having the effect you expect it to have. For instance, you may hypothesize that implementing a regular sleep schedule will decrease time spent lying awake in bed within three weeks. To test this hypothesis, you could ask your client to estimate the time they spent lying awake in bed on average over the past week, then teach your client how to maintain a regular sleep schedule and ask them again in three weeks. If they maintained a regular sleep schedule as prescribed and are spending less time awake in bed, then you could reasonably deduce that your intervention had its intended effect. If not, then you would need to revise your treatment plan. Perhaps your client did not implement the sleep schedule as planned or they did, but they used their phone right before bed. A disproven hypothesis means that your treatment plan or its delivery needs to change.

Sensitivity to empirical feedback is a crucial part of this principle. Making and testing predictions is insufficient. We must then incorporate what we have learned about our clients into intervention planning, altering or maintaining the course of treatment as appropriate (more on this in Chapter 7). For example, in a PBT case study, Ong et al. (2022) described doing a check-in after the client, Amy (pseudonym), had met her initial treatment goals. During this check-in, the therapist and Amy clarified Amy's current treatment goals and identified new variables to track over the course of treatment that were in line with her updated goals. Amy also made major life decisions in the second half of therapy, which tested the resilience of her treatment gains. With the onset of new stressors, Amy noted that she was especially struggling with attentional flexibility, so treatment shifted to reviewing attentional skills and how to apply them in her new context.

Such a data-driven approach to therapy—listening and being responsive to input from clients—is at the heart of the Empiricism Principle. Just like in science, it's OK if our hypotheses are wrong—it means we're learning new information about our clients. However, it's not OK to stubbornly stay on a path leading nowhere in the face of contradictory evidence just because a treatment is *supposed to* work. Following the data requires humility, to recognize when something isn't working, and flexibility, to shift your conceptualization and treatment plan.

Implementing PBT Principles

If you're feeling like these principles are *a lot*, that's understandable. Especially if you're new to these concepts, it may feel like we're asking you to spin plates while riding a unicycle on a tightrope. As with most of what we'll cover in the book, when putting these principles into practice, we'll advise you to focus on one thing at a time and give yourself grace to be "imperfect." For example, if you choose to integrate the Workability Principle, spend your next session establishing goals with your clients, or plan your next session in line with your clients' goals—pick something realistic and go from there.

Think of implementing these principles like learning a new language. Starting with *bonjour* or *au revoir* may not seem too impressive, but over time, you'll learn how to say *j'aime manger du fromage*, which is a little more impressive. And eventually, you'll be listening to the *Tour de France* commentary in French. Similarly, using the EEMM to identify gaps in your case conceptualization may seem pedestrian, but you might end up uncovering factors key to your clients' recovery that neither of you thought to bring up. Every time you apply these principles, you're exerting your PBT muscles, and building strength takes time.

Because these principles outline ways of thinking about—rather than doing—therapy, focusing on one principle at a time has the potential to shape many aspects of how you do therapy. For instance, implementing the Personalization Principle could include enhancing your case conceptualization with personal details about your client, learning more about culturally responsive therapy exercises, identifying personally meaningful outcomes to track, and so on. But again, take one step at a time.

We also encourage you to take some time to consider how you will enact these principles in a way that is consistent with your practice and true to your therapeutic style and orientation, because what these principles look like for one therapist is likely different from another. Personalization from a feminist framework may focus more on how the client is situated within their broader socio-cultural and political context, whereas a behavioral approach may lean more on clarifying stimuli that have unique effects on the client (e.g., what is reinforcing for one person may not be for another). Similarly, workability from a feminist perspective may be more strongly linked to empowerment and self-concept, whereas concrete observable goals may be more consistent with a behavioral approach. Thus, PBT may look different depending on the therapist, but the principles—in a sense, why you're doing what you're doing—are constant.

Chapter Summary

- When delivering PBT, keep in mind five core principles: (1) think in terms of process or function (Process), (2) consider all dimensions, levels of functioning, principles of change, and context-matching (EEMM), (3) tailor treatment to your clients not their diagnosis (Personalization), (4) do what works based on your clients' goals (Workability), and (5) use data to guide decision making (Empiricism).
- To see what these principles look like in treatment, see Appendix A, which provides a checklist of necessary ingredients for PBT.

4
Intake Interview

Purpose of the Intake Interview

For most clients, the first time you interact with them is in an intake interview where you gather information about their psychosocial history, presenting problem, and current environment. A process-based approach to an intake is similar in that it is also about gathering data, but the focus is on the *function* of the data. In other words, the content of the information is less important than whether the information fills certain knowledge gaps. At the end of your intake, you should be able to answer the following questions, which align with the five principles described in Chapter 3:

1. **Relationships among symptoms (Process)**: How do different aspects of the problem relate to each other? What might explain related problems (i.e., underlying process)?
2. **EEMM checklist (EEMM)**: Which EEMM dimensions and levels are most relevant to your client?
3. **Client variables (Personalization)**: What is unique about your client that influences their current presentation?
4. **Treatment goals (Workability)**: What does your client want to get out of therapy?
5. **Concrete examples (Empiricism)**: What evidence do you have to support your initial hypotheses?

Relationships Among Symptoms (Process)

Before you begin treatment, you need a case conceptualization that summarizes what you and your client see as their main struggles and how development and maintenance factors relate to them. Developing a case conceptualization is like sketching out a map before embarking on your journey.

A Process-Based Approach to Psychotherapy. Clarissa W. Ong and Eric B. Lee, Oxford University Press.
 DOI: 10.1093/oso/9780197696378.003.0004

While you can certainly start moving without a map, the map orients you to the terrain you're on and enables you to choose paths intentionally.

In PBT, we typically use a *network* to visually represent the client's presenting concern. We'll explain how to create a network in Chapter 5, but for now, all you need to be concerned about is linking the various aspects of your client's problem. In other words, you need to determine how clinically relevant variables relate to each other. These relationships should provide insight into why clients remain stuck (e.g., what reinforcers are maintaining unhelpful responses) and where it might be useful to intervene.

Let's say we have a client, Matty, who endorses low mood, oversleeping, feelings of worthlessness, constant guilt, and loss of interest in activities. With these symptoms, Matty could be assigned a diagnosis of MDD, but as we know, a diagnosis is a rather blunt instrument (as much as it may be helpful for billing and insurance). We can be more precise.

If we examine *how* these symptoms interact with each other, we might think of them as depicted in Figure 4.1 (only three are selected for illustrative purposes).

Figure 4.1 Possible relationships among Matty's symptoms (version 1).

Now, we are seeing Matty's story more clearly. Perhaps Matty lost interest in his hobbies, then felt guilty about his inactivity, leading him to feel worthless. In a sense, network building is a form of visual storytelling. We could even try out a different narrative, such as in Figure 4.2.

Figure 4.2 Possible relationships among Matty's symptoms (version 2).

Now Matty's story is about someone who generally struggles with low self-esteem, which may bring up guilt over his lack of self-confidence, and the associated distress may result in him no longer being able to enjoy his hobbies.

Crucially, understanding how these symptoms relate to each other guides treatment, as we usually want to focus on the originator of clients' struggles rather than downstream effects. Thus, in the first mini network, we would target anhedonia, with the expectation that reconnecting Matty with his hobbies and other activities will alleviate feelings of guilt and worthlessness. In the second network, we might target his feelings of worthlessness instead, predicting that guilt and anhedonia will decrease once Matty develops a more positive view of himself.

Of course, client networks are never as simple as what is shown in these mini networks. We are likely missing bidirectional relationships and self-perpetuating loops (more on those in Chapter 5). What matters at this point is that you're learning to focus on the *links* between problems and not just the *severity* of problems.

For therapists who are used to doing functional analysis or chain analysis, this way of thinking about antecedents and consequences bracketing a response of interest might already be familiar to you. Here, we use "response" instead of "behavior" to underscore the broad range of responses a person may have, including unobservable ones, like feeling guilt. A network is simply multiple antecedent–response–consequence sequences layered on top of each other. For instance, if we combine the two chains above, Matty's network would look like Figure 4.3 (note the bidirectional arrows).

Figure 4.3 Possible relationships among Matty's symptoms (version 3).

Antecedents, responses, and consequences are the building blocks of PBT networks, and each of these basic blocks can have multiple functions. An antecedent can be a consequence for a different chain, and a response can be an antecedent in another chain. Permitting multiple functions allows networks to represent complex relationships, which more closely model what we observe in real life, beyond unidirectional linear paths. For example, intrusive memories about a past traumatic event (antecedent) may precipitate self-harm (response), leading to attention from others (consequence). At the same time, attention from others (now an antecedent) may bring up a cognitive response in the form of "I don't deserve this," kicking off another chain.

To elaborate on these relationships further, we might even consider adding another variable—an underlying process—to explain how these responses are related. This step requires more inference, as clients may not directly report underlying processes. Hence, any such additions should be treated as hypotheses to be verified with more data. In Matty's case, perhaps he expressed that he finds himself messing up all the time, no matter how hard he tries. Even if he does not explicitly link this belief to his experiences of guilt and worthlessness, we could hypothesize the relationships shown in Figure 4.4.

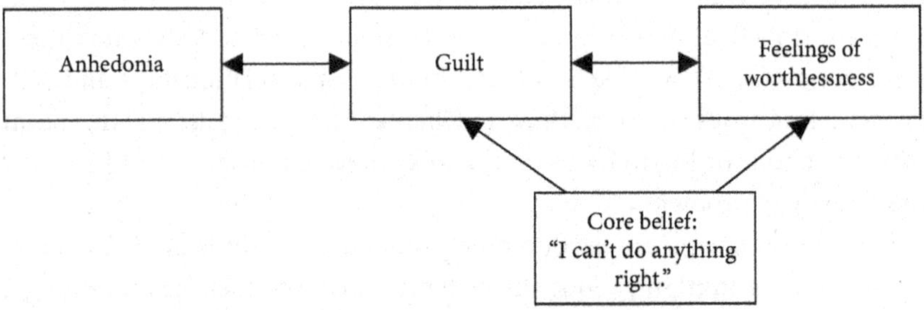

Figure 4.4 Hypothesized process underlying Matty's symptoms.

Notice that in this version of the network, we now have a potential treatment target (core belief that he cannot do anything right) that may be helpful for addressing guilt and feelings of worthlessness more efficiently.

EEMM Checklist (EEMM)

As you consider how symptoms relate to each other, you also need to be sure that you're not missing key aspects of your clients' presenting problems. It's common for clients—and humans in general—to overemphasize one aspect of their struggles, such as believing that their lives would be better if they were less impulsive or in a loving relationship. Yet, it behooves us to ask about other dimensions and levels that may be contributing to clients' problems. For instance, we may ask our clients questions like the following:

1. What emotions show up when you're feeling impulsive? (Affect)
2. What kinds of thoughts come up whenever you make a mistake? (Cognition)
3. What are you thinking about right before you "lash out in anger"? (Attention/Cognition)
4. What would a "better life" look like for you? (Motivation)
5. What do you do on a typical "unproductive" day? (Overt Behavior)
6. How do your relationship problems affect how you see yourself? (Self/Relationships)
7. How did your family talk about emotions growing up? (Affect/Context)

8. How has your sleep been? (Biophysiology)
9. What kind of movement or activity do you engage in? (Biophysiology)
10. How does the medication you're taking affect your functioning? (Biophysiology)
11. How might cultural differences contribute to conflicts in your relationship? (Relationships/Culture)

Not all dimensions or levels are clinically relevant—or at least core enough to the problem—to warrant further consideration. In addition, not all variables are within your ability to change. For instance, if you're not a prescriber, there's nothing you can directly do about your clients' medication regimen. If systemic oppression contributes to your clients' chronic trauma, there's not much you can directly do to mitigate large-scale injustices—at least in the short term.

Nonetheless, it's important to at least assess the dimensions and levels to know what you are including and excluding and why. Like creating an invitation list for a party, you're probably fine excluding most people, but you definitely don't want to forget the VIPs. In other words, the EEMM checklist is not about including all dimensions and levels; it's about considering each one and making a conscious decision about whether to include them in your case conceptualization.

Client Variables (Personalization)

A crucial aspect of regarding your clients as people rather than problems to be solved is acknowledging their humanity. This means appreciating your clients' identities: how they interact with each other, how visible they are, the extent to which your client relates to them, how they affect the way the world treats your client, etc. In addition, it's worth examining other aspects of your clients' context that influence how they experience their problem and treatment, such as their strengths, (dis)abilities, family history, and preconceived notions of mental health.

Just like different actors playing the same character bring new energy to the role, clients with identical problems may experience and interpret their problems in their own way and benefit from different treatment approaches. For example, if Matty believes that his feelings of guilt and worthlessness are his choice and that he just needs to "snap out of it," some psychoeducation about the environmental determinants of emotions may be helpful. If Matty has a long history of meditation practice, teaching him how to generalize mindfulness skills to his current struggles may facilitate positive change. If Matty holds a minoritized identity (e.g., Black man in the U.S.), then understanding how cultural oppression or intergenerational trauma might be contributing to his struggles or how his identities strengthen his resilience may be indicated.

Treatment Goals (Workability)

Ultimately, treatment is about meeting your clients' goals, so you need to clarify objective, measurable treatment goals at the outset. At all points in treatment, you and your clients should know what you are working toward in treatment and how to tell if you're on the right track. For instance, being happy is a slippery treatment goal. How happy is happy enough? How would you reliably measure the level of your happiness your clients are experiencing? In contrast, a behavioral goal associated with being happy, like hosting a dinner party or joining a frisbee league, is easier to check off a list. If you don't know your destination or checkpoints, focus on identifying them.

It's not enough to know the problems you want to eliminate, because a void or absence of symptoms doesn't automatically confer a meaningful existence, even if it has some positive effects. Imagine someone who is highly afraid of leaving their home. Successful treatment may result in a reduction of this fear, such that the person is able to go outside and do activities. But if the therapist never discovers what their client wants to do once they are outside their home, then merely being outside may be unfulfilling. After all, the point is not to eliminate fear per se, but to help the client engage in the life they have missed out on due to avoidance of fear.

Find goals that make your clients excited about living. The magic wand or lottery question can be helpful for this: "If I had a magic wand and could wave away your problems or if you won a billion dollars in the lottery, what would you be doing?" Even if your clients cannot realistically achieve those goals (e.g., quit my job and sail the world), you can work with your clients to extract values from their dream goals: "What would quitting your job and sailing the world mean for you?" Perhaps your client values freedom or adventure. These values can then be used to identify more manageable goals, such as finding a new job or going on a weekly hike.

Concrete Examples (Empiricism)

Throughout your assessment, ask your clients for specific examples with concrete details. We often ask clients, "If you were [e.g., feeling sad, arguing with your child], what would that look like?" This question prompts clients to list observable behaviors associated with abstract or ill-defined constructs, which can clarify the nature and severity of symptoms. For instance, we might ask a client, "When you say you 'blew up' at your partner, what did that look like?" We may get a range of answers from "I raised my voice, but honestly, my partner didn't seem to notice" to "I threw a vase at the wall, but it was away from my partner."

These descriptions facilitate hypothesis testing, a central feature of PBT. If your hypothesis is that your client's "uncontrollable anger" is contributing to relationship conflicts, then you need to know what that anger looks like. If it's imperceptible or handled adaptively (e.g., "I express my frustration and ask my partner for space"), then the evidence might not support your hypothesis, whereas if your client's anger manifests in interpersonally hurtful ways (e.g., "I pick on my partner's insecurities"), then your hypothesis may be viable. The vagueness of abstractions precludes proper hypothesis testing; details matter.

In addition, getting examples from clients increases the likelihood that you and your clients are using the same terms in the same way. Just as we can never really know if someone else's experience of the color blue is the same as ours, we cannot assume that terms like "scared" or "better" or "happy" mean the same thing to you and your client. For example, many clients come to therapy and say they want to be "happy" or "healthy," and these terms seem relatively straightforward. However, when we probe a bit further, we have gotten responses like, "I don't actually know what being happy would be like" or "being healthy means that I will never have negative thoughts again." Unpacking these terms can be helpful for clarifying your clients' perspective and guiding psychoeducation on what clients can reasonably expect from therapy.

Moreover, getting your clients to connect subjective terms to objective behavior provides a treasure trove of information about their level of insight and how they interpret their struggles. A client describing themselves as an "OK student" for getting straight As vs. being close to dropping out tells you something about your client's personal standards or minimization of problems.

Intake Interview Vignette

To see how to put these guidelines into practice, we present some basic information about a new client, Yan (see Box 4.1).

> **Box 4.1 Case vignette for Yan**
>
> Yan is a 29-year-old Chinese American gay ciswoman. She is seeking therapy due to her ongoing struggles with "impulsivity." She frequently "acts without considering consequences," resulting in risky behaviors, including excessive spending, occasional binge drinking, initiating arguments with others, and procrastinating work projects. Due to these behaviors, she consistently feels regret, shame, and anxiety. These behaviors have negatively impacted her financial stability, relationships, job performance, and emotional well-being.

Let's review the five questions we would like to be able to answer with data from our intake interview.

1. **Relationships among symptoms (Process)**: How do different aspects of Yan's problem relate to each other? What might explain related responses (i.e., underlying process)?
2. **EEMM checklist (EEMM)**: Which EEMM dimensions and levels are most relevant to Yan and her struggles?
3. **Client variables (Personalization)**: What is unique about Yan that influences her current presentation?
4. **Treatment goals (Workability)**: What does Yan want to get out of therapy?
5. **Concrete examples (Empiricism)**: What evidence do you have to support your initial hypotheses?

What information is missing so far? We encourage you to work through each question before continuing on to the next part. Focus on what information you need, rather than on how you will get the information. Similar to treatment goals, we need to figure out our destination before we can plot our path. Identify key pieces of missing information below. It does not have to be elaborate; broad areas are fine.

<u>Missing Information</u>

1. Relationships among symptoms:

2. EEMM checklist:

3. Client variables:

4. Treatment goals:

5. Concrete examples:

Turn to the next page to see our thoughts.

Relationships Among Symptoms (Process)

The vignette paints a partial picture of how Yan's various symptoms relate to each other. We know that lack of consideration of consequences tends to lead to a range of impulsive behaviors that have negative consequences for her functioning (i.e., financial stability, relationships, work) and well-being (i.e., regret, shame, anxiety).

However, we do not know why Yan is stuck in this pattern, beyond her inability to consider consequences. So, we might be interested in what is contributing to her difficulties regulating urges or making decisions based on long-term rewards and what is maintaining her risky behaviors (e.g., pleasure from new purchases, social connection from binge drinking). How do regret, shame, and anxiety contribute to other parts of her problem? It's possible that the risky behaviors are negatively reinforced by the temporary removal of distress. Moreover, it's unclear what led Yan to seek therapy *at this point.* What changed?

Missing Information

- Antecedents and consequences of risky behaviors
- Relationship between regret, shame, and anxiety and other parts of Yan's problem
- Processes underlying multiple problems
- Changes in Yan's environment that precipitated treatment seeking

EEMM Checklist (EEMM)

To examine Yan's full context, we'll review the EEMM dimensions and levels (see Table 4.1).

Based on this table, we see that we don't know anything about Yan's thought patterns, sense of self, motivations, or biophysiological functioning besides potential effects of binge drinking. We may later decide that some of these dimensions or levels are less relevant to her presenting problem and exclude them, but at this point, we need to make sure we have not missed them in the first place.

Table 4.1 Review of Yan's clinically relevant problems against EEMM dimensions and levels.

Dimensions	Affect/Emotion	Difficulties regulating urges, regret, shame, anxiety
	Cognition	
	Attention	Does not consider long-term consequences/Focused on short-term outcomes
	Self	
	Motivation	
	Overt Behavior	Risky behaviors
Levels	Biology/Physiology	Effects of binge drinking?
	Relationships	Relationship conflicts
	Culture	Poor work performance, potential financial problems

Missing Information

- Thoughts or responses to thoughts that impair functioning or well-being
- Self-perception or responses to the self that impair functioning or well-being
- Reasons for acting (or lack thereof) that impair functioning or well-being
- Physical symptoms and health behaviors that impair functioning or well-being

Client Variables (Personalization)

We have scant information on Yan's identities, strengths, learning history, and interpretation of her impulsivity. We do not know what Yan sees as the most distressing aspect of her struggles or the central problem. For instance, the occasional binge drinking may be especially shameful for Yan if she subscribes to mores that disapprove of substance use, even if it's not the behavior most negatively affecting her functioning. Alternatively, she might have grown up in an environment where risky behaviors were modeled, and she may underestimate their impact on her well-being and functioning. This is the part of the case conceptualization that gives it life and allows us to appreciate Yan's complexity as a human.

Missing Information

- Yan's central identities and her relationship with them
- Yan's perception of her struggles
- Yan's strengths
- Yan's beliefs about treatment and what is "normal" with respect to mental health

Treatment Goals (Workability)

There is no indication of Yan's goals for therapy, so we would want to know what she wants to be different in her life by the end of treatment.

Missing Information

- Treatment goals

Concrete Examples (Empiricism)

Yan has provided examples of risky behaviors, which is helpful. However, they can still be defined more specifically. For instance, does "excessive spending" refer to spending $500 on new shoes after her old shoes got worn out or $5,000 on a piano that she plans to learn to play one day? How frequent is the "occasional" binge drinking? How long has she been engaging in these risky behaviors? With whom does she engage in these risky behaviors?

In addition, it might be worth exploring what Yan means when she says she "acts without considering consequences," given that it seems to underlie her risky behaviors: What does acting without considering consequences look like? What thoughts and feelings come up when she acts without considering consequences? Sometimes obvious questions beget unobvious answers.

Missing Information

- Details of risky behaviors, including severity, frequency, and duration
- What "acting without considering consequences" looks like

What Else?

There are many other variables we could have identified—some of them are probably on your list. However, returning to function, our objective was not to be comprehensive—after all, this is only our first time meeting Yan and we will have time to learn more about her over the course of treatment. Our goal was to identify missing information that, once obtained, would capture roughly 80% of what is needed to develop a case conceptualization (network) and treatment plan.

Review your list and see if it accomplishes this goal. That is, if you have all the information outlined in your list, will you have a solid starting point and direction? Was there anything we included that you did not? What changes would you make to your list after reading ours? Once you have all the pieces, we can put them together into a network case conceptualization.

Intake Troubleshooting

Finessing your PBT intake will take trial and error. You'll inevitably encounter situations that derail your well-intentioned plans. For example, clients may not be willing to share relevant information (e.g., details of traumatic event), experience high emotional distress that keeps them from opening up, lack insight to articulate their struggles, veer off on tangential paths, or even provide contradictory information. When you inevitably encounter such intake hiccups, fall back on your core clinical interviewing skills, like using open-ended questions to draw out information, providing consistent and appropriate validation to alleviate shame or perceived stigma, recognizing how your client's identities may be influencing their experience of the intake and you . . . the list goes on.

At the same time, there can be challenges more specific to a PBT intake. Sometimes, therapists may get overly focused on asking their prepared questions or fitting their client into the EEMM that they lose sight of the function of the interview. In particular, the latter is not functionally different from trying to shoehorn our clients into a diagnostic manual. If you notice yourself getting frustrated because you aren't getting the answers you want, take a second to regroup. You could even make a comment like, "It seems like I'm getting a bit off track here. Let me refer to my notes before we continue." We believe the rat is always right, so if you're not getting the answers you're seeking, you're probably not asking the right questions. Similarly, if you're getting caught up in the EEMM, simply observe the pull to make sense of your client—as if they were a puzzle to be deciphered—and pivot to being present in the room with them as a human to be listened to. Ultimately, we do care about gathering information to inform treatment planning, but not to the extent that we neglect our clients' humanity.

Relatedly, it's OK if you don't get all the information you need in one intake session. In fact, expect that you won't. There's no way any therapist will have perfect information on their clients—even if they did, that information would be outdated as soon as their clients walk out the door and continue living their lives. Once we acknowledge that we will inevitably fail to get all the data we would like to have, we can channel our energy toward clarifying which information to prioritize. You may have pre-prioritized your missing information, but as you learn more about your clients, you'll probably be pulled in multiple directions. Knowing which directions are immediately salient and which ones are red herrings (at this time) is a skill that will improve with reflection and experience. Even then, we can't be unfailingly omniscient. Still, be intentional about choosing which threads to tug on; understand why you're pursuing A and not B.

When prioritizing areas to pursue, we tend to highlight malleable barriers that prevent clients from achieving their goals. There are two reasons for this: (1) these are directly relevant to their goals and (2) we can do something about them in treatment. For example, if Yan's primary goal is to turn in work on time, then we might prioritize variables that get in the way of this (e.g., what leads to procrastinating, what does she do instead of work). To get a sense of those variables, we would in turn first need to define what the problem is and what her desired end state is. The processes underlying difficulties related to one goal are likely linked to those for a different goal (e.g., acting on impulsive urges), so even if you only cover one goal in your intake, you may still be able to develop a decent case conceptualization.

Therapists can also get caught up in the content of clients' answers rather than their function. In PBT, the focus is more on how various aspects of your client's life relate to each other (Process, EEMM, Personalization) and to their goals (Workability). An example of being overly concerned about content is asking about minute details of a traumatic event, beyond what is pertinent to treatment planning. Of course, specific details are sometimes important to treatment but pursuing details about a traumatic event for half an intake session without getting information on how the traumatic event is currently impacting your client's well-being and functioning or the relationship client would like to have with their past may not be prudent. Whenever you are asking a question or responding to your client's answer, return to how the question or data will inform your treatment plan. You only have so much time to get information to clarify your initial steps, so use it judiciously.

Chapter Summary

- When doing a PBT intake, consider what information you need, then ask questions accordingly (see Appendix B for a list of helpful intake questions).
- Generally, we recommend gathering data on how problems relate to each other and what might explain related problems, relevant EEMM dimensions and levels, client characteristics that influence their presentation, clients' goals, and concrete definitions of problems.
- The expectation for an intake is to have sufficient information to develop a working case conceptualization and treatment plan (see Appendix C for an intake template). The goal is to establish a tenable starting point, not to finish the race.
- Common challenges that come up during a PBT intake include trying to shoehorn clients into the EEMM, not getting all the desired information, and getting caught up in the content of clients' responses.

5

Network Case Conceptualization

Once you've collected data from the initial assessment or intake interview, the next step is to organize the data into a coherent network. This network serves as your case conceptualization and the basis for treatment planning. The purpose of the network is to clarify driving and maintaining factors for your clients' problems. This is done through layering antecedent–response–consequence sequences over each other, as shown in Chapter 4. The resulting network is a visual representation of the interrelationships of your clients' problems (and strengths), which you can build with your clients in session or share with them to ponder between sessions.

As a quick note, we're more concerned about the *function* of a network than the form it takes. So if you have a different way of clarifying driving and maintenance factors associated with your clients' struggles and find that method more helpful for treatment planning, use that. A network is a *tool* and is only as useful as its ability to serve its intended function. The reason we're walking through the steps for building a network here is that it provides a structured—somewhat formulaic—foundation on which you can build your own clinical conceptualization. As for someone new to cooking, it's helpful to initially follow the guidance of a recipe, so you don't forget any ingredients or the sequence of steps.

Once you grasp the principles of process-based case conceptualization through basic network building, it'll be easier to fashion your own tools that better fit your therapeutic style and orientation, just like you probably won't need a recipe after you've cooked basil fried rice dozens of times. You may even be tweaking the original recipe as you become more adept—wonderful, we would never say no to more carbs. What matters in the end is that your clients enjoy their meal, not whether you adhered to a specific recipe.

A Process-Based Approach to Psychotherapy. Clarissa W. Ong and Eric B. Lee, Oxford University Press.
 DOI: 10.1093/oso/9780197696378.003.0005

Function of Networks

Before we get into the detailed network recipe, let's see why this dish is worth making in the first place by looking at a simpler version of the final product. In the same way that "cheat" versions of complicated dishes can still be delicious (e.g., using baking mix vs. making cake batter from scratch), mini networks with a few ingredients have their place. For example, the network in Figure 5.1 shows a person who struggles with chronic back pain, avoids physical activity, and believes they are "useless." Without understanding how these variables relate to each other, we might aim to reduce pain, increase physical activity, or restructure the thought, "I'm useless." These methods are symptom-based: we try to decrease or eliminate the problems themselves. Undoubtedly, these options could be helpful.

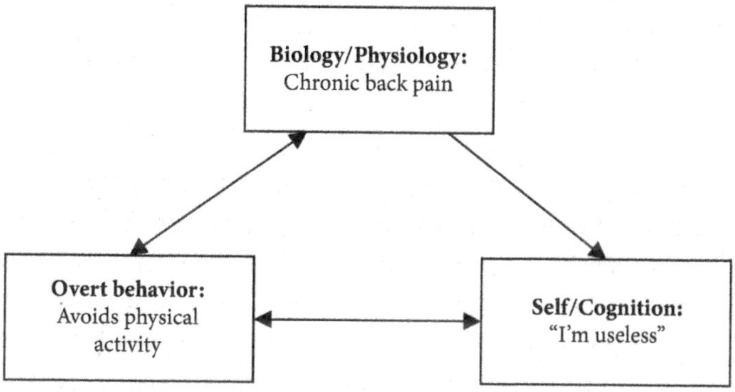

Figure 5.1 Mini network for someone with chronic pain.

However, from the three-ingredient network, we can appreciate this person's struggles more deeply. From the double-headed arrow between [chronic back pain] and [avoids physical activity], we see that their pain leads to avoidance of physical activity (which in turn results in more pain). From the double headed arrow between [avoids physical activity] and ["I'm useless"], we glean a similar mutually reinforcing relationship between avoidance and their belief that they are useless. Finally, the arrow from [chronic back pain] to ["I'm useless"] tells us that another contributor to the "I'm useless" belief is chronic pain. That's a good amount of information from three nodes and three arrows.

Using a process-based lens and considering how these problems are connected to each other, rather than reducing symptoms, we might shift toward altering the *relationships* among these problems. One way to do this is to target the *effect* of pain on physical activity and self-concept, or the *effect* of believing you are "useless" on behavioral avoidance. Another way to leverage these relationships is to target symptoms most likely to improve client well-being. For instance, increasing physical activity could have the dual impact of decreasing back pain and weakening the belief that they are "useless," even without directly targeting the latter problems.

We hope the three-ingredient version of the network shows that you don't always need a scrupulously technical recipe to make a decent dish to satisfy hunger pangs in the short term. So, if you feel intimidated by the eight-step recipe below, try making a few mini networks to get the hang of linking clinically relevant variables and thinking about how they influence each other. For practice, we've found it helpful to do simple networks on ourselves—focusing on a behavior we're trying to change—because we already have all the information we need.

For a more personal example, we've outlined what we think might be contributing to a behavior we're trying to change in Figure 5.2: procrastination. The variables ["I'm not in the right head space to write"] and [guilt over not writing] both have arrows going into [procrastinates book writing]. As we've identified ["I'm not in the right head space to write"] as a potential antecedent to procrastination, we might see if we can decrease the power of that thought using behavioral experiments (e.g., test and see if we can write without being in the "right head space") or defusion (e.g., noticing the automatic thought and letting it go). If we increase our time spent writing after this intervention, then we would say that the network has been clinically useful, especially if we haven't been able to decrease procrastination using other strategies.

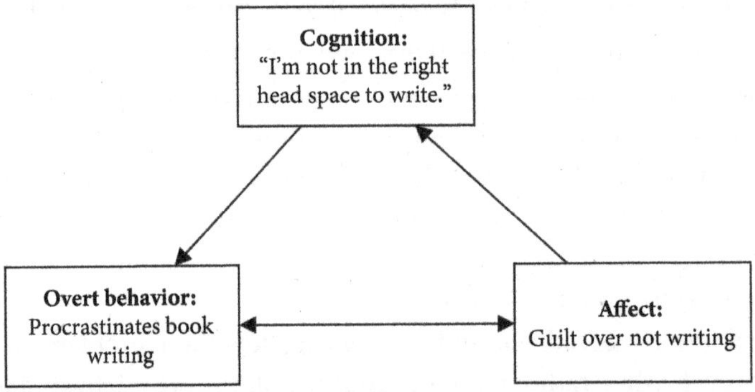

Figure 5.2 Mini network for someone procrastinating book writing.

Doing mini networks like the ones in Figures 5.1 and 5.2 will move you closer to process-based thinking. But whenever you get to the point where a baking mix just won't cut it, try the more complicated recipe below. It will be trickier than just mixing and stirring, but the flavors will be that much richer.

Developing a Network Conceptualization

The eight steps to network building we outline below are fairly detailed, so we suggest being familiar with them, such that you have a handle of the underlying principles, before initiating any network building with your clients. If not, you risk turning your therapy session into a lecture or study group. We provide a parallel list of questions in Appendix D to use with your clients during network building. The questions make more sense once you understand the principles of network building.

There are many ways to include your clients (or not) in these steps, and we generally recommend including them in some capacity: you could do all eight steps with your clients, do them by yourself then ask your clients for feedback on the completed network, or do a subset of steps with your clients. For example, if your clients have little insight into their problems, then starting with identifying clinically relevant variables (step 1) to increase awareness could be useful. Conversely, if you believe showing a completed network is more efficient for increasing awareness, then you could go straight to verifying the network with them. If your clients tend to find everything urgently important and is likely to include every problem in their network, then start with linking network variables (step 6) after you've identified the most relevant problems. That way, you can avoid getting mired in arguments about why your client's 50 problems must be represented in the network. On average, we've found it helpful to start with narrowing down relevant variables (step 3) after you've identified (step 1) and functionally defined (step 2) your clients' main problems. Either way, your network will change over time as you learn more about your clients, so it's OK if you get it "wrong" the first time. In fact, it almost certainly will be.

The Case of Mary

We'll walk through the steps of network conceptualization using the example of Mary. A summary of information gleaned from Mary's intake meeting is presented in Box 5.1.

Box 5.1 Case vignette for Mary.

Mary is a 63-year-old white ciswoman who has retired after teaching at an elementary school for over 40 years. She lives with her husband and has four children, all of whom live at least a four-hour drive away from Mary. Mary said that she does not have any friends; she considers the people in her yoga class to be "acquaintances" as she does not spend time with them outside class.

Mary reported constant worry about her children, health, and marriage; low mood; difficulty sleeping due to racing thoughts at night; accelerated heart rate at random times during the day; and feelings of restlessness. Her coping strategies for these symptoms include calling her children daily to check in on them, researching medical diagnoses and divorce laws, taking Xanax whenever she feels anxious, watching Korean dramas, and doing yoga. She said that she "can't stand" her life, because she feels miserable, lonely, and anxious "all the time." Mary shared how frustrated she feels about her husband's lack of contribution around the house and her financial dependence on him, which makes her feel trapped in her marriage.

During the intake interview, Mary repeatedly commented that she "deserves to suffer," alluding to past behavior about which she feels ashamed, but did not explain further, even when prompted. She said that her beliefs about suffering were most likely engrained in her due to her Catholic upbringing, which continues to influence her perspectives. Mary also stated that she finds life to be meaningless but would never take action toward suicide as she is afraid of going to hell, despite currently identifying as atheist. She remarked that even though she does not like her current life, she is unwilling to make changes, because she is "getting what she deserves." Her reason for seeking therapy is to feel less anxious and decide if she should divorce her husband.

Step 1: Identify Clinically Relevant Variables

The first step of network building is to identify possible candidates to include in your network, or *clinically relevant variables*. These may include cultural identities, strengths, social support, hobbies, behaviors, and symptoms. Clinically relevant variables would be anything related to why your clients are coming into therapy and what they want to get out of therapy. Hence, they are broadly defined.

As much as possible, we recommend using wording that fits your clients' perception of their problem to validate their experiences and allow the network to resonate with your clients. For instance, if your client describes certain intense physiological sensations as "panic attacks," you may want to use [panic attacks] in the network, even if they do not meet strict diagnostic criteria for panic attacks. In addition, direct quotes can be helpful for capturing clients' experiences, especially around core beliefs and self-labels, such as [core belief: "things will never get better"] and [sees self as "selfish and irresponsible"].

You may also include behavioral observations as clinically relevant variables, if they seem relevant to your clients' presentation. For example, if you have a client who is struggling with interpersonal problems and they consistently interrupt you or appear to be insensitive to your attempts to relate to them, those behaviors may be important to include in the network. Remember that a network is a hypothesis of what is occurring for your clients; a hypothesis naturally changes as you collect more data and can never be proven, only disproven.

In the highlighted version in Box 5.2, we identified 28 candidates for inclusion in the network. However, a network with 28 nodes becomes unwieldy quickly—there are 378 possible arrows in a 28-node network, even before we consider directionality. That's too many connections for the network to be reasonably interpretable. Indeed, a complicated network with extensive details may paradoxically make identifying a treatment plan more difficult.

Box 5.2 Case vignette for Mary with clinically relevant variables highlighted

Mary is a 63-year-old white ciswoman who has retired after teaching in an elementary school for over 40 years. She lives with her husband and has four children, all of whom live at least a four-hour drive away from Mary. Mary said that she does not have any friends; she considers the people in her yoga class to be "acquaintances" as she does not spend time with them outside class.

Mary reported constant worry about her children, health, and marriage; low mood, difficulty sleeping due to racing thoughts at night; accelerated heart rate at random times during the day; and feelings of restlessness. Her coping strategies for these symptoms include calling her children daily to

Continued

Continued

check in on them, researching medical diagnoses and divorce laws, taking Xanax whenever she feels anxious, watching Korean dramas, and doing yoga. She said that she "can't stand" her life, because she feels miserable, lonely, and anxious "all the time." Mary shared how frustrated she feels about her husband's lack of contribution around the house and her financial dependence on him, which makes her feel trapped in her marriage.

During the intake interview, Mary repeatedly commented that she "deserves to suffer," alluding to past behavior about which she feels ashamed, but did not explain further, even when prompted. She said that her beliefs about suffering were most likely engrained in her due to her Catholic upbringing, which continues to influence her perspectives. Mary also stated that she finds life to be meaningless but would never take action toward suicide as she is afraid of going to hell, despite currently identifying as atheist. She remarked that even though she does not like her current life, she is unwilling to make changes, because she is "getting what she deserves." Her reason for seeking therapy is to feel less anxious and decide if she should divorce her husband.

Step 2: Group Functionally Similar Variables

To whittle down the nodes, we can tidy up the preliminary pool of clinically relevant variables by grouping those that are functionally similar or likely to be driven and/or maintained by the same variables. Think about describing variables based on their function rather than form. Each node should be broad enough that it covers multiple instances of a pattern and is relevant to a range of situations, rather than tied to a specific context. So, instead of [avoids grocery stores], use [avoids crowded places]. Instead of [argues with spouse], use [argues when opinions are challenged]. If a node is too specific, it limits the scope of your intervention. For instance, if you only targeted avoidance of grocery stores, gains may not generalize to other crowded places. Similarly, if you only targeted relationship with a spouse, your client may continue to struggle with workplace interactions.

At the same time, you still need sufficient specificity, such that these nodes can be used as treatment targets. In the example of [avoids crowded places], that might lead you to use exposures focused on crowded spaces, so that's helpful. However, if we used an even broader category, such as [avoidance], we would not be able to use this node to identify a useful treatment target.

Same goes with [argues with others]—it becomes unclear which aspect of arguing needs to be addressed. Does the client need active listening skills, strategies to state their needs more directly, or something else?

As a general rule, if your node is defined so broadly that you have no idea where to start with an intervention (e.g., [avoidance], [argues with others]), you need to be more specific. Conversely, if your node is defined so specifically that even if you changed it and/or the arrows connected to it, your client's well-being would not significantly improve (e.g., [avoids grocery stores on Mondays], [argues with spouse about scheduling childcare]), you need to identify the broader underlying function or pattern. In short, you're looking for a Goldilocks node. Defining nodes functionally is important because it simplifies any resulting network while focusing on overarching processes that affect symptoms causing distress and functional impairment. In other words, it achieves clinical parsimony: the "right" network is the one that explains the same phenomenon with the fewest elements.

Returning to our case example, Mary engages in behaviors whose underlying function is anxiety regulation: calling her children daily to check in on them, researching medical diagnoses and divorce laws, taking Xanax, watching Korean dramas, and doing yoga. The reassurance seeking and distraction could be grouped together in an [emotion regulation strategies] node. Similarly, Mary reported two negative affect variables: low mood and miserable. These may also be grouped together as [low mood]. For now, we're going with this simplistic clustering, but as we learn more about Mary that may change. For instance, low mood and miserable might be experienced qualitatively differently by Mary and warrant their own nodes.

Table 5.1 shows our initial grouping of clinically relevant variables. You may choose to group them differently, and that's OK. Remember, these are hypotheses to be held lightly and that await verification with more data.

After this categorization, we are left with 16 possible nodes (listed below). At this stage, we have also noted the EEMM dimensions each node maps on to (see Chapter 2 for an explanation of these terms). Knowing the EEMM dimensions gives us a sense of the scope the nodes cover.

1. 63-year-old (Culture/Self)
2. White (Culture/Self)
3. Ciswoman (Culture/Self)
4. Retired (Culture/Relationships)
5. Lives with husband (Relationships)
6. Poor social support (Relationships)

Table 5.1 Grouping functionally similar variables.

Functionally Similar Variables	Category
Calling her children daily to check in on them Researching medical diagnoses and divorce laws Taking Xanax whenever she feels anxious Watching Korean dramas Doing yoga	Emotion regulation strategies
Low mood Miserable Lonely Does not like her current life	Low mood
Four children who live at least a four-hour drive away No close friends Frustrated with husband	Poor social support
Accelerated heartrate at random times Restlessness Anxious	Anxious symptoms
Worry about her children, health, and marriage Racing thoughts at night	Uncontrollable worry
Finds life meaningless Unwilling to make changes	Low motivation for change
Belief that she "deserves to suffer" Belief that she is "getting what she deserves" Shame over past behavior	Believes she "deserves to suffer"

7. Uncontrollable worry (Cognition/Attention)
8. Low mood (Affect)
9. Anxious symptoms (Affect/Biophysiology)
10. Difficulty sleeping (Biophysiology)
11. Emotion regulation strategies (Behavior/Affect)
12. Financial dependence on husband (Relationships)
13. Believes she "deserves to suffer" (Self/Cognition)
14. Low motivation for change (Motivation)
15. Catholic upbringing (Culture)
16. Atheist (Culture/Self)

Step 3: Narrow Down to 5–10 Clinically Relevant Variables

From these 16 nodes, we want to identify the 5–10 most relevant nodes. There's nothing magical about this number. We derived this range based on doing networks with our clients and learning which ones were most helpful for succinctly describing clients' problems, while still providing adequate information to formulate a relatively comprehensive treatment plan. You may deviate from this range, depending on what works for you, which will become clearer as you build more networks—like how you might learn to tweak a recipe. For now, we recommend sticking to the 5–10 range if you are new to network building.

Step 3 may be one of the trickiest steps in developing a network, because it's difficult to be *certain* that you're including the most helpful variables and excluding the least relevant variables. The good news is, you don't have to be sure—you can add or remove variables as you learn more about your client. In fact, you will likely be revising your network several times over the course of treatment.

What matters more for network building is that you're making informed hypotheses about what your clients are struggling with, verifying them with your clients, and presenting a coherent enough picture to begin identifying viable treatment targets. If you do this step with your clients, having them think through which aspects of their struggles are most salient can itself be an informative thought exercise.

An easy starting point for this process is the desired end point or Mary's treatment goals: feeling less anxious and deciding whether to divorce her husband. Having this direction can be helpful for anchoring your network conceptualization and ensuring it's sensitive to Mary's needs. Now, we can concentrate more on variables associated with these two goals, which leaves us with 12 variables:

1. Retired (Culture/Relationships)
2. Lives with husband (Relationships)
3. Poor social support (Relationships)
4. Uncontrollable worry (Cognition/Attention)
5. Low mood (Affect)
6. Anxious symptoms (Affect/Biophysiology)
7. Difficulty sleeping (Biophysiology)
8. Emotion regulation strategies (Behavior/Affect)
9. Financial dependence on husband (Relationships)
10. Believes she "deserves to suffer" (Self/Cognition)
11. Low motivation for change (Motivation)
12. Catholic upbringing (Culture)

We excluded variables related to age, ethnicity, gender, and current religious affiliation, given that they do not appear to be *directly* relevant to her treatment goals. Remember, we are looking for the most obvious connections to keep things simple. Avoid overthinking, which can lead to more indirect paths in your network, making it convoluted. For instance, it is possible that being an older ciswoman living in a patriarchal society, Mary has internalized sexist and ageist beliefs about women's need for partnership, especially later in life, which might dissuade her from choosing to divorce her husband. However, based on the data we have thus far, Mary's decision seems to be more directly impacted by her concerns about her financial stability, Catholic upbringing, and beliefs about deserving to suffer in her marriage.

For your initial network, go for the obvious answers. In later sessions, we may discover that her "older ciswoman" identity in fact plays an important role, and we can update the network then. Anyway, in real life, we would be regularly verifying these hypotheses with Mary. So ideally, Mary would give us feedback if the network is missing something crucial.

We included factors likely *correlated* with her demographic identities but more clearly linked to her goals: retired status, poor social support, and lack of financial independence. In addition, we included her Catholic upbringing, even though she does not currently identify as religious, because this historical factor may still be affecting her behaviors (e.g., protective factor against suicide) and influencing her views on divorce.

In Table 5.2, we listed factors we think are most obviously associated with each of Mary's treatment goals.

You may disagree with our set of 12 variables, and that's expected. You have your own learning history and theoretical orientation that differ from ours, so you probably have an alternative interpretation. As long as your identified nodes are aligned with data provided by Mary, are supported by a theoretically coherent rationale, are linked to her treatment goals, and reflect the simplest reasonable explanation, go with what makes sense to you.

After relevance to treatment goals, we'll consider another aspect of workability: which nodes will be most helpful for meeting those treatment goals and improving well-being? For example, they can be intervened upon (malleable) or have the strongest impact on well-being and functioning. Based on this, we generally want to limit the number of unchangeable or impotent variables, though it is still important to take context into account because it informs treatment planning.

Overall, a network must contain some or mostly manipulable antecedents, so that it has treatment utility. If all identified antecedents

Table 5.2 Clinically relevant variables related to Mary's treatment goals.

Anxiety	Decision to Divorce
Uncontrollable worry (Cognition/Attention)	Retired (Culture/Relationships)
Low mood (Affect)	Lives with husband (Relationships)
Anxious symptoms (Affect/Biophysiology)	Poor social support (Relationships)
Difficulty sleeping (Biophysiology)	Financial dependence on husband (Relationships)
Emotion regulation strategies (Behavior/Affect)	Catholic upbringing (Culture)
Believes she "deserves to suffer" (Self/Cognition)	*Believes she "deserves to suffer" (Self/Cognition)*
Low motivation for change (Motivation)	*Low motivation for change (Motivation)*

Note: Variables in italics are hypothesized to be related to both treatment goals.

are unchangeable (e.g., past events), our network will only explain how the client arrived at their present position but will not indicate how to intervene in the present. Similarly, if variables are changeable in theory but not through therapy, they are also rendered less helpful in treatment planning. For example, Mary could in theory come out of retirement or attain financial independence from her husband, but primarily focusing on these variables in the network won't translate to effective treatment. On the other hand, [poor social support] is easier to impact because it can be altered through interpersonal exposures, social activity scheduling, or social skills training.

Based on the vignette, we also differentiated between more and less impactful variables on well being and functioning (see Table 5.3). Mary's main complaints center around worry, anxious symptoms, and low mood, so they seem particularly impactful. In addition, she spends significant time on emotion regulation strategies and repeatedly echoed beliefs about deserving to suffer in her intake interview. Because low motivation for change appears to be keeping her stuck, we classified that as relatively more impactful. In contrast, Mary did not emphasize [difficulty sleeping] or [poor social support], so even though these are likely to impact her network, we considered them less impactful.

With respect to difficult-to-change variables, financial dependence on her husband and her Catholic upbringing seem most impactful on Mary's well-being, because Mary explicitly said that the former makes her feel like she cannot leave her husband, whereas her Catholic upbringing may inform her views on divorce—it appears to shape her views on other issues, like suicide—and are related to her beliefs around suffering. Conversely, being retired may exacerbate the problem of financial dependence but is not the crux (e.g., if she was retired and financially independent, being retired would not be an issue). Similarly, living with her husband may contribute to more frustration in her life but does not directly affect her divorce decision.

Now we'll exclude the variables that are more difficult to change and less impactful on well-being (bottom right cell of Table 5.3), leaving us with 10 variables:

1. Uncontrollable worry (Cognition/Attention)
2. Low mood (Affect)
3. Anxious symptoms (Affect/Biophysiology)
4. Emotion regulation strategies (Behavior/Affect)
5. Believes she "deserves to suffer" (Self/Cognition)
6. Low motivation for change (Motivation)
7. Difficulty sleeping (Biophysiology)

Table 5.3 2×2 grid considering impact and malleability of potential treatment targets.

	Easier to Change	More Difficult to Change
More Impactful	Uncontrollable worry (Cognition/Attention) Low mood (Affect) Anxious symptoms (Affect/Biophysiology) Emotion regulation strategies (Behavior/Affect) Believes she "deserves to suffer" (Self/Cognition) Low motivation for change (Motivation)	Financial dependence on husband (Relationships) Catholic upbringing (Culture)
Less Impactful	Difficulty sleeping (Biophysiology) Poor social support (Relationships)	Retired (Culture/Relationships) Lives with husband (Relationships)

8. Poor social support (Relationships)
9. Financial dependence on husband (Relationships)
10. Catholic upbringing (Culture)

We could probably prune this list further. However, we've already determined that these variables are more relevant than the excluded ones and we are within the 5–10 limit, so we'll stop here. Typically, trying to optimize your selection at this stage hinders network building, making it difficult to move on to the crucial step of connecting the nodes.

Step 4: Check for Comprehensiveness

After reducing the nodes, we still want to make sure we're considering the range of EEMM dimensions and levels, so we'll briefly check our final set of nodes against the EEMM (see Table 5.4). Notice that we've counted [uncontrollable worry] as cognitive and attentional, because we could either target the content of the worry (Cognition) or the amount of focus Mary gives to the worry (Attention). The same goes for other double-counted nodes. In this case, we have covered all the dimensions and levels. Your network does not have to cover every dimension and level, as long as you have considered each of them with respect to your clients' goals.

Table 5.4 Review of Mary's clinically relevant problems against EEMM dimensions and levels.

Dimensions	Affect/Emotion	Low mood Anxious symptoms Emotion regulation strategies
	Cognition	Uncontrollable worry Believes she "deserves to suffer"
	Attention	Uncontrollable worry
	Self	Believes she "deserves to suffer"
	Motivation	Low motivation for change
	Overt Behavior	Emotion regulation strategies
Levels	Biology/Physiology	Anxious symptoms Difficulty sleeping
	Relationships	Poor social support Financial dependence on husband
	Culture	Catholic upbringing

Remember, that a network should be as simple as possible and as complex as necessary to meet your clients' goals. A network won't represent your clients' full story, and it never will—even a 24-hour biopic can't accomplish that. Thankfully, it doesn't need to. Its job is to aid treatment planning so that the intervention delivered improves your clients' well-being. Ultimately, a network should be clear—even if at the expense of being comprehensive—rather than overwhelming.

Step 5: Convert Variables to Visual Nodes

To build a network, we first need to convert the nodes into their visual form. There are three points to note when drawing your nodes:

1. Use rounded rectangles or ovals for unchangeable moderators or contextual variables that provide the backdrop for Mary's struggles, such as (Catholic upbringing) and (financial dependence on husband); right-angled corners represent malleable nodes (see Figure 5.3). Tip: Ovals tend to make the distinction clearer, especially if you're mapping the network by hand with your clients.

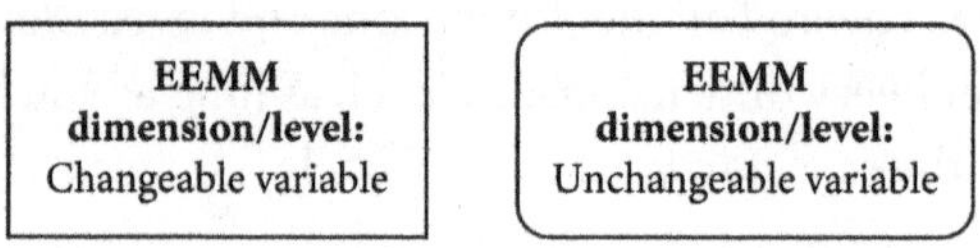

Figure 5.3 Examples of how to depict changeable and unchangeable nodes.

2. Label the dimension or level associated with each variable in bold (or uppercase letters if you're doing this by hand).
3. Optional: If there are variables you believe to be particularly severe in the network in terms of distress and impairment, enlarge those boxes as a visual reminder of those higher levels of intensity. This can be helpful for guiding where to focus attention in treatment. In Mary's case, anxious symptoms, worry, low motivation, belief that she deserves to suffer, and use of emotion regulation strategies appear to be especially prominent, so we have made them bigger in Figure 5.4.

Following these steps produces the nodes in Figure 5.4. Network drawing templates can be found in Appendix E. The templates each contain a legend to help you remember what the various node shapes and arrowheads mean. In Figure 5.4, we made the size of each node correspond to its severity to show one way you can account for severity in a network. For example, we can quickly glean that [believes "I deserve to suffer"] and [uses emotion regulation strategies] are key players in Mary's presenting problem and may be worth paying extra attention to. However, trying to incorporate too much information in your network risks making it less interpretable, so use your judgment as to how intense you want your network to be.

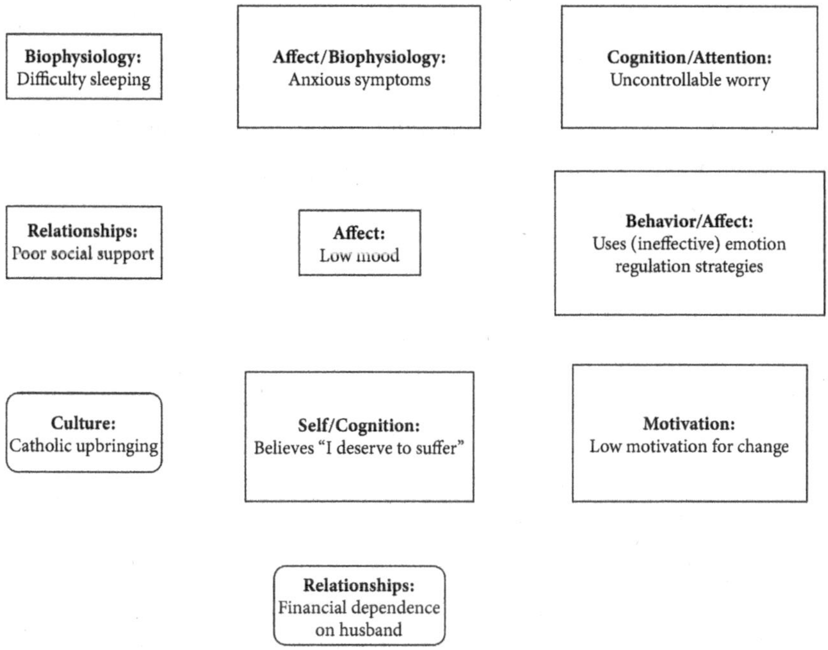

Figure 5.4 Nodes in Mary's network.

Step 6: Connect the Nodes

Now that you have all the pieces, you (and your clients) can start to arrange them into a coherent story. The size of the arrowhead corresponds to strength of the relationship and opacity corresponds to the direction of the effect (solid for increase, blank or open for decrease; see Figure 5.5).

If you want to designate *immediate* effects, such as how procrastination decreases anxiety in the short term, try using dashed lines instead of solid lines (see Figure 5.5). Networks typically focus on relationships over time to illustrate overall stuck patterns, so solid arrows represent longer-term effects by default. However, depicting immediate consequences (e.g., negative reinforcement of avoidance) can be helpful for us and our clients to understand why they continue to do what they do, even when it doesn't seem to be benefiting them in the long run.

Moreover, two nodes may have different relationships with each other, depending on the timescale (e.g., avoidance decreases anxiety immediately but likely feeds anxiety over time), so having a way to differentiate timescales is helpful. Dashed arrows are most useful when these immediate effects are crucial to your case conceptualization (e.g., substance use). However, they can complicate a network without providing much utility when used recklessly. We won't be using the dashed arrows for Mary's network to keep the steps as straightforward as possible, but you'll see them in Chapter 8, in the case of Ruby.

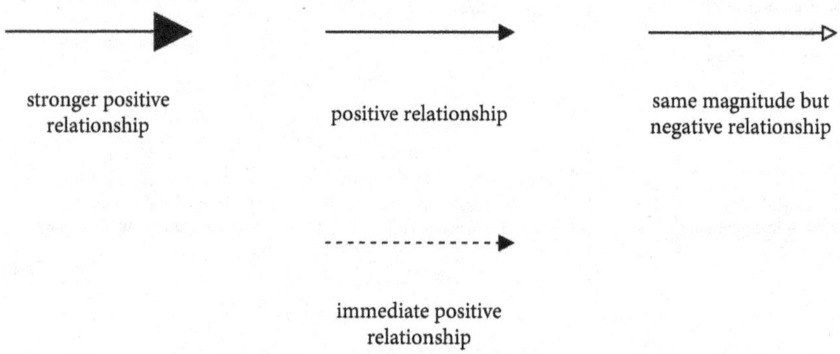

Figure 5.5 How to interpret arrows in a network.

Note: Other arrows are in reference to the top center arrow for positive relationship.

When connecting nodes, focus on one node at a time, identifying all arrows emanating from each node. It doesn't matter too much which node you start with, given that you'll be reviewing each one in turn, but we've found that it's usually easiest to start with the variable that you or your clients perceive to be the primary driving force of their problems or what is keeping them stuck. For Mary, this would be either [believes "I deserve to suffer"] or [low motivation for change], so we could select either one to begin.

Then, continue with the nodes that are connected to the original starting node. Again, the order does not matter too much. This helps to keep the network visually organized and minimizes arrows crossing, which can make the network difficult to interpret. As you connect the nodes, remember to go for obvious links. Given how our minds work, we can probably find a way to link any node to any other node and provide a compelling justification.

However, for networks, follow the law of parsimony and only include arrows that require the fewest assumptions.

Once you've connected all the nodes, check if you have any right-angled rectangles that *don't* have any arrows going into them. This means you may be missing a driving factor for that node (the antecedent in the antecedent–response–consequence chain). See if you can identify possible antecedents for it. A node without antecedents doesn't provide a lot of information on how it can be changed, so it's less useful. It also likely wouldn't be a problem if there was nothing continuing to keep it active, so there must be something driving it. Rounded rectangles will almost always only have arrows going out of them, because they're by definition unchangeable. The occasional instances when arrows go into rounded rectangles are when we know something else in the network is meaningfully influencing the unchangeable variable. For instance, if Mary engaged in compulsive buying, that may exacerbate [financial dependence on husband], even though she would still be dependent on her husband without the compulsive buying.

In the following pages, we show how we built Mary's network one step at a time. As recommended in *Learning PBT* (Hofmann et al., 2021), we used the draw.io program, which is freely available as a browser interface at https://app.diagrams.net/ or for download at https://github.com/jgraph/drawio. However, you can draw your network by hand or use different software. Before proceeding to the next page, try connecting the nodes in Figure 5.4, then compare your network to ours.

1. **[believes "I deserve to suffer"]:** We'll start with [believes "I deserve to suffer"], as it appears to be a central part of Mary's struggles (see Figure 5.6). We hypothesized that this self-belief would lead to low motivation to change, as Mary explicitly attributed her unwillingness to change to these beliefs. In addition, although not stated by Mary, it seems reasonable to assume that this self-punitive stance would contribute to low mood and misery.

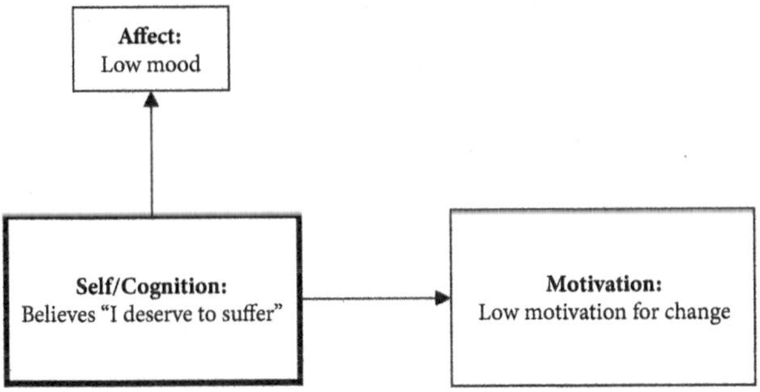

Figure 5.6 Step 1 in Mary's network building.

2. **[low motivation for change]:** We hypothesized that [low motivation for change] would reinforce Mary's beliefs about deserving to suffer (bidirectional arrow) and contribute to her low mood (see Figure 5.7). In addition, her unwillingness to change may lead her to use the same coping strategies again and again.

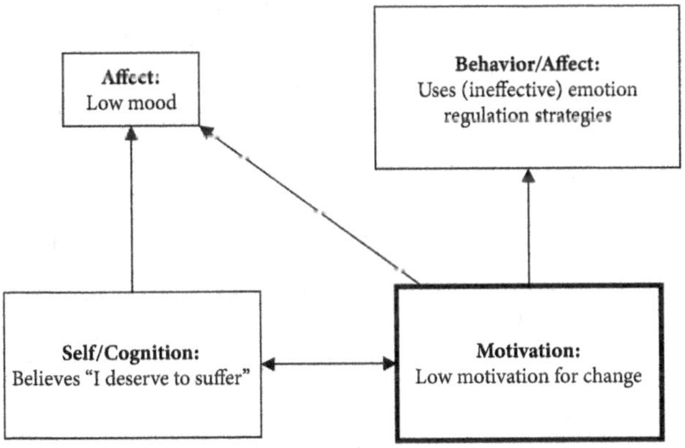

Figure 5.7 Step 2 in Mary's network building.

3. **[low mood]:** We added an arrow back to [low motivation for change] (second bidirectional arrow), as low mood generally depresses motivation (see Figure 5.8). In addition, Mary reported using emotion regulation strategies in response to negative affect, so we included an arrow going from [low mood] to [uses (ineffective) emotion regulation strategies].

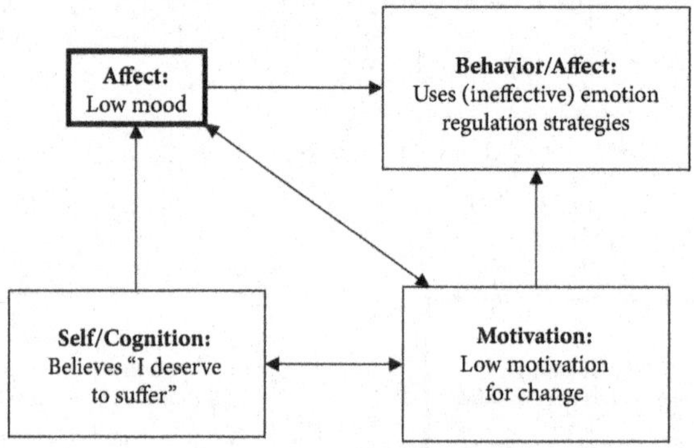

Figure 5.8 Step 3 in Mary's network building.

4. **[uses (ineffective) emotion regulation strategies]:** We hypothesized that using ineffective emotion regulation strategies would exacerbate Mary's symptoms over time, even if they provide immediate relief, given that Mary continues to experience low mood, anxiety, and worry, despite frequently engaging in reassurance seeking and distraction. Thus, we added arrows from [uses (ineffective) emotion regulation strategies] to [low mood], [anxious symptoms], and [uncontrollable worry] (see Figure 5.9). Although there is no strict rule on what timescale to use in these networks, because we're looking for patterns that impact Mary's *long-term* well-being, we'll focus on longer-term relationships, such as how using ineffective emotion regulation strategies is likely to exacerbate symptoms in the long run.
5. **[anxious symptoms]:** Similar to [low mood], [anxious symptoms] likely prompt Mary to use emotion regulation strategies, so we added an arrow from [anxious symptoms] to [uses (ineffective) emotion regulation strategies] (see Figure 5.10). In addition, [anxious symptoms] likely contribute to [low mood] and [uncontrollable worry], especially since Mary reported worrying about her health. We also know that some of these physiological symptoms make it difficult for Mary to fall asleep, so we'll link [anxious symptoms] to [difficulty sleeping].

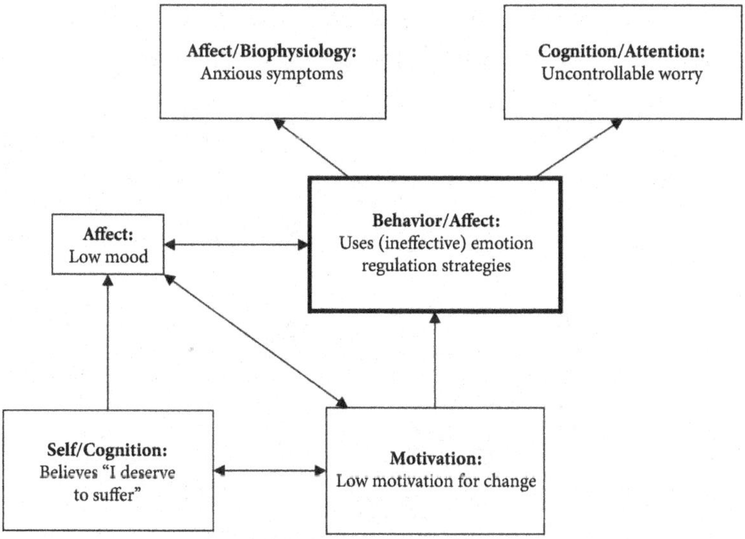

Figure 5.9 Step 4 in Mary's network building.

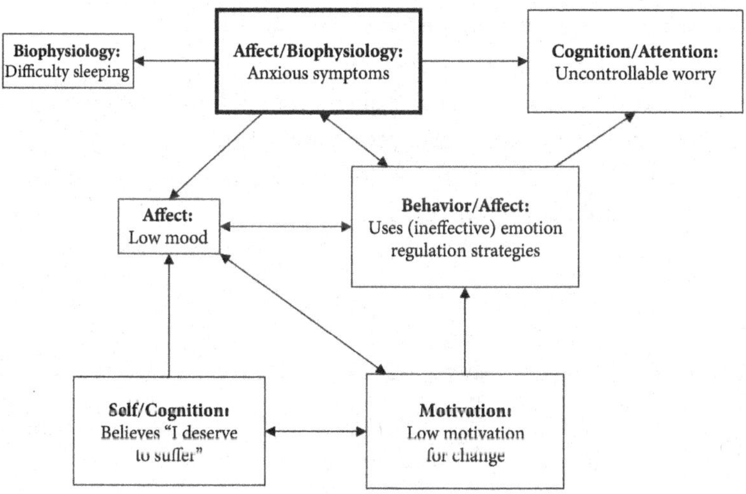

Figure 5.10 Step 5 in Mary's network building.

6. **[uncontrollable worry]:** Because worry likely increases anxiety, we added an arrow from [uncontrollable worry] to [anxious symptoms] (see Figure 5.11). In addition, given that Mary is kept awake by "racing thoughts," we directed an arrow from [uncontrollable worry] to [difficulty sleeping]. Finally, we hypothesized that Mary uses

emotion regulation strategies to manage worry, so we added an arrow from [uncontrollable worry] to [uses emotion regulation strategies].

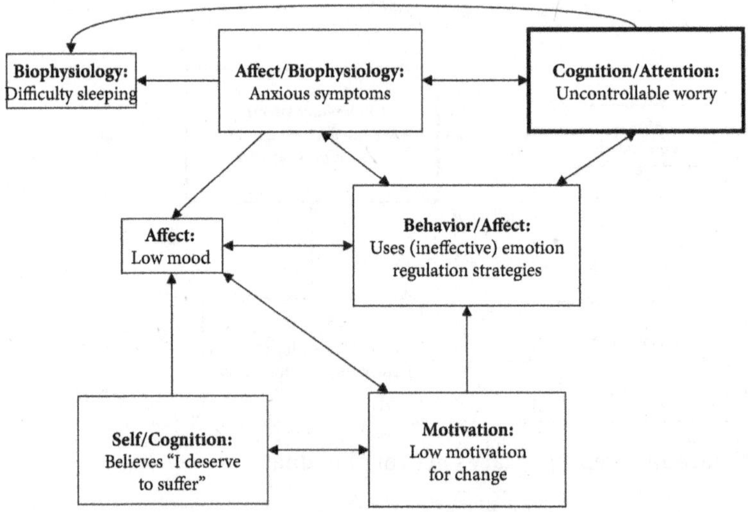

Figure 5.11 Step 6 in Mary's network building.

7. **[difficulty sleeping]:** Even though Mary did not directly report this, poor sleep tends to impact mood and anxiety, so we hypothesized that [difficulty sleeping] would increase [anxious symptoms] and [low mood] (see Figure 5.12).

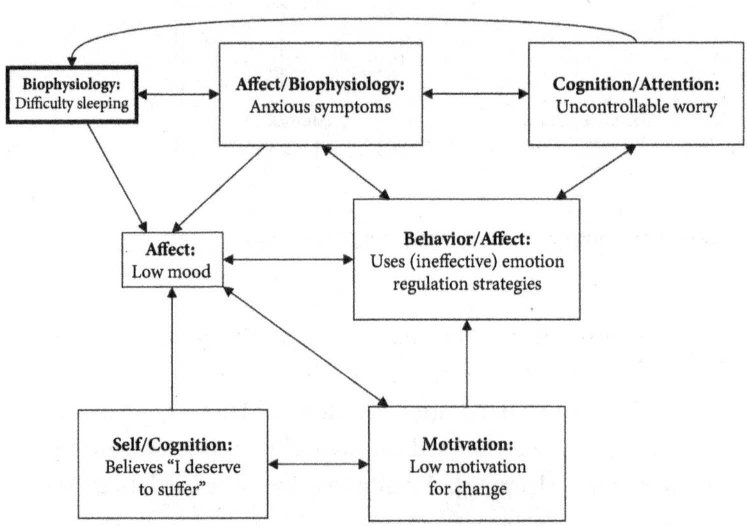

Figure 5.12 Step 7 in Mary's network building.

8. **(Catholic upbringing):** Per Mary's report, her Catholic upbringing shaped her beliefs about deserving to suffer, so we included an arrow to [believes "I deserve to suffer"] (see Figure 5.13). We did not discern any other obvious relationships between her Catholic upbringing and other variables.

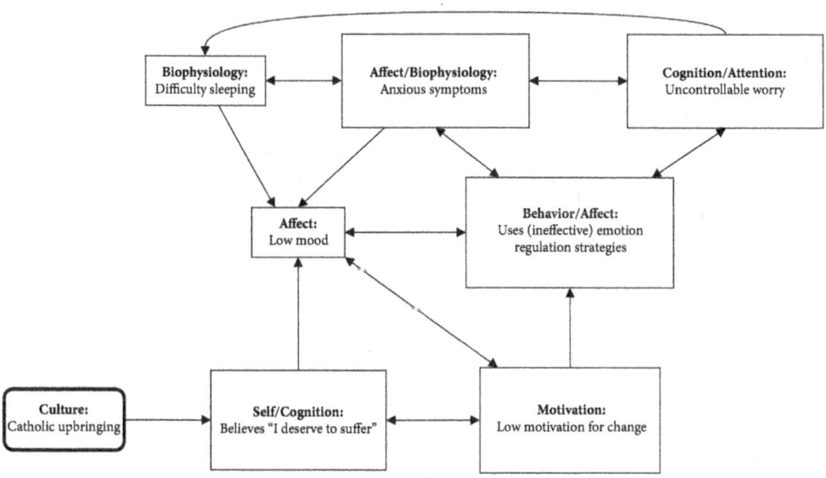

Figure 5.13 Step 8 in Mary's network building.

9. **(financial dependence on husband):** Mary's financial dependence on her husband makes her feel stuck and unable to change, so we added an arrow to [low motivation for change] (see Figure 5.14). Her lack of financial independence and self-efficacy in this domain may also reinforce beliefs that she deserves to stay in her current unhappy situation, so we added an arrow to [believes "I deserve to suffer"]. Furthermore, it's plausible that the potential of financial instability contributes to [uncontrollable worry], given that one of her main worry topics is her marriage.
10. **[poor social support]:** Mary's lack of strong social connections seems to most directly impact her low mood, especially loneliness, so we added an arrow from [poor social support] to [low mood] (see Figure 5.15). In addition, given that one of her main worry topics is her children, we hypothesized that lack of social support from her children increases her [uncontrollable worry]. Notice that we avoided overlapping arrows in our diagram to make it easier to follow the many hypothesized relationships, but this is not always feasible, as you will see in step 7.

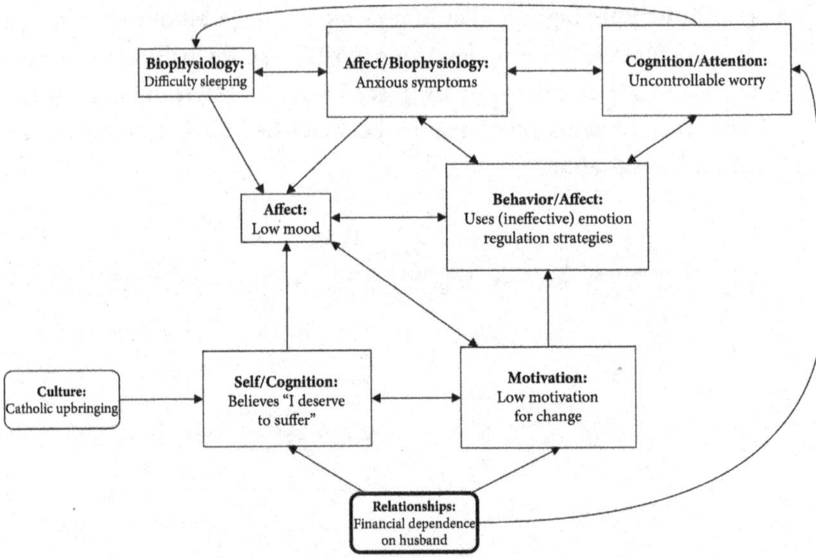

Figure 5.14 Step 9 in Mary's network building.

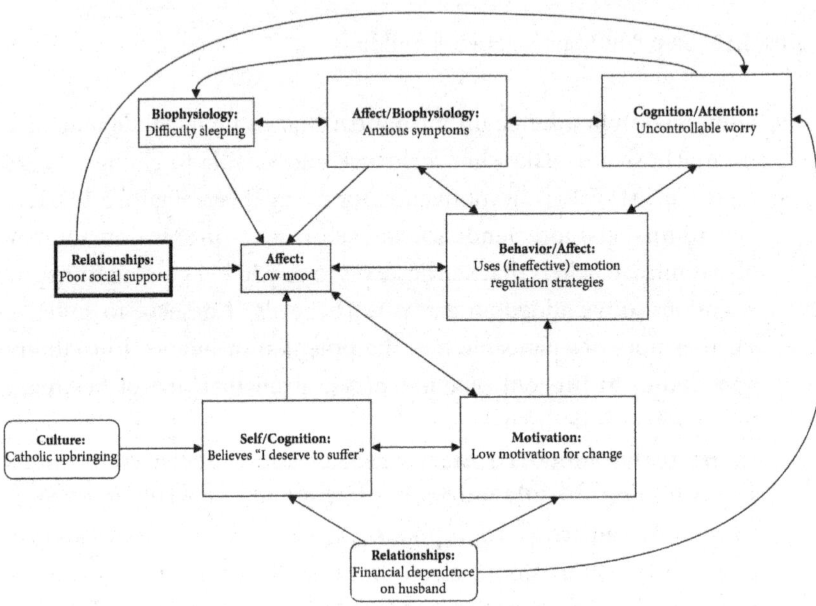

Figure 5.15 Step 10 in Mary's network building.

Step 7: Check for Missing Arrows

Next, we want to see if there are any right-angled rectangles without arrows going into them. Typically, this means we're missing antecedents. Rounded rectangles are context variables that are difficult or impossible to change, so they don't always need to have arrows going into them.

It looks like [poor social support] is the only malleable node missing incoming arrows. So, let's consider which nodes are likely to contribute to social disconnection or isolation. We might reasonably hypothesize that believing she deserves to suffer and low motivation to do things differently discourage Mary from seeking support or meaningful connections with others, so we'll add those two arrows (see Figure 5.16).

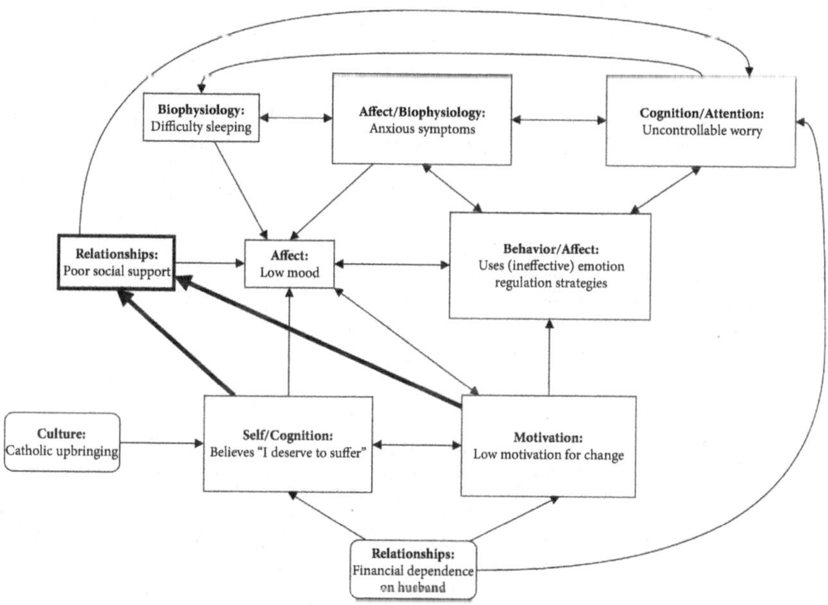

Figure 5.16 Addition of missing arrows (bolded) going toward [poor social support].

Step 8: Adjust Arrowhead Size

Next, we adjust the arrowhead sizes. Remember that the arrowhead represents the strength of the relationship between variables. A bigger arrowhead means that variable X has a stronger influence on variable Y, whereas a smaller arrowhead means that X has a weaker influence on variable Y. For the sake of simplicity, we'll stick to small, medium, and large arrowheads—sometimes, even just small and large arrowheads are adequate. Be careful not to miss the forest for the trees; if you get too bogged down by arrowhead sizes, you'll quickly lose sight of the point of your network in the first place.

Returning to Mary's vignette, we know that her emotion regulation strategies are strongly affected by her symptoms, so we would emphasize those relationships (see Figure 5.17). We also know that her sleep is significantly impacted by her anxious symptoms and worry, and that her belief that she is "getting what she deserves" has an especially strong influence on motivation, so we'll increase the size of those arrowheads as well.

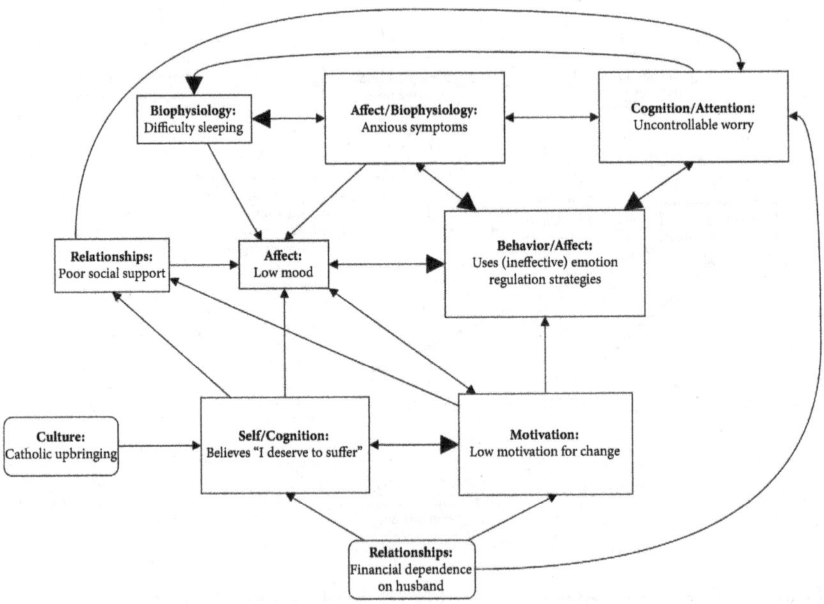

Figure 5.17 Adjusting the size of arrowheads in Mary's network.

With this preliminary network, we are getting a more nuanced picture of Mary's problems. We see that her life is dominated by anxiety, worry, and the belief that she deserves to suffer (based on outgoing arrows and size of nodes), which are in part maintained by continued use of unhelpful coping strategies, having few social connections, and financial dependence on her husband.

Interpreting a Network

To use a network for treatment planning, we need to be able to efficiently parse its contents and extract clinically relevant information. Otherwise, it's just a mess of boxes and arrows. The quickest way to do this is to identify networks within the network—*subnetworks*—that are self-perpetuating. This means there is a positive feedback loop that can continue indefinitely without any external input, such that the subnetwork is self-contained and self-sustaining. Typically, these subnetworks contain 3–5 variables and can be understood as a functional analysis of one aspect of your clients' problems. We identified two main subnetworks in Mary's network.

Subnetwork 1: Cycle of Ineffective Emotion Regulation Strategies

The first subnetwork describes the mutually reinforcing effect between Mary's use of ineffective emotion regulation strategies and her psychological symptoms, such as anxiety and worry (see grey boxes in Figure 5.18). For instance, the more she worries, the more she uses unhelpful strategies, which in turn increases her worry over time. In addition, we see that sleep difficulties are both an antecedent and consequence of some of these symptoms, such that the less sleep she gets, the worse her symptoms are, which makes it more difficult for her to get the sleep she needs.

Subnetwork 2: Self-Fulfilling Prophecy of Suffering

The second subnetwork concerns Mary's perceived stuckness. Her belief that she deserves to suffer leads her to feel miserable and unmotivated to change, both of which feed each other. In turn, the less Mary is motivated to change, the more her low mood worsens and the more her belief that she "deserves to suffer" is reinforced—restarting the positive feedback loop (see Figure 5.19).

These subnetworks get special attention because they are the *engines* of the overall network, keeping it stable over time. They summarize Mary's primary sources of suffering and tell us how her problems are maintained. If we want to disrupt—*perturbate* in technical terms—Mary's network, we'll need to destabilize at least one of these subnetworks. In other words, these subnetworks bring our attention to which variables may be most useful to target in treatment.

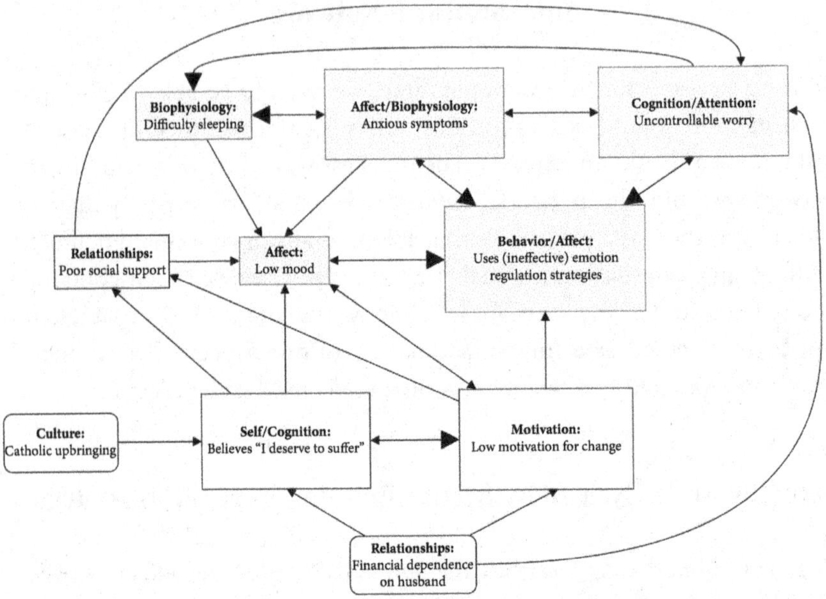

Figure 5.18 First subnetwork in Mary's network, highlighted grey.

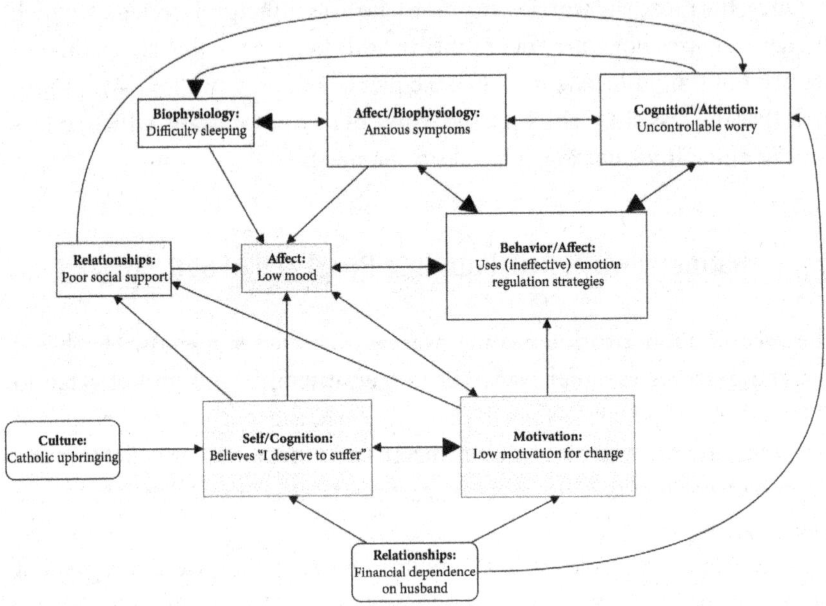

Figure 5.19 Second subnetwork in Mary's network, highlighted grey.

Verifying Network with Clients

If you do not complete the network with your clients, present it to them at this point to get their feedback. Because networks are not always immediately intuitive, it can be helpful to first walk your clients through the network and explain the notations used, especially highlighting cyclical subnetworks. Indeed, we've found that seeing the network only in its completed form—as opposed to piecing the nodes together step by step—can be daunting.

As you go over the network with your clients, ask them if it's missing any arrows, if there are arrows that shouldn't be there, which arrowheads should be bigger or smaller, and so on. Clients with some insight into their struggles usually provide helpful responses to these questions, and you can use their feedback to make further adjustments to the network. Ideally, the resulting network should resonate with your clients and help them see the links among their problems more clearly. That is, your clients should recognize themselves in the network.

In Mary's case, she might tell us that her anxiety and low mood exacerbate each other and that her use of emotion regulation strategies decreases her motivation to change because of the short-term relief they provide. With this new information, we can add two more arrows to her network (see bolded arrows in Figure 5.20): (1) [low mood] → [anxious symptoms] and (2) [uses emotion regulation strategies] → [low motivation].

This information confirms the crucial role of the two subnetworks identified in Figures 5.18 and 5.19, as it indicates that these subnetworks are even more entrenched than we had hypothesized. Generally, the more bidirectional arrows, the more stuck a problem is.

"Finalizing" the Network

This last step is about zooming out and checking to see if your network is serving its purpose: to visually depict your case formulation and inform treatment planning by clarifying driving and maintaining factors associated with your clients' problems. We use "finalize" in quotes because the network comprises multiple hypotheses that are constantly being tested. As such, hold it lightly. Here, "finalize" means using your network as a jumping off point for treatment planning.

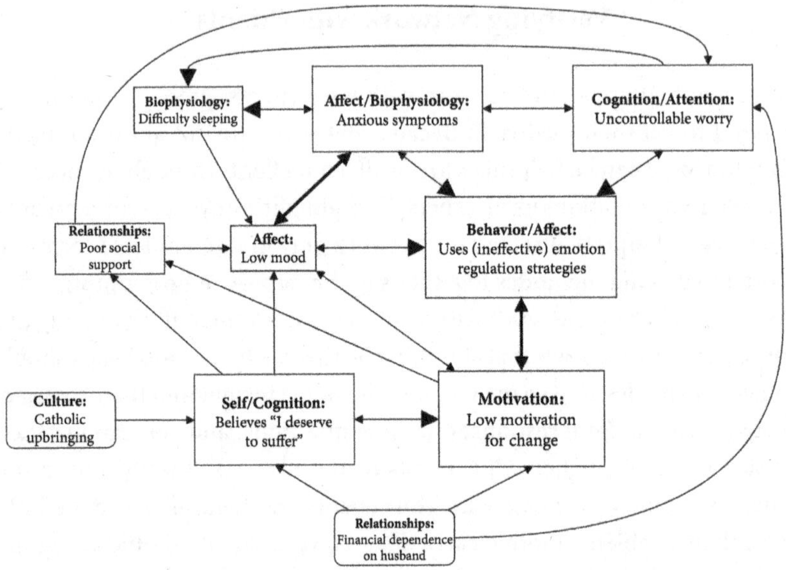

Figure 5.20 Addition of missing arrows (bolded), per Mary's feedback.

Ask yourself the following questions:

1. Would someone who doesn't know my client be able to grasp my client's primary presenting concern based on the network?

For Mary's network, you be the judge. We think her "final" network does a good job showcasing her two core struggles and how they interact with each other, particularly via [low mood] and [uses (ineffective) emotion regulation strategies], but we're biased because we came up with the network.

2. Can I/my client identify treatment targets from the network?

Returning to the subnetworks, we can easily identify multiple treatment targets implicated in the self-perpetuating cycles, including [uses (ineffective) emotion regulation strategies], [believes "I deserve to suffer"], [anxious symptoms], and the relationships among them. We will discuss exactly how to select among many potential treatment targets in Chapter 6.

3. Can I/my client identify why they are stuck from the network?

In addition to the subnetworks, reasons Mary is stuck may have to do with immutable contextual factors: (Catholic upbringing) and (financial dependence on husband) constantly provide fresh energy activating the rest of her network, especially via her core beliefs about suffering and low motivation. Thus, even if Mary learns effective emotion regulation strategies or improves her sleep hygiene, her core beliefs and low motivation will likely persist. Unless these contextual variables change—which as we have discussed, is unlikely or impossible—or more likely how she responds to them changes, the network will continue operating as usual.

Collaboration with Clients

As you develop your network conceptualization, be as collaborative as possible with your clients, unless clinically contraindicated. Including your clients in network building gives you access to firsthand information from them and empowers them to play an active role in their treatment. So, invite your clients to provide their own interpretation of events and check in with them frequently about how you are conceptualizing their struggles. As you do so, bear in mind your goals as a therapist and your clients' treatment goals and evaluate how effective collaboration is against these goals. Possible therapist goals include

- Increasing client buy-in
- Providing person-centered care
- Verifying your understanding of clients' problems
- Encouraging client autonomy
- Empowering your clients to participate in their own care

There are several ways to collaborate on network conceptualization. You could build the network together with your clients on a whiteboard, drawing nodes and arrows as your clients tell you about their problems. You could draft a network after the intake, then bring it to your clients and get their feedback. You could even have clients develop their own network and then compare it with yours. Most commonly, we've found it helpful to first list relevant nodes in consultation with your clients *before* trying to connect them, rather than try to connect nodes while identifying them at the same time.

When introducing networks to our clients, we say something similar to the content presented in Box 5.3.

Box 5.3 Example spiel when introducing networks to clients.

You've shared what you're struggling with and what you want to work on, which is a great start. The next step is for us to understand how your problems are connected. Usually, our problems don't occur in isolation. There's a reason you feel so stuck. If it was just about [binge eating], you'd probably have figured something out by now. My guess is that [binge eating] is connected to other problems in your life, like a bug caught in a spiderweb. If we can't see the spiderweb, we would just ask the bug to fly away—which would be me telling you to just stop [binge eating]—and you know better than anyone that that doesn't work. But, if we can see the whole spiderweb and learn skills to dismantle it, we'll have a better chance of getting you unstuck.

For example, you said that you tend to [binge eat] whenever you feel [stressed]. If that's the case, then we would want to learn ways to cope with [stress] more effectively, rather than focus solely on [binge eating]. In fact, if [stress] is the main driver of [binge eating], then it's possible that we could reduce [binge eating] even without talking about it at all, at least in theory. What are your thoughts about that?

The caveat here is that, in our experience, collaborating on networks is most fruitful when your clients are psychologically minded and have insight into their struggles. For instance, sometimes clients are unaware of the negatively reinforcing function of behaviors like reassurance seeking and instead believe their behaviors are wholly driven by logic or values. Other times, the very problem clients are seeking treatment for interferes with network building, such as when a client who struggles with needing to do things exactly right insists on spending multiple sessions getting the network "right" before they're willing to begin treatment. In these cases, collaboration will likely end up being counterproductive at the outset. Withdrawing the network at this point may also hurt rapport.

Instead, in these cases, we recommend increasing collaboration on case conceptualization as your clients develop insight or skills to undermine treatment-incompatible behaviors. Alternatively, you could use their response as a teaching moment to show your clients how their network is being activated in that moment (e.g., "Notice how you want to make sure we're doing the network right, and we're getting stuck on whether we should use uppercase or lowercase letters. It looks like being stuck is making you feel frustrated. Does this pattern show up in other areas of your life?"). In general, use your clinical judgment and test the waters by briefly discussing relationships among your clients' problems to assess their level of insight and receptiveness.

Network Troubleshooting

Real life probably won't be as straightforward as the linear sequence we have laid out above. You and your clients may disagree on aspects of the network, you might struggle to define network variables with sufficient precision and breadth, your clients may insist on including 20 variables in their network, and so on. Broadly, these issues fall into two buckets: (1) technical/logistical limitations and (2) clinically relevant processes.

The first bucket has more to do with your level of familiarity with network building; developing this takes time. Learning any new skill typically involves at least three steps: watching someone do it, practicing it yourself, and getting feedback. Hopefully, this chapter is that first step, but there are still two steps to go. You'll need plenty of practice—again, we recommend making mini networks for a behavior you'd like to change. You also need feedback on the clinical utility of your network based on the degree to which it facilitated behavior change. In therapy, this feedback may come from your clients directly (e.g., "This network is missing an important link") or from how your clients progress in treatment. All this to say: the first bucket of challenges will decrease with practice and experience, but they are an unavoidable part of learning.

An especially common issue in the first bucket is creating overly complicated networks that make sense only to you. Based on our experience, there are two main reasons for this. One has to do with clinical skills—specifically, the ability to parse relevant information efficiently from a deluge of data. Keeping networks to a manageable size partly relies on the same skill that leads to intake reports getting shorter over the course of a therapist's career. With experience, therapists get better at knowing which information is more salient earlier on and more accepting of making changes later. We have observed that newer clinicians tend to include too many variables, perhaps because everything seems relevant or they fear making mistakes. However, making and learning from mistakes is part of growing as a therapist.

The second reason comes from a place of deeply caring for clients and wanting to ensure that they are seen as a whole person and not flattened into a placid case conceptualization. While we agree with the sentiment—and indeed, any case conceptualization should respect our clients' humanity—we are constrained by clinical utility. That is, the network conceptualization that fully represents our clients' personhood is unlikely to be the one that aids treatment planning. Instead, it might be more helpful to think about case conceptualization in phases, such that we are working on one piece of our clients' problems at a time, but the backdrop of each phase is the arc of their therapeutic journey—just like cleaning an elephant a body part at a time doesn't mean you're disregarding the elephant as a full animal. If you allow yourself to be shaped by feedback from your clients, you'll naturally learn what scope of a network is helpful for which clients, while maintaining your value of empathy for your clients.

The second bucket of challenges is harder to define, because the underlying issue can vary greatly. For example, if you and your clients disagree on aspects of the network, the issue could simply be a misunderstanding or miscommunication and your ability to be transparent and communicate effectively will resolve the problem. But if the disagreement is more entrenched and there's strong resistance, there might be a clinically relevant process going on. Perhaps the therapist is unwilling to be receptive to their client's feedback once they've formulated their hypotheses. We say process here because rigidly holding on to certain views could be a pattern for the therapist. It could be replicated across clients or even in other sessions with the same client. It's also possible that a client has an oppositional interaction style, and the disagreement is not about the network. If an argumentative pattern shows up in other parts of the client's life, it may be impacting their relationships and so could be relevant to therapy. There are multiple other explanations we could come up with, but the idea is that, sometimes, problems with the network are not about the network—just like fights about putting away the dishes are not always about putting away the dishes. Thus, in the face of network roadblocks, maintain a curious stance, be willing to self-reflect, and check in with your clients on how they're interpreting any misalignment.

Networks Across Therapeutic Approaches

In this chapter, we presented a more CBT-oriented network with respect to how we have defined which variables to include and how they relate to each other, such as identifying low mood and a core belief as primary drivers in Mary's network. However, a network is a tool, so therapists with other theoretical orientations might use networks differently. For instance, therapists who place a heavier emphasis on how formative developmental experiences impact current functioning may use more rounded rectangles to represent contextual factors. Conversely, therapists who are more concerned with interpersonal stressors may include more information on Mary's social environment in the network.

Regardless of theoretical orientation, step 4 in our network building sequence ensures that therapists are reviewing the EEMM to check that they have not neglected any crucial aspects of their client's presentation. Because a network is essentially a visual representation of multiple A → B relationships and is variable-agnostic (i.e., any clinically relevant variable can be included in a network), any clinician who thinks about their client in terms of interrelated variables (e.g., A → B → C → A) can readily fit network building into their case conceptualization.

The same goes for interpreting a network. Therapists can use the network to clarify the engines of their clients' struggles by identifying self-perpetuating subnetworks and use their theoretical orientation to guide treatment planning. The primary function of a network is to clarify and elucidate, but it is not prescriptive. A network may point to self-perpetuating subnetworks but whether they are included in the treatment plan is up to you and your clients. Thus, there is plenty of room for clinicians to exercise their clinical creativity once they have a clearer picture of how their clients' struggles are linked to each other—more on treatment planning in the next chapter.

Chapter Summary

- A network showing the relationships among your clients' problems can be a helpful tool for identifying treatment targets.

Continued

Continued

- Make sure your network is comprehensible and relevant to your clients' struggles and goals.
- When interpreting a network, look for self-sustaining subnetworks. These usually reflect core stuck areas for your clients.
- A network is a visual hypothesis, so hold it lightly. Use data to revise your network as needed.

6

Treatment Planning

This chapter covers the principles of process-based treatment planning. We also describe how treatment may vary depending on the therapist and their clients. As is true with the other principles we outline in the book, those underlying intervention planning may lead to different plans depending on context, even if the principles themselves are the same. We'll use a case example to illustrate this point. A treatment plan template summarizing the ideas discussed in this chapter can be found in Appendix F.

Admittedly, we pack a good amount of information in this chapter. It's difficult to illustrate the flexible and winding path of treatment planning with a neat linear narrative. Thus, to maximize learning from this chapter, we recommend extracting big-picture ideas the first time you go over it. Resist getting bogged down in details and attend to the overarching principles. When you have a grasp of these high-level ideas and have clients in mind whom you'd like to try them out with, return to this chapter and read the relevant sections again—this time, focus on how to apply the principles to your specific clients.

The Case of Hermine

Box 6.1 Case vignette for Hermine.

Hermine is a 34-year-old software engineer who was laid off from her job at a "big tech" company after working there for 5 years. She has been working for a start up company for the past 2 months. She identifies as cisfemale, Black American, and bisexual. She reported close relationships with her family whom she described as "high achieving": her mother is an attorney, her father is a professor, and her brother is a medical resident. Hermine

Continued

A Process-Based Approach to Psychotherapy. Clarissa W. Ong and Eric B. Lee, Oxford University Press.
 DOI: 10.1093/oso/9780197696378.003.0006

Continued

said that she constantly feels like she needs to prove herself because she didn't attend graduate school, unlike the rest of her family.

She recently ended a 7-year relationship after she found out that her ex-boyfriend had been sending explicit direct messages to other women on social media. Following the break-up, she has avoided their mutual friends and associated hobbies (e.g., board game nights, Ultimate frisbee), because she is concerned about running into her ex, even though she still wants to participate in these activities. To cope with loneliness and work stress, Hermine has been using marijuana daily, which has affected her concentration at work. Hermine received supportive counseling while she was in college and has had no other experience with therapy. Hermine's treatment goals are to re-engage in hobbies, reduce marijuana use, and learn more effective ways to cope with work stress.

Interpreting the Network

Based on the information in Box 6.1, we created a network for Hermine, as shown in Figure 6.1 (see Chapter 5 for steps for network building and how to interpret a network).

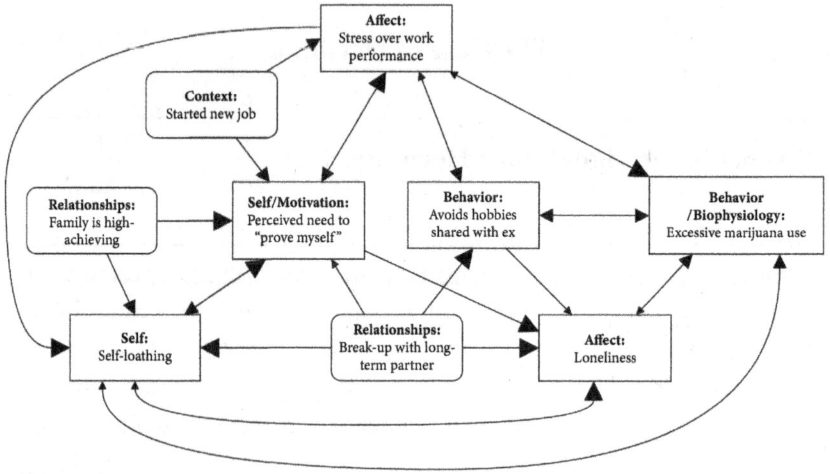

Figure 6.1 Hermine's network

The network in Figure 6.1 presents a fairly focused summary of Hermine's struggles based on her stated treatment goals. It illustrates the roots of her need for striving and self-loathing, as well as how her recent break-up feeds into these longer-term struggles. For example, we see that her family background, starting a new job, stress over performing well at her new job, self-loathing, and recent break-up bolster her perceived need to prove herself. In particular, the achievements of her family members and self-loathing are hypothesized to be major contributors.

In addition, the network shows how some of Hermine's problems are maintained. For instance, avoiding hobbies and using marijuana for emotion regulation exacerbate her work stress, which reinforces Hermine's need for striving. In turn, Hermine's need for striving increases the pressure she puts on herself to perform well at work. Yet, the more work stress she experiences, the more she relies on these unhelpful coping strategies, keeping her stuck in a problematic loop.

Broader cultural considerations may also inform her case conceptualization. For instance, software engineering in the U.S. is dominated by white men (Rangarajan, 2018). If Hermine is the one of the few Black people—let alone Black *women*—at her company, that may exacerbate her sense of loneliness and fuel her perceived need to prove that she belongs. Furthermore, the systemic discrimination of Black Americans in the U.S. and concomitant racist messaging about Black inferiority may contribute to Hermine's self-loathing (Wilkerson, 2020). At this point, these are hypotheses, as we do not know how much Hermine endorses these perceptions, and we will need more data from Hermine to verify them.

Identifying Treatment Targets

The Four Criteria

There are many "right" treatment targets, with varying levels of malleability and impact on well-being. What is considered "right" depends on the criteria you use to evaluate treatment utility. Are you looking for a target that is easiest to change? Or one most relevant to your clients' goals? Or one centrally implicated in the network? Regardless of what you choose to target, have a coherent rationale for your decision and tie it to your clients and their goals.

Our objective at this point is not to find the magic target that will transform Hermine's life in 10 sessions of therapy. In fact, it is unlikely that changing one node will significantly destabilize her network. Rather, the objective is to start getting Hermine unstuck from unhelpful patterns. Similar to building a network, you can identify treatment targets with as much client input as is helpful. Anecdotally, we have found that doing this step with clients increases buy-in and gives us useful insight into which areas they are most motivated to work on.

At the end of this exercise, we want 2–3 possible targets on which to base our treatment plan. With too many targets, treatment may become unfocused and confusing for clients (and the therapist). It would be like trying to teach a tennis novice the forehand, backhand, serve, volley, and smash in the first few lessons. Instead, trust that you'll eventually get to the targets you need to get to, which is why it's more helpful to ensure that your clients establish a solid foundation at the outset on which to build a strong and sustainable game.

We recommend considering these four main criteria when selecting treatment targets (see Appendix G for corresponding decision tree):

1. Centrality in the network or to outcomes
2. Cultural responsiveness
3. Malleability (in response to treatment)
4. Relevance to clients

As a quick note, while there are many "right" targets, there are also many "wrong" ones that may endanger clients or directly harm them, such as encouraging a client to disclose their trauma to family members who have historically invalidated them or ignoring life-threatening behaviors. In the latter case, such behaviors should be prioritized.

Centrality

Centrality broadly refers to relevance to the network and/or personally meaningful outcomes. In other words, which nodes, if changed, would make a meaningful difference in your clients' lives? These outcomes could be realized in the short term (e.g., solving a specific problem) or long term (e.g., making another node more malleable to facilitate subsequent treatment).

One place to start is the most central node in Hermine's network. Conceptually, this corresponds to the "source" of your clients' problems. In network terms, this could be the node that has the most arrows coming out of it, regardless of size of the arrowhead, or it could be the node with the largest cumulative arrowhead weight coming out of it, regardless of the number of arrows. Generally, the most central node should be the one that is most likely to disrupt the network, should it disappear.

In Hermine's network, the boxes with the most arrows emanating from them are **[excessive marijuana use]** and **[stress over work performance]**, at four each. In terms of arrowhead weight, **[stress over work performance]**, **[perceived need to "prove myself"]**, and **[self-loathing]** appear to be the most central. Although [perceived need to "prove myself"] and [self-loathing] each have three outgoing arrows, the heavier weight on their arrows makes them comparably central to [stress over work performance] in terms of their impact on the network.

A second way to think about centrality is with respect to meaningful outcomes: which node is causing Hermine the most distress or most interfering with her functioning? For instance, Hermine may be most distressed by her marijuana use if she will be drug-tested prior to being "confirmed" as a new employee, so even if it's not the most central node in her network, it's the most central with respect to her functioning. In addition, consider targeting nodes that will positively impact treatment goals and well-being rather than merely reduce distress. In PBT, change should be intentional and directed to a specific purpose (variation and selection). Change for the sake of change (variation without selection) is not always useful.

You can also think about centrality in the long term, which might lead you to select nodes that are likely to have positive effects throughout the network over time or that would set your client up to maximally benefit from treatment later on. For instance, for Hermine, cultivating a reliable source of positive reinforcement through values-consistent hobbies may establish a psychologically healthy foundation and social support system from which she will be better able to face her deeper struggles with self-esteem and loneliness.

Cultural Responsiveness

Cultural responsiveness broadly refers to taking into account clients' cultural background in clinical decision making. This could range from behaviors seemingly as insignificant as how you ask your client about their identities during the intake to more notable ones like choosing which interventions to use. The function here is to be *aware* and *respectful* of your clients' identities and what they mean to your clients in every space in which you interact with them—be it sending appointment reminders, making small talk in the waiting area, or delivering treatment.

In this context, we note cultural responsiveness as it relates to selecting treatment targets. In other words, we want to be respectful of Hermine's identities and their importance to her when determining which node(s) to include in our treatment plan. In Hermine's case, we may consider addressing [stress over work performance], given its central role in her network and relevance to her treatment goals. But what if the work stress primarily stems from microaggressions from coworkers who frequently express concerns over her "professionalism" and talk over her in group discussions? In that case, what would it mean for us to teach Hermine how to cope with a toxic work environment? At best, we would be invalidating Hermine's struggles. At worst, it would make us complicit in Hermine's oppression, as we would be implicitly asking Hermine to accept racist behavior as normative and encouraging her to adjust to her oppression. Thus, it is always helpful to pause and ask yourself what message you may be sending with your treatment plan.

Taking a more culturally responsive stance, we might instead validate that feeling stressed is a reasonable response to an unfair situation and empower Hermine to change her environment instead of her response to it. Thus, we would target **(microaggressions at work)** (which would be added to the network), rather than the stress caused by them per se. By appropriately acknowledging the backdrop for Hermine's anxieties, we opt out of the gaslighting cycle where those in power tell members of minoritized groups they are overreacting or being sensitive. As another example, if your clients are neurodivergent and struggling with interpersonal interactions, it may not be culturally responsive to jump to social skills training. Doing so may signal to your clients that they are the problem (for not being socially adept), rather than our society and its dogged insistence on treating "common" and "correct" synonymously.

At the same time, to the extent that racism and other forms of discrimination cannot be fully avoided or eliminated, we recognize that individual coping skills for the resulting chronic distress can be helpful. It's part of learning to adapt to difficult circumstances and being resilient. Thus, we are not advocating never teaching individual skills. Rather, a combination of validation, acknowledgment of the role of contextual factors, teaching skills to change one's context, and teaching individual coping skills may be more useful.

Malleability

Just because a node is central and/or consistent with culturally responsive practice doesn't mean it's the most practical to target. With Hermine, for example, immediately targeting [self-loathing] may be a challenge, especially if this is an especially vulnerable area she's reluctant to share with a new therapist. Similarly, it may be difficult to directly change the stress she faces at work, because she might actually be in a high-pressure environment: there might be factors related to misogynoir (i.e., misogyny directed toward Black trans- and ciswomen, Bailey, 2021), she may be on probation and need to pass a performance evaluation before being "confirmed," or there may be high expectations set on her performance. When a node is difficult to change, going after it may not be workable until other parts of the network are weakened first.

As such, another criterion to consider is malleability: which nodes can you realistically change at this point in treatment given certain fixed parameters? These parameters include

- Treatment setting
- Clinician (or clinician's supervisor) competence
- Client insight
- Client environment
- Client strengths and resources

For instance, if you're working in a short-term partial hospitalization program, what is changeable will be different from that in a self-pay private practice where you may be working with your clients for years. Similarly, if your clients have parents who are willing to financially support them, their financial resources may be more robust than others who do not have access to intergenerational wealth. If clients have received CBT before and found it useful, it may be easier to work with them on irrational cognitions than it would be with clients who have limited psychological insight, and so on.

Nonetheless, you could still see if these parameters are indeed fixed, especially if changing them would make a significant difference to your clients' well-being. For instance, if you work in a primary care setting that only offers patients a set number of sessions but see private clients outside that setting, you may be able to offer some patients additional sessions. If you don't know how to work with a problem but can connect to a supervisor with relevant expertise, then your competence may change as well. Similarly, if your client is facing financial stressors but could ask their family members for financial support, that option may be worth exploring, especially in the short term.

For Hermine, even though she wants to decrease marijuana use—one of her stated treatment goals—it could be the only behavior that decreases loneliness and anxiety in the short term (i.e., is negatively reinforced), making it difficult for Hermine to change marijuana use until alternative sources of reinforcement are established. Hence, in Hermine's network, **[avoids hobbies shared with ex]** may be easier to change, given that Hermine expressed a desire to engage in these activities and the issue of meeting her ex-boyfriend can be problem solved (e.g., finding alternative spaces for the activities, asking friends not to invite her ex-boyfriend). Furthermore, reintroducing hobbies may led to contact with positive reinforcement, making this behavior more likely to be retained. Having a new source of positive reinforcement could also render using marijuana less motivating, making it easier to decrease marijuana use.

Conversely, problems like [perceived need to "prove myself"] and [self-loathing] may be more intractable, as they are maintained by her current unchangeable context (i.e., family, new job, recent break-up). That is, even if Hermine learned skills to more effectively handle her perceived need to excel, her environment will continue to exert pressure on her to care about striving and achievement, making it difficult to maintain these changes outside the therapy room, especially early on in treatment. This goes back to the idea of establishing a sound foundation for skills before moving to more entrenched targets, just as you might teach the forehand and backhand before a serve in tennis.

Relevance to Clients

This criterion has to do with the question, "Which nodes do my clients care about changing?" One way to identify these nodes is to consider the variables most relevant to your clients' treatment goals, which would be what they care about, by definition. For Hermine, these would be **[avoids hobbies shared with ex]**, **[stress over work performance]**, and **[excessive marijuana use]**. Ideally, we would target these nodes by either decreasing their severity or weakening their links to the rest of the network, and Hermine would achieve her goals.

However, in reality clients don't always select treatment goals most relevant to healthy change, and achieving the goals they care about would only be part of the clinical picture. This occurs when treatment goals fail to reflect the problems most significantly impacting client well-being, which could be due to poor insight (e.g., clients being unaware of the processes underlying their suffering, clients downplaying the severity of bigger problems) or unwillingness to confront larger problems (e.g., it is easier to deal with marijuana use than deep-seated self-hatred).

Where there is avoidance, we generally recommend addressing it. This may not mean undermining the avoidance and encouraging approach behaviors, because the avoidance may have an important self-protective function and blithely dismissing it could be harmful to your clients and/or compromise rapport. Instead, addressing avoidance may be shining light on the aversion your clients have to a distressing topic, even as it tries to operate in the shadows. Even if they're not ready to face this problem in the moment, bringing awareness to its presence may influence your clients' response to it over time.

In Hermine's case, her treatment goals omit problems related to [self-loathing] and [loneliness]. This matters because even if she no longer struggled with work stress, marijuana use, and avoidance of hobbies, she would likely continue to suffer from self-loathing, loneliness, and the constant sense that she is not good enough. In these cases, it may be helpful to explore why your clients are ignoring nodes that—from your perspective—are crucial for improving their well-being.

Review of Selected Targets

Once you have considered the four criteria, you will likely find some overlap among targets identified for each criterion. For Hermine, **[stress over work performance]** and **[avoids hobbies shared with ex]** show up twice, providing some convergent validity to aid our decision making. If you did this step with your clients, you could ask them which factors stand out to them as treatment targets. You could even ask your clients which criterion they care about the most and choose based on that. There are many ways to weigh the criteria and be persuaded one way or another.

Ultimately, bear in mind the function of this exercise: to make an informed decision about which two or three treatment targets to start with and begin developing a treatment plan. Nothing is set in stone. You can even change your treatment target next week if new data suggest that is most beneficial to your clients. As long as you have a cogent rationale supporting your treatment plan and your clients' blessing, you're doing it "right."

Client Feedback

In situations where there is strong disagreement between you and your clients on which nodes to target, we suggest being transparent about your motivations as a PBT therapist, which are to support your clients in healthy variation, selection, and retention vis-à-vis contextual demands. Working together on a network conceptualization at the outset or sharing the one you developed with your clients may help them understand your perspective and why you identified the nodes you did. Modeling this transparency may also help your clients be more forthcoming about the reasoning behind their disagreement. You may have missed certain variables in your initial assessment or misinterpreted information obtained from your clients.

Regardless of how you choose to approach such disagreements, avoid imposing your conceptualization on your clients or dismissing their concerns as due to "low insight." Instead, be curious about the discrepancies, so you can better understand why you and your clients see the situation differently. For instance, a client may be adamant about working on their drinking, whereas you perceive the drinking to be related to situational problems that can be remedied (e.g., being unemployed). But if you leaned in and probed, you might learn that your client has a core belief that they "cannot control their future," a thought that likely influences how they respond to other problems in their life and should be factored into your case conceptualization.

Developing a Treatment Plan

For Hermine's treatment targets, we have tentatively selected

- [stress over work performance]
- [avoids hobbies shared with ex]
- [excessive marijuana use]

These targets are consistent with Hermine's treatment goals, include central nodes, and seem to be most malleable at this point. We also don't have evidence that any of them are inconsistent with culturally responsive treatment. Of course, these targets can change over time, as we gather more data working with Hermine. For instance, if work stress is primarily due to racist company practices, we would adjust the plan accordingly.

Building Blocks of Treatment: Treatment Kernels

The next step is to determine *how* we plan to change these nodes or their links to other nodes in the network. In PBT, nodes and arrows between nodes are targeted using treatment components or *treatment kernels*. Treatment kernels refer to the smallest active ingredients in treatment packages that have been shown to independently affect outcomes. For example, we know that, on average, behavioral activation improves depressive symptoms, even without cognitive restructuring, and the same goes for cognitive restructuring without behavioral activation (Ciharova et al., 2021). We also know that, on average, acceptance-based skills improve OCD symptoms, even without explicit exposures (Twohig et al., 2010). Thus, behavioral activation, cognitive restructuring, and acceptance skills may be considered treatment kernels—you could even break them down more—though this doesn't automatically mean that the kernel will fit your specific client.

Kernels can target one EEMM dimension, such as attentional training (Attention), or multiple EEMM dimensions, such as exposures (Affect/Emotion, Cognition, and Behavior). The dimension being targeted can also depend on how the kernel is delivered. In the case of exposures, if you use an inhibitory learning framework, you may emphasize cognitive variation, whereas using a habituation framework may facilitate affective variation. Conversely, if exposures are done in a values-based way as in ACT, they may entail motivational variation. Kernels can also span different EEMM levels, such as adhering to a regular sleep schedule (Behavior and Biology/Physiology) and interpersonal effectiveness skills (Behavior and Relationships).

As a reminder, we're always thinking about the *function* or effect of kernels, not just their content, so categorizing them into their "correct" dimension or level is secondary. Rather, each treatment kernel should support variation, selection, or retention in some way, ideally as these principles of change map onto your clients' treatment goals. To show how we define and think about treatment kernels, a non-exhaustive list of common treatment kernels and their associated EEMM dimensions and levels are presented in Appendix H.

We won't offer comprehensive heuristics that prescribe exactly which kernels work best for which clients in their unique circumstance because of how different clients and therapists are. However, we provide a list of questions and accompanying decision trees for node and kernel selection in Appendix G, so you have some structure for decision making. In general, the idea is to select among evidence-based kernels you are competent at delivering, while considering what works for your specific clients with respect to their personally meaningful outcomes.

At the same time, you don't have to be the one delivering every kernel to your clients. For instance, you may refer your clients to a psychiatrist to see if they would benefit from psychotropic medication (Biology/Physiology) or to a couples therapist if they're experiencing relationship problems (Relationships). Workability means doing what works for your clients in the long term, not taking full responsibility for their well-being.

Selecting Treatment Kernels

Once you and your clients have identified treatment targets, the next step is to select kernels that will change those targets efficiently and effectively. The criteria for kernel selection somewhat overlap with those for selecting treatment targets. You're still considering *relevance of the kernel to your clients* and whether the kernel is consistent with *culturally responsive* practice. In addition, an appropriate kernel is one that can change the node of interest, is supported by available evidence, and you're able to deliver competently. Here are the five criteria we recommend for kernel selection (see Appendix G for corresponding decision tree):

1. Relevance to target node
2. Evidence base
3. Cultural responsiveness
4. Relevance to clients
5. Ability to deliver kernel effectively

Relevance to Target Node

In the first place, any kernel you select should map on to the target node and/or arrows linked to it. The EEMM Principle is helpful here. Use the EEMM to identify the dimension(s) and level(s) your kernels need to encompass given the treatment target. For example, if you're targeting a core belief about the self, kernels linked to Cognition and/or Self, compared to Attention or Motivation, would be more relevant. If the target has to do with interpersonal interactions, the kernel should contain a Relationships element.

In addition, determine which principles of change to focus on based on where your client is stuck. Should your kernel vary responding, select for helpful responding, or encourage retention of adaptive responding? If your client uses the same coping strategies again and again, you might want a kernel that increases variation. Whereas, if your client has found a useful strategy but applies it infrequently, a retention-focused kernel may be more effective.

Evidence Base

There are two parts to this criterion. First, check that the selected kernel is evidence-based, or only select from evidence-based kernels to begin with. Evidence-based means data in the literature indicate a kernel is independently effective for improving symptoms, functioning, or well-being—or it's part of a treatment package that does. This is the foundation of PBT that keeps it from becoming a free-for-all endeavor unmoored from science.

At the same time, aggregate data have clear limitations, given that group-level data—from humans who are different from each other and from themselves at different timepoints—do not generalize to particular people (Molenaar, 2004). In other words, we cannot assume that group-level findings (e.g., on average, everyone improved) from clinical trials apply to our clients. This weakness is in fact a major factor driving the person-centered stance of PBT. Furthermore, the data we do have are based on fairly homogeneous samples (Grau et al., 2022; Mendoza et al., 2012; Williams et al., 2010), meaning that even if group-level data were reliable, they still fail to adequately represent large swathes of the population, usually those with minoritized identities.

These limitations lead to the second part of this principle: in addition to the extant literature (largely based on group-level research among majoritized participants), it's crucial to integrate *idiographic empiricism*, applying empirical principles like experimental manipulation and hypothesis testing in your work with clients. For instance, you might assess an outcome of interest prior to and after implementing a kernel and see what effects that kernel has, accounting for external variables that may also affect the outcome of interest. If you have reliable idiographic data to suggest that a specific kernel is responsible for improving your clients' well-being, you shouldn't discount that kernel just because it has "mixed empirical support" in the literature. After all, what works on the group level doesn't always work for particular people and vice versa.

Cultural Responsiveness

A culturally responsive kernel is one that considers the cultural identities important to your clients and makes them feel seen and respected. The function is to validate and respect your clients' identities and experiences, but the form a culturally responsive kernel takes can vary widely. For example, the notion of "letting go" or "simply observing" thoughts and feelings in mindfulness-based approaches is incredibly powerful for many people. Yet, encouraging "letting go" may be iatrogenic (i.e., cause harm, usually unintentionally) for some minoritized clients by reinforcing a narrative of involuntary helplessness. Whereas, reframing these exercises as *choosing* to let go or *freeing* the self from difficult thoughts and feelings may be more empowering for these clients (Payne, 2022).

Culturally responsive practice extends to what happens outside of session as well. For instance, when providing therapeutic resources for clients, it is important to consider if those resources resonate with your clients and their identities. The overarching idea is that whatever you do as part of treatment must consider your clients in their cultural context. As an example, African American study participants reported that listening to guided meditation from a "white voice," where they were expected to follow instructions without resistance, brought up feelings of oppression and increased the salience of racial trauma (Watson-Singleton et al., 2019). Thus, when sharing guided meditations—or other resources—for between-session practice, clinicians should provide clients with options featuring diverse voices and perspectives, so they can select the ones that work for them. Generally, being aware of the cultural—not just therapeutic—valence of kernels is crucial.

Relevance to Clients

As much as our clients live in a cultural context, they are unique individuals who see the world in their own way, which could be wildly different from someone else who shares their exact same identities. In contrast to cultural responsiveness, this criterion focuses more on the specific values, goals, circumstances, needs, and wants of your clients, recognizing that they are more than their cultural identities. However, to the extent that cultural identities are relevant to who your client is as a person—and they invariably are—this and the previous criterion have some overlap.

To be relevant, kernels should resonate with your clients' understanding of their struggles and what will help them, be informed by their history and values, and leverage their strengths and resources. In other words, select kernels that your clients will buy into or engage in as much as possible. For example, if your clients value harmony, you may lean toward teaching relationship building skills, such as GIVE from DBT, as opposed to skills more aligned with individualistic goals, such as assertiveness training. If your clients have a long history of meditation and find it beneficial, they may respond better to a mindfulness-based cognitive kernel like defusion rather than cognitive reappraisal.

You could even directly ask your clients for feedback on the kernels you're using or planning to use. If your clients reject a kernel, be curious about why. It's possible that you have not adequately presented the rationale for the kernel and psychoeducation is needed. Alternatively, your clients may have tried something similar in the past and disliked it. In which case, it would be important to clarify whether you will indeed be delivering the same kernel. For instance, when our clients say they have done exposures in the past, they don't always describe what we think of as exposures. Regardless, gaining a deeper understanding of your clients' preferences and perspectives can only help you make better informed decisions in treatment.

Clinical Skill

Your ability—or your supervisor's ability to help you—to adeptly deliver a kernel is tied to the Workability Principle. Even if you're aware of a cutting-edge kernel that seems perfectly suited for your clients, the kernel will only be as useful as you are skilled at delivering it. As such, treatment planning is not about choosing the "correct" kernels; it's about choosing *effective* kernels. As you gain experience and knowledge, the kernels at your disposal will increase over time, so what counts as workable is fluid.

It's even possible for you to update your clinical repertoire in the short term. For instance, if another therapist or supervisor in your clinic happens to be skilled in the kernel you've selected, you could seek consultation or supervision from them to ensure you're delivering it competently. Of course, this repertoire expansion is likely more feasible for "simpler" kernels, such as doing a guided meditation or a values card sort. More complex kernels—such as a thorough chain analysis—may require more time and training.

Ordering Treatment Kernels

A common question we get at this point is, "How do I know which node to target or kernel to deliver first?" The short answer is you won't know. How could you? Expecting yourself to know exactly where to start treatment with clients after an intake session is setting an unrealistic standard.

Nonetheless, you can make an *informed* decision. Some of the criteria for this decision overlap with those for *Identifying Treatment Targets*. As such, you could start with the kernel that targets the most central node to maximize initial impact (centrality), or the kernel you're most confident will lead to change to generate early momentum (malleability). You might even start with a broader kernel that targets multiple nodes at the same time, like a meditation kernel that might target affect and attention simultaneously. Again, there's no "right" answer, but some of the PBT principles can provide guidance.

The principles most relevant to deciding where to start treatment are Personalization, Workability, and Empiricism. The Process and EEMM Principles are more helpful for selecting nodes and kernels. For ordering, we're largely thinking about setting you and your clients up for success over time. Here are three questions to ponder:

- **Personalization**: What are my clients most bought into or most motivated to start with? This maximizes the probability that your clients will be engaged in treatment from the outset and could help to establish rapport.
- **Workability**: What's going to make treatment most effective in the long term? Sometimes, doing what our clients want isn't the same as helping them. For instance, if your clients are highly avoidant, they may consistently choose goals that are too easy for them, depriving them of the opportunity to engage in new learning. Therefore, you also need to consider the long game. For clients who avoid discomfort any chance they get, you might be wary of reinforcing their

avoidance and instead target motivation for treatment. Labeling their avoidance and enhancing motivation may not be what your clients care about, but it could be the most sustainable route to improving their well-being.

- **Empiricism**: How do I know if what I'm doing is working? We can hypothesize all we want, but without data, hypotheses are just abstract ideas floating in the ether. So, should you allow some avoidance at the beginning to leverage rapport later or confront avoidance from the beginning to eschew reinforcing a maladaptive pattern? Test it out. Pick an approach, identify what outcomes will tell you if it's working, and collect data to ascertain its effectiveness. Then, adjust accordingly. Empiricism saves you from needing to know the right answer before trying.

Selecting an Initial Kernel for Hermine

We'll use Hermine's case example to illustrate kernel selection and ordering. Let's first reorient to her treatment goals:

- Learn more effective ways to cope with work stress
- Re-engage in hobbies
- Reduce marijuana use

The nodes we chose to target were

- [stress over work performance]
- [avoids hobbies shared with ex]
- [excessive marijuana use]

With respect to which node to start with, [stress over work performance] was directly relevant to her treatment goals and one of the more central nodes in her network. For the sake of the example, let's say Hermine indicated that she was most motivated to work on [stress over work performance], and managing this stress would significantly improve her well-being and functioning. Thus we'll target [stress over work performance] first. Let's review the kernel selection criteria to decide which kernel(s) to try out (see Appendix G for decision tree):

- **Relevance to target node**: Stress itself is more of a symptom than a process, so we may also want to consider the processes underlying Hermine's stress (i.e., examine arrows linked to the target node). For Hermine, stress is primarily driven by her perceived need to prove herself as worthy, thus we could take this antecedent into account when choosing a stress-focused kernel. That means we're looking for a kernel that covers Affect (for stress) and, ideally, Self and/or Motivation. A kernel that integrates mindfulness and self-compassion, such as a self-compassion meditation, may be especially helpful for Hermine.

  In addition, we might want to clarify which principle of change is relevant here. From Hermine's network, it seems like she repeatedly relies on the same avoidance-based strategies (e.g., marijuana use, avoiding hobbies), suggesting a problem with variation. Thus, we would want a kernel that teaches a new skill to induce variation.
- **Evidence base**: Meta-analyses have found that mindfulness- and self-compassion-based interventions reduce stress symptoms (e.g., Burton et al., 2017; de Abreu Costa et al., 2019; Ferrari et al., 2019; Virgili, 2015; Wilson et al., 2019). Admittedly, as much as these data we cite are imperfect (e.g., group-level, relatively homogeneous), they are what we have and, for now, they provide a starting point for our decision making. We will later want to use idiographic data from Hermine to verify whether a mindfulness approach works for her.
- **Cultural responsiveness**: Given Hermine's identity as a Black woman, acceptance-based approaches may be tricky if they're not paired with empowerment strategies, because they might implicitly signal that she needs to "just accept" the stress—an invalidating rhetoric often espoused to members of minoritized communities. Of course, this does not preclude the use of self-compassion meditation, just that we ought to be mindful of how we deliver it. We might even want to gather more information on the source of Hermine's work stress and determine if structural factors (e.g., discriminatory workplace policies) are contributing to it, to better consider Hermine in context and ensure that any kernel we use acknowledges the intersecting role of racism, sexism, and biphobia on Hermine's work stress.

It may be especially critical for Hermine to engage in clinical decision making to bolster her autonomy, given that she is part of communities (i.e., Black American, women, LGBTQ+) who have been historically—and continue to be—disenfranchised and ignored by the medical profession (Carter, 2022). As such, a collaborative approach to kernel selection and delivery may be indicated.

- **Relevance to client**: We also need to know which kernels resonate with Hermine most strongly. Is she interested in mindfulness-based approaches? Does she like the structure of worksheets, which might align with her engineering background? Which approach does she feel most hopeful about? For example, if Hermine has undergone several meditation courses or expresses openness to trying meditation, then we might lean toward a mindfulness-based kernel to leverage her existing skills or interests. Furthermore, we may recognize that a self-compassion kernel could lay the groundwork for changing other nodes that will be important to target in the long run, such as [perceived need to "prove myself"] and [self-loathing].
- **Clinical skill**: Do we have the skill to deliver self-compassion meditation as a kernel? Let's say that we have done many guided meditations, but not one that is specifically about self-compassion. The skill of delivering a guided meditation may be generalizable here, and we would need to practice a self-compassion-focused one before doing it with Hermine.

In terms of what kernel selection looks like in the therapy room, it varies, depending on how involved your clients are. To make kernel selection more collaborative, you could ask your clients what kinds of approaches they think might be helpful for changing the treatment target after providing psychoeducation on evidence-based options and what previous coping strategies they have found helpful or unhelpful. Alternatively, you could independently consider how each kernel might land with your clients (if you choose not to ask them directly) before delivering the selected kernels, using their response to gage if you're on track. Either way, you're considering your clients in context and using evidence to test your hypotheses.

As you can tell, there are myriad factors to consider when selecting kernels. Depending on Hermine's perspective and preference or even clinician skill, cognitive restructuring could have been just as feasible (Ezawa & Hollon, 2023). Like most aspects in PBT, the decision-making process matters more than the solution. Indeed, you're not expected to divine an answer and fix all your clients' problems. That's not how therapy works. Instead, be intentional: ensure that the moves you make in treatment are backed by a defensible clinical rationale and pay attention to how your clients respond before choosing how to proceed. After all, every chess match is different, and you will only get better by playing more games (refer to Chapter 1 for full analogy).

Assessment During Treatment

Once you have selected and begun delivering the kernel, assess. Part of PBT is continually assessing how your clients are doing with respect to their goals over the course of treatment to test your hypotheses about whether the intervention is working as planned. This longitudinal assessment is part of the idiographic empiricism underlying personalized process-based care. For instance, if we expect Hermine's work stress to decrease after three weeks of practicing regular self-compassion meditations and that doesn't happen, we have to return to the drawing board and troubleshoot. Perhaps Hermine is not implementing the homework as discussed, or we need to add another affective kernel to strengthen the intervention effect. Kind of like with cooking, keep tasting as you go and adjust along the way. Too bland? Add salt. Too sweet? Add some acidity.

Ideally, longitudinal assessment would be entirely automated for you and your clients. For example, your clients get regular prompts on their smart device, and you get a neat visual summary of their data before each session. While this is technologically possible, it's not always feasible, depending on the profile of your clients and the treatment setting you're in. If you mostly see clients in a lower income bracket, they may be more concerned about paying their bills than completing daily surveys on a smartphone. Alternatively, you may be working in a setting that lacks the resources and infrastructure to make automated assessment a reality.

With the Workability Principle in mind, we describe general guidelines you can use to make your assessment plan. We encourage you to take what's helpful and leave what's not. That's the beauty of principles. They provide the skeleton, but you decide what shape the body takes. (The treatment plan template in Appendix F also provides some guidance on assessment planning.)

Know Your Reasons

Before anything else, know *why* you're conducting assessment for your particular clients. How will it help with treatment planning and their treatment goals? It's insufficient to simply administer default clinic measures and look at sum scores. We also need to integrate those data into treatment delivery and verify that these data actually improve client outcomes.

It's especially helpful if you have plans for what to do depending on what you observe. For example, if you notice anxiety increasing, you might then ask about the presence of new stressors or troubleshoot strategies learned thus far. Stating this intention ahead of time makes it that much more explicit why assessment matters and shows that you understand exactly how the data your clients provide will impact treatment.

Know Your Variables

Besides the why, clarify *what* you are assessing. Typically, we're interested in variables related to our clients' well-being, functioning, treatment goals, or treatment targets (i.e., nodes). They may include quality of life, work impairment, spending time with family, and time spent worrying about health. Ultimately, we care about variables that are *personally relevant* and *meaningful* to our clients. These can be measured in a multitude of ways, from one-item questions to clinician-observed behaviors.

Personalizing assessment doesn't mean throwing out standardized measures. Standardized measures may very well resonate with your clients. The key here is to ascertain that they match your clients' needs rather than assume they do. For instance, some clients with anxiety may not endorse symptoms listed on the Generalized Anxiety Disorder–7 (GAD-7) scale, perhaps because they engage in significant avoidance or other coping strategies such that they hardly experience physiological symptoms of anxiety, or they are overly focused on their poor sleep (which the GAD-7 does not explicitly assess) and ignore other signs of anxiety. In these cases, an alternate form of assessment or psychoeducation to increase understanding of how their anxiety manifests may be needed. For others, the GAD-7 may perfectly encapsulate their struggles with anxiety.

A hybrid (and oxymoronic) standardized-personalized measure is the PBAT (first mentioned in Chapter 3; pbatsupport.com), which was designed according to PBT principles (Ciarrochi et al., 2022). The PBAT provides a pool of items you and your clients can pick and choose from. This stands in contrast to standardized measures that dictate the same items for everyone, regardless of the problem. The PBAT is intended to be used flexibly to maximize relevance to clients and provide clinically useful data. Even if you ultimately use items different from those in the PBAT, the PBAT can be a helpful starting point if you and your clients are stuck on what kinds of variables to track.

A critical consideration for assessment is that your clients understand how variables are being defined. Let's say you and your client choose to track spending time with their partner. You may be thinking of this variable as spending *quality* time with their partner, with the expectation that your client is present and responsive during that timeframe. However, your client could be counting all the time spent with their partner (e.g., watching TV on the couch), regardless of whether they are present-focused. In this case, more time spent with their partner might not actually reflect progress. Thus, it is crucial to ask your clients how they understand the variables being tracked before embarking on longitudinal assessment.

Furthermore, it's important to define variables such that you can reliably track changes over time. For instance, "sleep" is not a terribly useful variable, because it's so loosely defined. Instead, "hours of sleep" would be more concrete, or even something subjective like "sleep quality" may be helpful so long as your clients are able to define it consistently over time. Otherwise, a score of 3 at the start of treatment will not mean the same thing as a score of 3 at the end of treatment. For this reason, it's usually more reliable to track an objectively measurable variable, such as percentage of homework assignments submitted before the deadline (for procrastination). Nonetheless, life is largely comprised of subjective experiences, so objective variables may not have the same salience as subjective ones. As such, the skill lies in finding a variable that is meaningful to your clients and can be reliably assessed over time.

Another domain to consider is context. We often focus on assessing what's going on within our clients to the extent that we may forget to assess what's going on around our clients. For example, your client's new roommate might snore loudly, negatively impacting their sleep quality, or your client could have been assigned a new project at work and is feeling overwhelmed by the added responsibilities, which keeps them awake at night. Understanding clients' context gives us a deeper appreciation of the function of their responses and clarifies how to precipitate change. In the case of the snoring roommate, you may want to assess how often and how much the snoring is affecting your client and devise a plan accordingly.

Reading this, you may realize that you're already doing some longitudinal assessment, such as when you ask your clients about what they did over the past week or how much they engaged in their between-session assignments—that's great. The next step is to track how these variables change over time, not just their level at a specific timepoint. This means asking about the same variable, measured in the same way, at regular intervals. These longitudinal trajectories provide crucial data on the effects of treatment, which you need to test your hypotheses.

Know What You Want

As obvious as it sounds, we also need to be clear about what we expect to find from assessment. In other words, you must clarify hypotheses about what effects your kernel is supposed to have (e.g., define what counts as treatment progress a priori). If you're working with a client on thought monitoring, your client may report an increase in negative thoughts initially, simply because they are paying more attention to them. In this case, an increase in negative thoughts may actually reflect that treatment is working. Similarly, if your client is engaging in more approach-based behaviors after avoiding feared stimuli for a long time, their distress and mood may worsen in the short term, and that may indicate increased willingness.

Another reason why it's important to clarify the desired effect of the kernel a priori is that the desired effect influences how you deliver it. For instance, an exposure kernel may look quite different if you are targeting rule following ("let's see what happens when you break the rule") vs. distress intolerance ("practice sitting with the distress").

Having a sense of *when* you expect to see change can also be helpful for knowing when to change course. You may expect behavioral change to come more quickly than changes in self-perception, for example, so you would not conclude that self-compassion kernels are ineffective because your client continues to experience self-critical thoughts after two months. However, you may expect to see an increase in self-kind behaviors within two weeks.

Broadly speaking, you want to see some combination of variation, selection, retention, and context sensitivity in your assessed outcomes. Are your clients engaging in new behaviors? Do your clients know if what they're doing is working based on their goals? Are they forming helpful habits? Can they figure out what is most effective in different situations? Helpfully, the PBAT provides items that map onto these concepts (e.g., "I stuck to strategies that seemed to have worked" [retention], "I was able to change my behavior, when changing helped my life" [context-matching]).

Know Your Limits

There is ideal and there is reality. If you're a full-time therapist with a caseload of 40 clients, preparing personalized assessments and worksheets for every client or analyzing intensive longitudinal data to produce dozens of empirically derived networks is unfeasible. Indeed, trying to realize all these ideas may increase your frustration and paradoxically decrease your willingness to try any of the longitudinal assessments we described.

Instead, we recommend starting small, something you're 99.9% confident you'll be able to stick to for at least a month. Perhaps prepare a check-in question for one client that is tailored to what you've been working on to test whether treatment is going as planned. "How much time did you spend looking at your ex's social media profiles this past week?" "How many times did you explicitly state your needs with your friends this week?" In our view, it's more clinically useful for these questions to be personally relevant than precise, because at the end of the day, our priority is for our clients to live their best lives, not provide granular data.

Once you get in the habit of asking your client the same question, branch out by preparing a question for a second client, or reflect on how you will adjust treatment based on responses from your first client. It's OK to go slowly. Doing PBT is not an all-or-nothing endeavor; it's about thinking in a process-based way, which proceeds gradually.

The Short Version

For clinicians with large caseloads or limited time, the preceding content might feel like a lot to take in and use with your clients. In fact, we would probably spend several classes reviewing these ideas with our students and supervisees. Thus, if you don't feel equipped to implement every single principle immediately, that sounds about right. In our experience, learning how to do PBT is an iterative, evolving journey, and we don't see ourselves ever saying, "We know PBT now." In the same vein, we don't expect you to go from wherever you are to 100%. Think of the journey more as adding 3% or 10% with each read. Once you've established some new skills, return to the book and add another 5%.

To facilitate incremental learning, we've simplified the list of steps outlined in this chapter in Box 6.2. If you're already familiar with the relevant PBT principles, this may serve as a useful checklist as you go about treatment planning. If you're still learning the principles, use these steps as a map of the forest, so you don't get too stuck in the trees. Either way, be patient with yourself. Take your 2%, or 7%, or 13% for now, then come back when you're ready for more.

Box 6.2 Simplified steps for process-based treatment planning, delivery, and evaluation

1. Develop network conceptualization of client (detailed in Chapter 5).
2. Identify potential treatment targets (see Appendix E for decision tree guide).
3. Identify treatment kernels for targets (see Appendix E for decision tree guide and Appendix H for example kernels).
4. Select a kernel to start with, particularly considering the Principles of Personalization, Workability, and Empiricism (see Appendix G for example of a treatment plan).
5. Select a variable to regularly assess that will tell you if your kernel is working as designed.

Updating the Network

As you implement kernels and your clients change their patterns of responding, update your network using the data you've collected from your clients. Your updated network could include kernels, skills acquired or new responses, and remaining active nodes. Nodes that are no longer a problem—for example, they are no longer present or influencing other nodes—can be dropped from the network for parsimony. Conversely, new stressors can be added, if they currently influence your clients' presenting concerns. Be wary about making a network that is so complicated it becomes useless. The rule of comprehensive parsimony still applies.

With Hermine as an example, let's say we used self-compassion meditation and pleasant activity scheduling kernels. We signify them as treatment kernels by using dashed lines to outline the nodes (see Figure 6.2). Then, if we have data indicating that Hermine has learned to **[mindfully observe difficult emotions]** and **[treat herself more kindly]** (e.g., by cutting herself slack and setting more realistic expectations), we can add these new nodes to her network (see italicized nodes in upper right corner of Figure 6.2).

Notice that these new responses have an *inhibitory* (open arrows) effect on [stress over work performance] and [perceived need to "prove myself"]. This means that when Hermine practices mindful observing, her stress and/or its power in the network decreases. Similarly, if we know that pleasant activity scheduling has increased Hermine's **[engagement in hobbies and other leisure activities]**, we can add that node to the network. In turn, we see that when Hermine engages in fun activities, her avoidance of hobbies shared with her ex decreases. In this version of her network, Hermine has stopped excessive marijuana use entirely, so it has been dropped from the network. You could even adjust the size and direction of the arrows if the relationship between nodes changes. For instance, we reduced the size of the arrowhead from [stress over work performance] to [avoids hobbies shared with ex] to show that [stress over work performance] has a weaker effect on [avoids hobbies shared with ex] now compared to the start of treatment.

Revisions to the network are based on data gathered over the course of treatment. The data could be from standardized measures, subjective self-report, or even clinician observations, depending on your assessment plan. To represent hypothesized relationships, we use dotted arrows, such as if we predict that engagement in leisure activities will decrease Hermine's feelings of loneliness (see Figure 6.2). If you're using dashed arrows for immediate effects in your network, you could use wavy instead of dotted arrows (especially if you are drawing networks by hand) to maximize the contrast among different types of arrows. Subsequently, we will need to assess these variables to determine if our prediction is accurate. Being able to map treatment response via the network is helpful for showing the precise effects of treatment and their downstream impact. Furthermore, given that one of the goals of PBT is to end up with a stable healthy network, having a "live" network over the course of treatment clarifies how close your clients are to that point and what other parts of the network need to be changed.

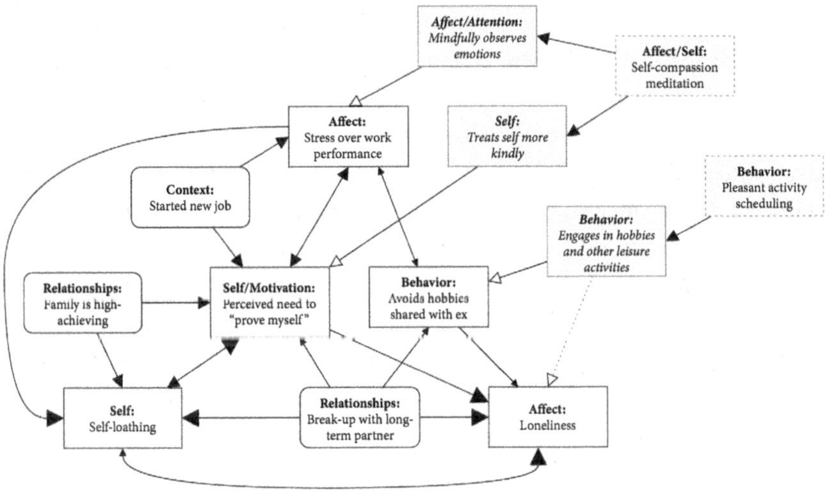

Figure 6.2 Hermine's updated network over the course of treatment.

Writing Session Notes

As an administrative note, PBT is less concerned with the minutia of therapy, such as how your session or progress notes are structured. However, for therapists newer to PBT, we recommend including fields for *target node* and *kernel used* at minimum. Including a *target area of change* (evolutionary principles of change plus context-matching) could be useful as well. Having these fields will remind you of the focus on treatment and, over time, alert you to overlooked nodes, dimensions, or areas of change. For instance, if you notice that most of your sessions have been focused on Affect and you haven't seen expected gains despite trying multiple kernels, it may be worth considering if other dimensions are getting in the way (e.g., Self: negative self-concept). We provide a basic PBT-informed progress note template and completed examples in Appendix I.

Of course, there will be sessions where no obvious node is being targeted or no discrete kernel can be identified. Even then, having these fields can situate your interpretation of the session in a PBT framework. For instance, such a session might occur if your client has a specific stressor they want to talk about, and the session ends up looking like supportive counseling infused with reflection and validation. After a session like that, you might conclude that you failed to deliver a kernel.

However, if you paused to reflect in terms of your client's network, EEMM dimensions, and principles of change, you might realize that your client was being more open to their emotions (Affect) by allowing themselves to feel strong feelings in session and labeling them as they showed up. Your positive response to their openness in the form of validation may have naturally reinforced their open stance (selection). In this case, the target node could be [avoids painful emotions related to trauma] and the kernel could be interpersonal reinforcement of novel affective responding from functional analytic psychotherapy (Tsai et al., 2015). Understanding what transpired in session through this lens could make you more intentional and sensitive to when target nodes show up in future sessions—regardless of their form—and more likely to deploy a kernel to induce healthy change.

A Note on Generalizability

An ironic feature of a personalized approach built on principles is that it can be highly generalizable. Consider operant conditioning, the process of learning through which behaviors are modified by attendant consequences, such as reward and punishment. Operant conditioning is personalized in that we can use this learning principle to change particular people's behavior and generalizable in that the same principle is relevant across individuals—as long as we apply it functionally. This means we are contemplating what is rewarding or punishing to particular people (money vs. praise, silence vs. criticism) and then using this information to determine what consequences to deliver to change specific people's behavior. In contrast, a formal application of operant conditioning might look like giving everyone money to positively reinforce behavior. We can instinctively see why such a formal application won't work: some people don't care about money or already have too much of it.

The same is true for process-based treatment. If we apply PBT formally, such as by always selecting the most central node to target in everyone's networks or going with the kernel your clients have background knowledge in, it will not be generalizable. This is why we emphasize principles and function repeatedly in this book. PBT is not about what you do, it's about *how* and *why* you do it. To take a functional approach, the Workability Principle is most helpful, because it anchors us in the question, "What is going to work for my clients?" This is an inherently personalized question, because its focus is your clients, yet generalizable because we can ask this question for all our clients.

Chapter Summary

- The first step in intervention planning is to identify treatment targets (nodes). Consider centrality, cultural responsiveness, malleability, and relevance to your clients (see Appendix G).
- Then, select treatment kernels for the target node that are evidence-based, culturally responsive, relevant to your clients, and within your clinical skillset (see Appendix G).
- Assess relevant variables throughout treatment, so you can verify your hypotheses and gage client progress. Stick to what is feasible and sustainable.
- In session notes, identify the target node, kernel used, and target area of change to keep yourself grounded in a PBT framework (see Appendix I).

7

Decision Making in Treatment

At this point, you've put in the hard work of assessment, conceptualization, and treatment planning; your clients are on board, and you're eager to begin treatment. This foundational work is crucial to successful treatment, and if everything goes according to plan, you won't need to adjust a thing. But as any therapist knows, things rarely go according to plan. More likely than not, you'll be faced with many more decision points throughout the course of therapy. To serve the needs of your wonderfully complex clients you'll need to stay on target by checking on their progress with respect to their goals (Workability), engage in continual assessment and monitoring of treatment goals (Empiricism), and make adjustments where necessary to tailor treatment to their specific needs (Personalization).

Our goal with this chapter is to illustrate how PBT principles can be flexibly applied to different decision-making scenarios in treatment. That said, we recognize that the nature of clinical work makes providing clearly delineated rules or answers to every possible scenario a fruitless endeavor. There's scant reliable evidence for recommended clinical decision-making steps; thus, our advice is largely anecdotal and based on our clinical experience. So, while some of these examples may appear authoritative or like they are the "right" answer, this is not the case. Our intention is to emphasize *how* to think about these concerns—rather than provide solutions to every possible problem—so you can apply these principles to your clients in your own way. Below we try to address some of the questions we've been asked most frequently as we have taught this approach.

Does Every Node Need a Treatment Kernel?

When first encountering a network-based case conceptualization, therapists often feel compelled to match a treatment kernel to each of the nodes. Treating a network as a to-do list of nodes to check off one at a time misses the point of network conceptualization and reduces our clients to a linear series

A Process-Based Approach to Psychotherapy. Clarissa W. Ong and Eric B. Lee, Oxford University Press.
 DOI: 10.1093/oso/9780197696378.003.0007

of problems to overcome. In reality, our clients' problems are much more complicated—they consist of multiple internal and external processes that reinforce one another and are maintained across contexts. Think back to Hermine in the previous chapter. If we treat her problems like a to-do list and ignore the relationships between them, we might end up with a treatment plan like this, with an intervention assigned to each of her problems:

- Stress over work performance → relaxation training
- Need to "prove herself" → cognitive restructuring
- Avoids hobbies shared with ex → values clarification
- Self-loathing → acceptance and self-compassion
- Loneliness → activity planning
- Excessive marijuana use → motivational interviewing

Now, this is a fine list of problems and evidence-based kernels, all of which likely would be beneficial to Hermine to some degree. But aside from greater precision, functionally speaking, there's little difference between using nodes as a checklist and matching protocols to diagnoses. We can do better; we can think in terms of networks and aim to destabilize the processes that are either self-maintaining or contributing to additional problems. In other words, we don't just want to shrink the network by deleting nodes; we want to dismantle the system altogether. We don't know how long Hermine will continue in therapy, and we want to make as big and sustainable of an impact in as little time as possible. In other words, we want to get the most bang for our buck and a to-do list mentality won't get us there.

In addition to the considerations discussed in Chapter 6 (i.e., relevance to target node, evidence base, cultural responsiveness, relevance to clients, and clinical skill), we might think about treatment kernels that have the potential to disrupt multiple areas of the network, rather than moving through the list one by one. For example, values clarification exercises could be tailored to explore not only how Hermine wants to meaningfully spend her time but also her self-identity, to target self-loathing. Values exercises could also build insight into behavioral deficits and activity planning as well as the feelings of loneliness Hermine reported. Our therapeutic techniques are flexible enough to influence more than a single node if we are thoughtful in *how* they are delivered.

Choosing a technique to match a process is not as mechanical as it's often made out to be. There aren't one-to-one methods to throw at people to "fix" their problem. For example, a hammer can be used to drive nails or to pull them. And in a pinch can be used as a paper weight, or a stirrer, or even a musical instrument. So, just because you use a hammer doesn't necessarily mean you can only manipulate nails. Likewise, we can't assume that doing an activity scheduling kernel with a client is the same as successfully targeting behavioral avoidance. Depending on how the exercise is framed and performed, activity scheduling can be used to increase values clarification (Motivation), values-based committed action (Behavior/Motivation), and/or contact with social reinforcers (Relationships/Motivation).

So, no, not every node needs its own treatment kernel. Our client case conceptualizations should be more than a list of separate problems to solve. Thinking in terms of process can help you to get to the heart of the problem, disrupt maintenance patterns, and simply put—be a more efficient and effective therapist.

When Do I Change to a Different Node? Or Do I Need to Change the Treatment Kernel?

This question tends to come up when there is a lack of progress in treatment, when you might feel stuck, confused, or frustrated because little is changing and there is little movement toward treatment goals. Within this lack of progress are data you can use to refine decision making. If you and your clients are happy with your case conceptualization and treatment plan—that is, you've decided on a node and associated treatment kernel—and there's still a lack of progress, we suggest considering the following questions before jumping to a different node or revising your treatment plan.

Do My Clients Buy into the Treatment Plan?

It's crucial that our clients have some buy-in for the interventions or kernels we present to them. We ask a lot of our clients—to face their deepest fears; to make space for difficult emotions and sensations; to practice new, uncomfortable skills; to share the most vulnerable parts of themselves; to keep commitments . . . Is it any wonder our clients are at times unsure or reluctant to fully engage in treatment?

In our experience, a well-considered network case conceptualization built and modified in collaboration with clients goes a long way toward helping them understand, buy in, and engage with treatment. It can help to refer to your network diagram in session and have clients explain to you what they see as the problem and where intervention might be most beneficial. Also consider whether the network has been tailored to their unique concerns. Have you captured their concerns using their language or are most of the nodes generic terms that could apply to any client? If your clients appear to grasp the rationale behind their treatment plan, move on to the next question.

Are My Clients Engaging with the Kernel?

Understanding the rationale for the kernel is one thing, engaging in the prescribed intervention is another. It goes without saying that a treatment kernel does no good if it's not practiced. Sometimes we assign homework to our clients, expecting them to engage in challenging exercises with little guidance, and we are surprised when they don't do the assignment or do it in a way counter to spirit of the exercise. If your clients are not engaging with a kernel outside of session, consider more in-session practice.

For example, if your chosen treatment kernel is mindful awareness in response to overwhelming feelings of anger, consider whether your clients have the requisite skills to engage with this kernel before assigning them to do it on their own. Their skill level can be easily assessed in session. Perhaps you can evoke anger through an imaginal confrontation with a loved one and walk through the steps of the intervention together in session. You can then observe how your clients respond and whether they are able to engage in the mindful awareness strategies in an effective manner. Often, in-session work like this clarifies how your clients are interpreting the kernel, which may be different from how you are thinking about it. Perhaps your clients become frustrated that the mindful awareness strategy "failed" because their anger didn't immediately dissipate. Or maybe your clients perseverate on the imagined scenario and have difficulty turning their attention to the mindful part of the exercise. Whatever the case, these insights can guide next steps: psychoeducation or more skills practice, changing the treatment target or the kernel, and so on.

Once you've established that your clients can effectively engage with the kernel in session, you will want them to transfer these skills to out-of-session contexts by engaging in between-session practice. Moreover, you want to ensure that they are following through on their commitments between sessions. Consider whether your clients have a way to track their practice. Are they using a notebook or phone app to monitor their practice? Are they monitoring what happens during the exercises and what goes well or what is challenging about them? These steps can provide data on whether the out-of-session practice is contributing to skill acquisition and change.

Finally, consider whether there are barriers that stand in the way of your clients' ability to engage in the kernel, beyond a lack of understanding. Even as behaviorists, we understand the tendency to attribute client behaviors to intrapersonal variables, like low motivation or forgetfulness. Yet, it is almost always more helpful to examine the role of contextual factors. Perhaps your client faces logistical concerns such as work or school schedules, transportation, lack of resources, or other constraints that need to be overcome in the first place. In these cases, problem solving to facilitate engagement in therapy may be necessary before dispensing your prepared kernels.

Have You Tried Different Versions of the Kernel to Target This Node?

Sometimes, no matter how hard we try, an intervention or exercise simply does not click for clients. Rather than repeating the same exercise again and again, perhaps with a different spin or angle, try another kernel. It is difficult to say exactly when to shift from "try harder" to "try different," but a general guideline could be referencing your original hypothesized timeline for change. For example, if your client struggles with the core belief that they don't deserve to get better, you might start with a defusion exercise, like visualizing leaves on a stream. If that doesn't land, then you could move to another defusion exercise, such as singing the core belief or saying it in a funny voice. If you had expected to see some shift in your client's relationship with the core belief within two or three sessions—even if it's just that they can now recognize it as a thought—yet observe no progress after six sessions, you might then check in with your client about trying a different strategy, such as cognitive restructuring worksheets or self-compassion exercises.

Have You Followed the Data (Empiricism)?

Have you observed your clients' responses and gotten feedback from them? Use these data to shape your decision making. Even the best-laid networks go awry, so over-relying on hypothetical case conceptualizations without consulting real-time updates is perilous. When the data from your living, breathing clients contradict your hypotheses, listen to the data. Be willing to change the focus and target a different node or to reconsider your network conceptualization entirely, if that will make treatment more effective for your clients.

Consider also whether your clients have successfully developed the skill targeted by the kernel and are using it in situations where they believe it will be helpful. If they have done both and practicing the skill appears to not have affected the node or network—as evidenced by no change in their functioning, well-being, or progress toward goals—then it's probably time for a change. Ultimately, you won't—in fact, you cannot—know what the "right" kernel will be at the "right" time. The best we can do is see our clients as fully as possible and be sensitive to how they respond to treatment, so you can meet them where they're at—that's the dance of therapy.

What If the Target Node Keeps Changing (aka "Problem of the Week")?

Sometimes our clients seem to have a new problem that pops up every time they come to session. These "problems of the week" often present as urgent issues that are genuinely important to clients; thus, they demand a delicate balance between addressing clients' immediate concerns and maintaining focus on overarching therapeutic goals. We want to avoid falling into the trap of playing whack-a-mole—smacking down problem after problem, week after week—without looking into the underlying circuitry that may be exacerbating and maintaining these problems in the first place. Otherwise, it would be like cutting off the heads of the Lernaean Hydra without taking the further step of cauterizing the remaining stumps. In fact, situations like these—where you need to identify the process(es) underlying seemingly varied problems in real time—present invaluable opportunities to put your PBT skills to the test.

Clients' narratives about weekly concerns tend to be content heavy, and, on the surface, may seem like a series of disconnected events or give you a problem to solve in session. However, if you pay attention with an eye toward process, these narratives are gold mines, rich with underlying psychological processes. When your client says, "I had a tough week. This happened . . . then this happened . . . then I did this . . . and they did this . . . then this happened," you have two jobs. First, think in terms of process. Do. Not. Get. Caught. Up. In. Content. We absolutely appreciate the allure of diving into the illogic of clients' interpretations or of brandishing a foolproof solution to annihilate the source of their stress, but resist the urge. The best therapists are far more than a sounding board or problem solver. Rather, they are interested in helping their clients gain the skills they need to solve problems on their own. This requires an intentional deemphasizing of the form or content of the problem—*what* it is.

Once you resist the temptation to go after content, your second job is to mine the content for those gold nuggets of process or function—*why* this problem is occurring, or *how* your client's responses are working (or not working) for them in that context. One way to think about this shift in framing is to reflect on interpersonal arguments you've had, especially in close relationships. For instance, you might have argued with your close friend about cancelling on you at the last minute for the third time in a row. Content-wise, sure, that's frustrating—no one enjoys being flaked on. But what was the argument *really* about? Perhaps it was about feeling abandoned, being seen as the second-best option, or even about your close friend drifting away from you. When we say process, we're asking, "What is this *really* about?"

Let's go back to Hermine from Chapter 6. Imagine she comes into session immediately after breaking up with her boyfriend. She's clearly stressed, her affect is dysthymic, and her speech is littered with negativity about the person she is: all the things she's done wrong to get to this position and failing to even get out of bed for work most days this week. Despite her low mood, she speaks about her problems with an urgency that pulls for you to find a solution—a way out of this mess—as soon as possible. She recounts everything that led up to the breakup. Who said what, how she felt, the mistakes she made, how frustrated she is about everything, and so on and so forth. So, what are you to do? How do you help most effectively?

Remember your first job: as compelling as the content of her story is, let it go. Avoid getting caught up in who was right or wrong, what was fair or unfair. This doesn't mean that you don't care about Hermine or her breakup. Rather, it indicates that you are interested in a deeper, more thorough understanding of her problems; an understanding that will lead to a more comprehensive case conceptualization and treatment plan that will do more than whack this mole.

Next, do your second job: focus on the function of what you are seeing in session. Instead of asking content-focused questions like, "What did he say after that?" or "What are you going to do now?," we might instead ask, "When you felt that way this week, what happened next?," "What kind of thoughts/emotions came up during/after the argument?," or "What do you do with those thoughts/emotions?" Notice where these function-focused questions lead us. Answers to these questions provide building blocks for antecedent–response–consequence chains. Before you know it, we're off to the races building a network case conceptualization.

Another consideration when clients come in with a problem of the week is that they may, even unknowingly, be deflecting attention from more challenging therapeutic work. For example, clients may be reluctant to engage in exposure exercises and the problems of the week function as avoidance. On a content level, it may seem that your clients are going through an especially stressful time—which could still be true. But, by thinking about process, we might also consider adding avoidance or distress intolerance to our case conceptualization and treatment plan. The content of clients' stories contains clues about which processes might be most relevant to their problems. The art of PBT lies in listening not just to the story but to the processes underlying the story.

What Do I Do When My Clients Have a Crisis in the Middle of Therapy?

When clients experience a crisis or other meaningful stressor in the middle of therapy, it can feel like a curveball, disrupting your treatment plan. By meaningful, we mean something different from a "problem of the week." A significant stressor would impact your clients' functioning or well-being in a major way (e.g., onset of depressive mood or suicidal plans, missing work for two weeks straight). Of course, what counts as major requires clinical judgment. Regardless, when something you and your clients deem significant occurs, here are some steps to take.

Re-assess Treatment Goals

Returning to the Workability Principle, we need to ground therapy in our clients' treatment goals. It would be entirely reasonable to assume that your clients would now want to shift focus to this new problem, but we need to ask them to know for sure. Check in with your clients about how this new stressor impacts their treatment goals. Do they want to set short-term goals related to the problem? Does it change where they want to be at the end of treatment? Sometimes, clients just want us to know what's going on in their lives, without needing us to provide the solution.

Update Your Network

Networks, just like the clients we serve, are dynamic and ever-changing. Pull out your network case conceptualization and see where this new stressor might fit. If it's an external event, you could add it as a context node in a rounded rectangle or oval (see Chapter 5 for details). Then, lean on your curiosity: How does it relate to their existing problems? Are there current processes that might be relevant to this new issue? Does the problem interact or exacerbate existing nodes, or is it entirely separate? Stay focused on processes and consider the full picture to place this event within the larger context of the client's network.

If the stressor introduces problems or processes not previously identified, add these to your network—most likely as regular rectangles, which represent malleable responses. This will affect the overall case conceptualization and treatment plan. Thus, these revisions might result in setting new goals and introducing new kernels to the treatment plan.

Go Back to the Drawing Board

If after this, the stressor has led to fundamental changes in the client's presentation, you may be best served by a blank piece of paper and developing a brand-new network case conceptualization. For instance, if your client's primary presenting problem was interpersonal conflicts with their parent and their parent dies, your network would probably shift dramatically.

Work with your client to explore their new life context. What nodes from the original network are still relevant? What nodes need to be added to tell the story of their current situation? What relationships between nodes from the original network remain the same, have changed in magnitude or direction, or have disappeared? Ultimately, you'll want to walk through the network building and treatment planning steps, just as you did at the start of therapy. Doing so may also help your client make sense of the upheaval in their life and clarify how to proceed.

Temporarily Shift Gears

Sometimes a new stressor doesn't fit into your clients' current network. Perhaps the stressor is orthogonal to the original problem and any attempts to incorporate it into the network only end up making an entirely separate network that does not meaningfully interact with the other. This usually happens when clients experience an acute or short-lived stressor they have the fundamental skills to cope with, even as they feel overwhelmed and helpless.

In these cases, you may elect to temporarily focus on this second network. This might involve the use of problem-solving strategies to brainstorm solutions, evaluate pros and cons, or explore potential resources relevant to their new stressor. We advise caution when employing this gear shift, as you still want to keep track of the original conceptualization and treatment plan. We recommend setting clear boundaries to ensure that you don't get lost on treatment detours, such as setting a session limit for discussing this problem.

At the same time, be wary about dismissing "orthogonal" problems too readily—it always comes back to context. It's possible that your current network represents the "easy" problem, and the new stressor triggered more deep-seated struggles (e.g., related to past trauma) that your clients have yet to divulge in therapy. Bear in mind the Personalization Principle. What do your clients need from you at this juncture? How do their unique backgrounds and histories inform what this new stressor means to them?

What If My Clients Want to Change Their Treatment Goals?

Times like these are perfect to practice thinking in terms of process. When clients say, "I want to work on something different," consider the form of the statement (i.e., the actual request) and its function (i.e., what the request is *really* about). Process-based thinking encourages you to appraise reasons behind the desire to shift goals that may not be immediately apparent. Perhaps clients are confused by the current treatment kernel, don't see how the intervention applies to their problem, are having difficulty trusting the therapist, are fearful of making changes in a particular area of their life, or any number of possible reasons. If, after some exploration, you both agree that the desire to change the treatment is driven by a factor such as fear, avoidance, confusion, etc., then add this new factor to your network. Clearly, it's significant enough to influence your client's perception of their treatment goals.

As an example, let's say you begin working with your client on interoceptive exposures to decrease avoidance of exercise due to elevated physiological arousal. To track the introduction of this kernel, you add it to your network. In Figure 7.1, [interoceptive exposures] has a hypothesized inhibitory (negative) effect on avoidance.

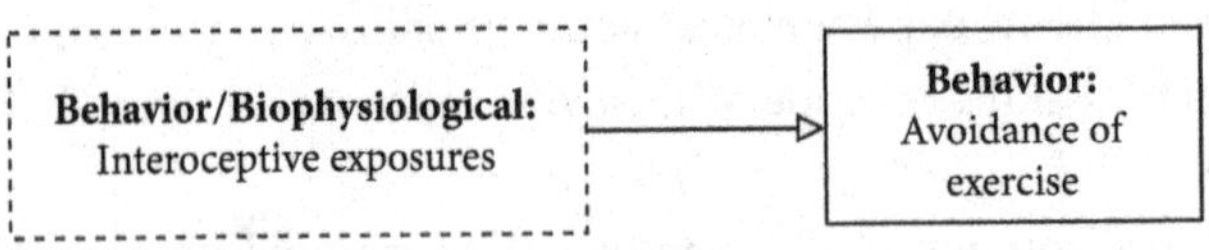

Figure 7.1 Mini network for client avoiding exercise with treatment kernel.

As you do more interoceptive exposures, you notice your client begins to give reasons why they can't do their exposures. They didn't have time this week, or they weren't sure how to follow the instructions. After examining the underlying process, both of you identify [fear of dying] as a barrier to treatment. You can then update your network again to reflect this new clinically relevant variable. In the revised network in Figure 7.2, [fear of dying] has an inhibitory effect on exposures and excitatory (positive) effect on avoidance of exercise.

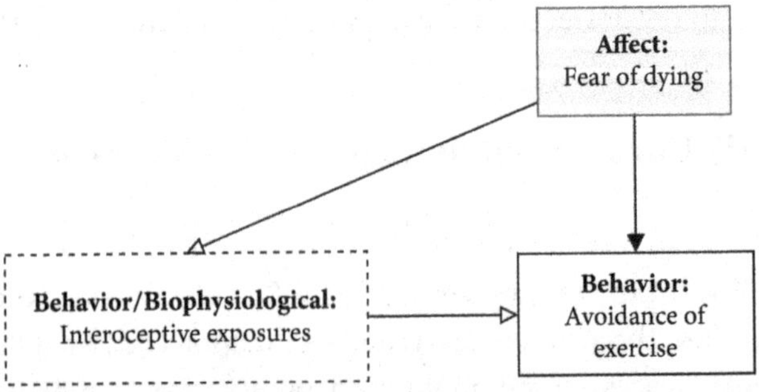

Figure 7.2 Mini network for client avoiding exercise with treatment barrier.

Rather than change treatment goals, by including the underlying antagonist in the network, you and your client acknowledge the function of changing treatment goals as avoidance (of fear of dying) and can collaboratively revise the treatment plan as needed. In this case, perhaps the client would benefit from easier exposures, exploration of existential fears, or a better understanding of the rationale for exposures. It may also be helpful to remind your client of the motivation behind their original treatment goals. Why did they want to work on exercising more? What brought them into therapy in the first place? Bringing your client back to this headspace may help them recognize that the person who now wants to alter treatment goals is exactly the person who has kept them stuck all this time.

If, after thorough exploration, you and your client agree that the new goals are meaningful, values consistent, and not driven by one of the aforementioned factors such as avoidance, you may want to revise the treatment plan to incorporate these new goals into your current case conceptualization. This may result in a reorganization of which nodes are emphasized and which associated treatment kernels would best serve your client's needs.

How Do I Know When to End Treatment?

Determining the appropriate time to conclude therapy is a surprisingly difficult task. Again, there's no "right" answer. Progress in treatment tends to be nonlinear, with ups and downs along the way. There aren't bright red lines that delineate adaptive from maladaptive behavior. Clients are often unsure about their own progress and whether they can maintain it outside of treatment. Despite these challenges, PBT offers some guidance.

Adaptive, Self-Sustaining Networks

Because PBT is about more than eliminating a problem or learning a new skill, we must look for evidence of deeper, longer lasting, and meaningful change in our clients' networks, specifically changes in their networks from pre- to post-treatment. Your initial network case conceptualization is a map of your clients' presenting concerns. An objective of PBT is to disrupt this

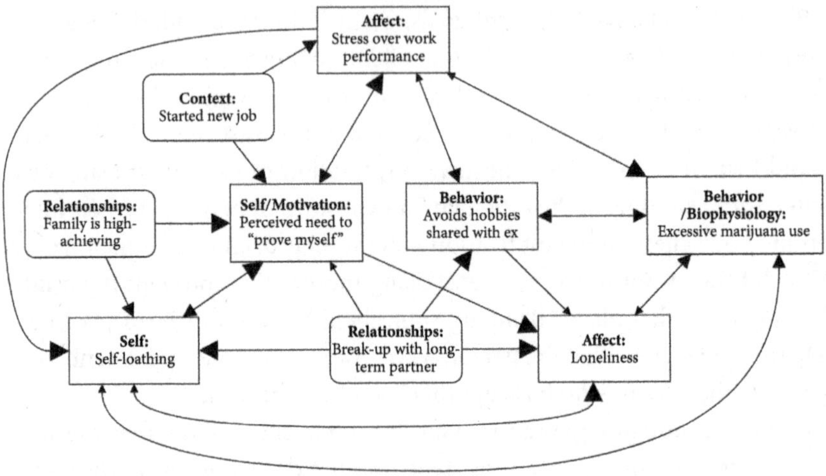

Figure 7.3 Hermine's network (again).

maladaptive network and help your clients build a stable, adaptive network that facilitates goal attainment.

Recall Hermine's network at the start of treatment (see Figure 7.3). In this state, her network was maladaptive; it consisted of multiple processes that were sustaining unwanted behavior, affect, and self-perceptions. Her need to prove herself led to stress, which led to self-loathing, which fed loneliness, which resulted in excessive marijuana use. It was like an engine that created its own fuel, never stopping. When a network is in this state, we can safely say that treatment is not complete.

Compare this to Hermine's network as she learns skills in treatment (see Figure 7.4)—it's becoming a different, much more adaptive engine. She's practicing self-compassion and meditation and seeing a reduction in her stress, loneliness, and perceived need to prove herself. She is using pleasant activity scheduling, which is impacting her feelings of loneliness and engagement with hobbies. Moreover, she has stopped using marijuana to avoid these unwanted internal experiences.

Closely examining the network, it's clear there is still more work to be done. There remains a less-adaptive engine consisting of pressure from family to be high-achieving, driving feelings of self-loathing and a continued need to prove herself. These factors contribute to persistent stress and loneliness that are likely affecting important areas of her life and getting in the way of her goals.

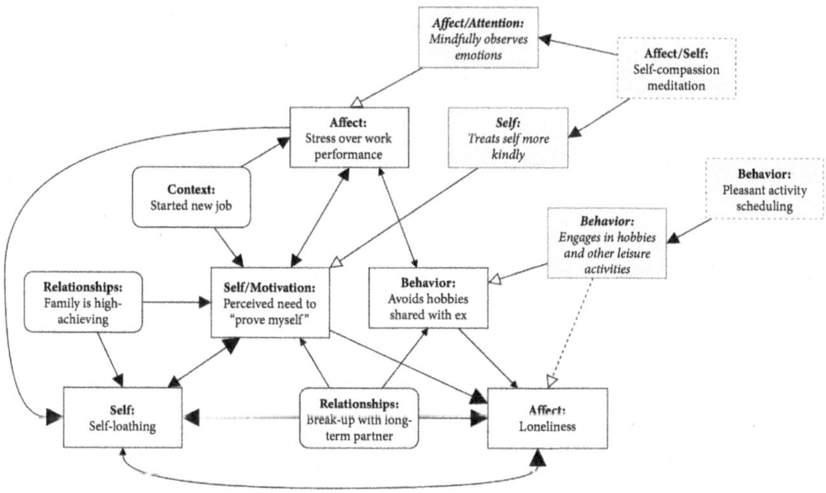

Figure 7.4 Hermine's updated network over the course of treatment (again).

If we fast forward some more, we can observe a potential outcome for Hermine that has resulted in a more adaptive network (see Figure 7.5). Now, Hermine has embraced a daily mindful meditation practice and has become skilled at observing her emotions from a distance, not allowing them to dictate her behavior as they used to. This skill, paired with a more compassionate stance toward her internal experiences has transformed her past need to prove herself into a more intrinsically motivated and confident self-conceptualization. This is evidenced by her use of new language in session (e.g., "this is for me," "I'm good enough") and behavior outside of session (e.g., participating in the local Ultimate frisbee league).

Hermine's new network is self-sustaining, and she has integrated pleasant activity planning into her routine. On top of this, two of her contextual stressors have changed with time. She has become much more experienced and comfortable at her job, finding success and satisfaction at work that were previously absent. The initial pain from the break-up with her long-term partner has subsided (reflected by smaller arrowheads), and she has learned more effective ways of coping with the related difficult thoughts and emotions that still pop up from time to time. Furthermore, her stress over performing well at work has become a cue for her to practice mindfully observing her emotions.

Notice how these new factors are the driving force of Hermine's adaptive network. Of course, she still experiences stress at work, times when she

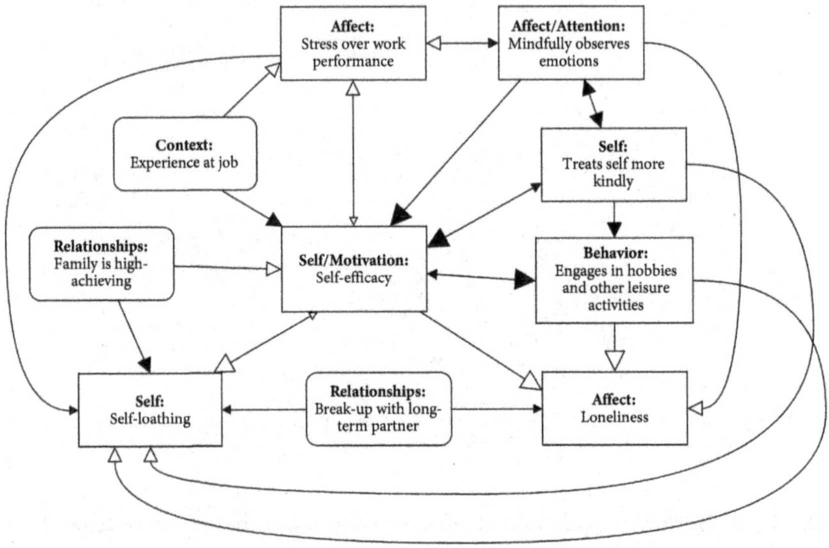

Figure 7.5 Hermine's potential adaptive network.

feels lonely, and self-loathing. We wouldn't expect therapy to strip Hermine, or anyone, of the fullness of their lived experience. But Hermine is now much better equipped to handle these human experiences that previously caused so much suffering. You can see how the skills she has learned (i.e., self-kindness, mindful awareness) have significantly increased self-efficacy. In turn, this has reduced the impact of unwanted internal experiences (i.e., stress, self-loathing, and loneliness), while increasing her motivation to engage in valued leisure activities. Moreover, her skills enhance each other, such that, for example, the more Hermine is able to mindfully observe her emotions, the more she is able to treat herself kindly and vice versa. At this point, we would call this an adaptive, self-sustaining network that is likely resilient to future stressors. Assuming Hermine reports that she has met her treatment goals, we would wrap up therapy at this time.

Contextual Variables

A stable adaptive network should retain its form, even in the face of stressors, just like a self-sustaining maladaptive network usually retains its form even after many sessions of therapy. Kind of like how a stress ball returns to its original shape even after you sit on it. Generally, contextual variables—rounded rectangles typically without arrows going into them—are crucial for supporting network stability, so look at the full EEMM picture when evaluating whether a client's network is sustainable. Areas of context to consider include a stable living situation, social support, a supportive work or academic environment, and access to resources for managing unforeseen future stressors.

Data-Driven Decision Making

As much as your clients feeling like they're done with therapy matters, the data you've been collecting over the course of treatment should support your and your clients' assessment of treatment progress and determination of an adaptive network. At the very least, the data you use to inform when to end treatment should include a few things. First, self-report data. Clients' own reports about their experiences are invaluable. Ask them what they have learned in therapy. Do they believe they have the resources and skills to maintain their treatment gains? We're including self-report assessments here too. What measures have you used to track progress? Evaluate their current scores and consider whether there are still areas for growth. In addition, there should be some consensus—convergent validity—between the therapist's observations and clients' self-report that they are ready to graduate from treatment and that progress can be maintained.

Clinical observations are a second source of data. What do you notice about your clients' behavior in session? How well have they followed through on between-session practice? How has their body language shifted over time?

Third, gather data about the stability of your clients' networks. How well do they hold up to stressors? Sometimes these stressors occur naturally during the course of therapy, and you can simply observe your clients' ability to adapt. Other times, you may need to intentionally approach a stressor by engaging in a novel exercise or evoking the stressor in the therapy room. The proof is in the pudding, as they say. If your clients successfully navigate new stressors using skills they have learned in therapy, it suggests a resilient adaptive network and readiness for ending treatment.

Mapping Your Treatment Route

At any given moment, there are innumerable options for how to proceed with clients. Do you attempt to bring up an unpleasant emotion? Do you reflect what your clients said back to them? Do you ask a question? Do you simply nod your head and allow for silence? We could go on and on. The same goes for the number of potential ways to conceptualize clients' problems and develop treatment plans. Like an explorer mapping a trail up a previously undiscovered mountain, the choices before us can be daunting and the path forward is often unclear. It can be overwhelming when you pause to think about it.

The most skilled therapists we know, much like any explorer worth their salt, are able to make space for the dialectic of respecting the vast and humbling ambiguity inherent in their work, while trusting that their mapping and decision-making skills will lead them to the summit. Like explorers, we're tasked with getting a lay of the land and creating a map, or conceptualization, that represents our clients and their struggles. Like any map of a mountain, it's not the actual mountain—it's a representation that is only as helpful as it's able to inform climbers how to successfully navigate to the top.

So, we take our best-guess map and hike without having hiked the mountain before. And we trust our map, so long as it gets us closer to the peak. Undoubtedly, we'll find errors in our map or learn that the trail has changed from what we once thought it was. We'll need to redraw and improve the map as we continue to hike, using the data at our disposal.

Now, you probably aren't an explorer, or at least not one who scales uncharted mountains. We certainly aren't. However, we would argue that your work is at least as intellectually challenging and filled with even more decision points than the challenges facing your average mountaineer. Thankfully, PBT principles are designed to develop the maps we need to effectively guide our clinical decision making. These principles empower us to effectively address the endless number of questions and choices that face us. Without a doubt, the questions we've addressed in this chapter are not exhaustive, nor are the answers definitive. After all, the heart of any effective therapy—certainly one using a PBT approach—lies not in having all the answers, but in asking the right questions and flexibly and compassionately engaging with your clients.

Chapter Summary

- When making decisions about which nodes to target, think big picture and long term. What will have the greatest and/or most sustainable impact? What has the highest likelihood of disrupting the network as a whole?
- Before making changes to your treatment plan, do some troubleshooting and identify factors that might be getting in the way of treatment engagement.
- Do not let your clients' content overwhelm your sessions. Instead, use content to dig deeper into process. Ask, "What is this problem about?" rather than "How do we solve this problem?"
- At the end of treatment, adaptive networks should be self-sustaining and resilient in the face of stressors.
- You'll never have all the answers and always be faced with some doubt about which nodes to include in a case conceptualization and which kernels to use for a given problem. PBT principles can guide your decision making and help you flexibly adjust your plans as needed.

8

Putting It Together

Final Case Example

It's showtime. Time to take everything you've learned and apply it to a new client, step by step. We'll discuss our rationale and choices at each point, but we encourage you to make your own decisions before reading ours. Shift your focus away from getting the "right" answer. Instead, use this chapter to flex your PBT muscles. Think *functionally* about the case and consider potential paths that would be *workable* for this client. We offer two potential paths, but there are likely many effective ways to approach case conceptualization and treatment planning.

The Case of Ruby

Box 8.1 contains a case vignette for Ruby. For this client, we imagine treatment being done on a weekly basis in an outpatient private practice setting. We'll approach the case from a modern CBT perspective informed by ACT, given our theoretical background and area of expertise, but use your own knowledge, skills, and theoretical orientation to inform your decision making. For example, where we go toward exposures and cognitive restructuring, you may veer toward polyvagal exercises or chairwork.

Box 8.1 Case vignette for Ruby

Ruby is a 45-year-old Indian American woman who works at an insurance agency in New England. She enjoys her job but worries she will be let go as there have been recent layoffs in her sector. She was the first in her family to attend college and has been highly successful in school and her career. However, Ruby's achievements are shadowed by a lingering sense of not

A Process-Based Approach to Psychotherapy. Clarissa W. Ong and Eric B. Lee, Oxford University Press.
© Oxford University Press (2025). DOI: 10.1093/oso/9780197696378.003.0008

belonging, stemming from a childhood history of being bullied and feeling out of place due to her race and ethnicity.

Growing up attending predominantly white schools, she often felt like an outsider. Her parents are devout Muslims and hold traditional patriarchal views. Ruby reported feeling overlooked and undervalued as a girl and now as a woman, especially compared to her two brothers. She identifies as Muslim and derives strength and purpose from her religious practice. However, she describes herself as "far less traditional" than her parents, hiding many of her less orthodox beliefs from them for fear of rejection. She feels conflicted between being the person her parents want her to be and forging her own path, stating, "I'm 45 and still haven't figured out who I am."

These early experiences embedded a deep-rooted fear of being abandoned and alone, manifesting in persistent anxiety and overworking. She has constant thoughts that "everyone will leave me," which leads to excessive reassurance seeking in her relationships (e.g., "Do you really love me?," "Are we OK?"), overwhelming her partners. She is single and cycles between using dating apps daily and then deleting them from her phone for weeks. Recently, after a few meetings, her date expressed that he no longer wanted to see Ruby and mentioned that he was not attracted to her. Since then, Ruby has been plagued by thoughts that her dark skin tone is "ugly."

This rejection led to what Ruby describes as "higher than usual" levels of anxiety, fearing that she is unattractive and will be alone forever. At times, Ruby finds her heart racing and her head spinning and feels as though she is losing control and her grip on reality. She finds herself unable to concentrate, avoids social contact, and has completely stopped her once-consistent daily jogging routine. In addition, she now spends most of her day procrastinating work, worrying about her future and what others think of her, looking up relationship advice, and scrolling through her friends' social media accounts. At night, she stays up in bed, watching videos on her phone and trying to "zone out" from the world. Despite a strong desire to sleep, she experiences insomnia and only gets a few hours of quality sleep a night.

As Ruby enters treatment, her goals are broad, wanting to "get [her] life back together," figure out a "life direction," and to "stop feeling so scared

Continued

Continued

and anxious all the time." Additionally, she is hoping for advice on how to find a partner.

Intake

The following pages present an example of a completed intake form (a blank form can be found in Appendix C). Information gathered from the intake will be used to select potential nodes of interest and begin building a network conceptualization.

Presenting Problem (EEMM/Empiricism)

Table 8.1 shows Ruby's struggles organized along the EEMM dimensions and levels.

Table 8.1 Ruby's presenting concerns organized along EEMM dimensions and levels.

EEMM Dimension/Level	Client's Description	Specific Examples (What Does This Look Like?)
Affect/Emotion	"Higher than usual" levels of anxiety	Frequently asks partner if relationship is going well or avoids dating altogether
Cognition	Believes, "everyone will leave [her]," feels as though she is losing control and her grip on reality	Reassurance seeking
Attention	Difficulty concentrating, significant time spent worrying about future and what people think of her, tries to "zone out" from the world	Takes longer than usual to complete simple tasks (e.g., email), uses phone in bed till 2–3 a.m.

EEMM Dimension/Level	Client's Description	Specific Examples (What Does This Look Like?)
Self	"I'm ugly," perceives dark skin as unattractive, "I'm 45 and still haven't figured out who I am"	Blames self for problems, downplays accomplishments, deletes (and re-downloads) dating apps regularly
Motivation	Wants to figure out "life direction," wants to "zone out" from the world, desire to sleep, desire to stop feeling anxious	Difficulty articulating needs and desires even when prompted, uses phone as distraction, avoids usual activities of jogging and socializing, frequent use of "should" statements
Overt Behavior	Avoids social contact, procrastinates work, uses phone in bed	Ignores texts from friends, uses phone for at least one hour before going to bed and upon waking
Context	Living in mostly white New England as an Indian American, first-generation college student, recent layoffs in her sector, parents hold patriarchal views	Parents have expressed disappointment that she's "still not married"
Biology/Physiology	Racing heart, head spinning, dizzy, insomnia, paused jogging routine	Takes frequents breaks from work to "reset," sleeps for ~ four hours a night
Relationships	Rejection and invalidation as a child and adult, was bullied, perceived favoritism from parents	Other children gave her racist nicknames, parents spend more time talking to and about her brothers
Culture	Muslim faith important to her, being single as a 45-year-old woman and stigma associated with that	Attends mosque weekly, performs all five salah daily, avoids discussing her single status with others

Note: Some of the specific examples listed here are based on behaviors we might observe in session rather than directly reported by Ruby, such as difficulty articulating needs and desires even when prompted.

Relationships Among Problems (Process)

We identified four target problems to capture Ruby's primary struggles (see Table 8.2). Given what we know about her current situation and treatment goals, we believe these four targets capture most of her concerns.

Table 8.2 Identifying antecedents and consequences associated with Ruby's target problems.

Target Problem/Symptom	Antecedent	Consequence
Fear of rejection in the context of relationships	History of rejection and invalidation, perceives self as "ugly"	Seeks reassurance from partners, avoids dating for periods of time
Avoids socializing with friends	Desire to stop feeling anxious, worries about what others think of her	Feels less anxious in the short term, spends more time in bed on phone, worries about what others think of her
Difficulty sleeping	Racing heart, head spinning, dizzy, uses phone in bed before sleeping	More anxiety throughout the day, blames self for problems
Anxiety	Stress at work, being rejected, core belief that everyone will leave her	Avoids socializing, spends time in bed on phone, difficulty sleeping

Client Variables (Personalization)

In Table 8.3, we consider variables unique to Ruby that may be influencing her presenting concerns.

Table 8.3 Mapping unique client variables to Ruby's struggles.

Area	Client's Description	Relationship to Problem
Client Identities	Middle-aged, Indian American Muslim woman, hardworking employee, kind friend, caring daughter	Social and parental pressure to marry causes stress, internalized racism related to fear of rejection and low self-worth, mismatch of values/norms with parents leads to unclear goals and values

Area	Client's Description	Relationship to Problem
Strengths	Continued dating even when it was difficult before recently giving up, has good support system (friends, family, coworkers)	Lost contact with support as social avoidance has increased
Interpretation /Understanding of Problem	Feels that the problem has been "bubbling up" since childhood, history of rejection and feeling unsupported, recognizes that avoidance is part of the problem	Uncertainty over ability to change (related to low self-worth)
Treatment Expectations	Realistic view of therapy: "I'm ready to put in the work"	Motivation may be helpful to leverage against uncertainty about future change
Reason for Seeking Treatment Now	Feeling like she has "hit rock bottom," recently told by date that he was not attracted to her—huge blow that has significantly increased symptoms	"Confirmation" that her worst fears are true, increasing intensity of problems and compromising her ability to function

Treatment Goals (Workability)

In Table 8.4, we've provided plausible and measurable versions of Ruby's treatment goals and identified outcomes to evaluate progress toward those goals, to illustrate what to do with this part of the treatment plan in Appendix C. Later in the chapter, we'll discuss her goals in different scenarios and how we plan to track them.

Table 8.4 Ruby's treatment goals.

What is the specific goal?	How will it be measured?	Is it attain-able?	Why is this goal important to the client?	What is the timeline for completion?
Use coping strategies in response to anxiety	Fortnightly anxiety measure	Yes	"It's getting in the way of everything"	12 weeks

Continued

Table 8.4 *Continued*

What is the specific goal?	How will it be measured?	Is it attain-able?	Why is this goal important to the client?	What is the timeline for completion?
Socialize with friends again	Did she do it today? Yes/no	Yes	Needs her support system, misses friends	2 weeks
Sleep for six or more hours per night	Number of hours of sleep per night	Yes	Believes it will improve other problems and symptoms	4 weeks
Go on a date	Did she do it this week? Yes/no	Yes	Wants to find a partner	6 weeks

Network Case Conceptualization

Node Selection

Now that we've gathered some information from the intake, we'll move to case conceptualization, starting by following the steps from Chapter 5 to select which nodes to include in our network. For this example, we'll use a simple table to streamline node selection that combines steps 1 (identify clinically relevant variables), 2 (group functionally similar variables), and 3 (narrow down to 5–10 clinically relevant variables). Before looking at which nodes we considered, excluded, and ultimately selected, fill out Table 8.5 using the information from Ruby's vignette.

Table 8.5 Blank table for node selection with rationale.

Node Excluded	Node Selected	Why/Why Not

Node Excluded	Node Selected	Why/Why Not

See Table 8.6 for what we came up with (yours will probably look different). We first identified 21 potential nodes. Next, we whittled them down by combining functionally similar variables (e.g., feeling that she doesn't belong and core belief that everyone will leave her) and excluding those that appeared to be more distal, less relevant to treatment goals, and/or were causing less distress relative to other potential nodes. This left us with 10 nodes to build our network.

Table 8.6 Completed table for node selection with rationale.

Node Excluded	Node Selected	Why/Why Not
Layoffs in her sector		Distal factor, not in forefront of Ruby's mind compared to relationships and anxiety
First-generation college student		Distal factor, not as central to Ruby's identity compared to her faith, ethnicity, and gender
Decreased exercise		Seems to cause less distress and impairment than selected nodes
Concentration difficulties		Seems to cause less distress and impairment than selected nodes
History of invalidation		Functionally similar to history of rejection
History of being bullied (related to race)		Functionally similar to history of rejection
Parents' lack of support		Functionally similar to history of rejection
	History of rejection	Combines functionally similar nodes
Feeling that she doesn't belong		Functionally similar to core belief that everyone will leave her
Fear of abandonment		Functionally similar to core belief that everyone will leave her
	Core belief: "Everyone will leave me"	Described as a significant cause of anxiety
Single status at 45 years old		Cultural pressure from family and society to be married, overlaps with mismatch between her values/norms and her parents' values/norms and low self-esteem

Continued

Table 8.6 *Continued*

Node Excluded	Node Selected	Why/Why Not
	Mismatch between her values/norms and her parents' values/norms	Important background context likely relevant to motivation
Panic-like anxiety symptoms		Functionally similar to anxiety
Worry about future and what others think of her		Overlaps with anxiety and low self-esteem, less directly relevant to treatment goals
	Anxiety	Causing significant impairment; related to treatment goals
Belief that she is unattractive because she has dark skin		Functionally similar to internalized racism
	Internalized racism/low self-esteem	Readily seen in session, many examples outside the therapy room (it is pervasive), appears to be related to other problems Note: We added "low self-esteem" to this node to capture how internalized racism is affecting Ruby
	Reassurance seeking	Negatively affecting relationships
	Rejection from dates	Proximal contextual variable related to anxiety and core belief that everyone will leave her
	Avoids social activity	Relevant outcome related to her ability to move forward, which is a treatment goal
	Excessive time in bed and on phone	Avoidance related to other nodes (e.g., difficulty sleeping)
	Difficulty sleeping	Critical to overall functioning, Ruby explicitly stated she wants to improve sleep

Node Review

Before we begin building our network proper, let's check to make sure we didn't miss anything (step 4: check for comprehensiveness). To the EEMM (see Table 8.7)!

Hmm . . . there are two blanks in Table 8.7: Attention and Motivation. Let's consider these in turn. First, attention. Ruby mentioned concentration

Table 8.7 Review of Ruby's clinically relevant problems against EEMM dimensions and levels.

Dimensions	Affect/Emotion	Anxiety
	Cognition	Core belief: "everyone will leave me"
	Attention	
	Self	Internalized racism/low self-esteem
	Motivation	
	Overt Behavior	Excessive time in bed and on phone Avoids social activity Reassurance seeking
Levels	Biology/Physiology	Difficulty sleeping
	Relationships	Reassurance seeking History of rejection Rejection from dates Mismatch between her values/norms and parents' values/norms
	Culture	Internalized racism/low self-esteem Mismatch between her values/norms and parents' values/norms

difficulties; however, we chose to exclude that node because, based on our current information, it seems to cause less distress and impairment than other reported concerns. For now, we'll take note of this omission and monitor whether it becomes more relevant in future sessions.

We could also consider other common attentional processes that might be relevant to Ruby. For example, does she have a hard time being present and aware of her surroundings or her own emotions or bodily sensations? Does she display behaviors in session such as readily noticing threatening stimuli and/or ignoring safety signals that might be a sign of attentional bias? As of now, we have not seen these behaviors and Ruby has not reported them. Thus, we'll leave the Attention row blank for the time being. As a reminder, we're going for the core of Ruby's struggles, which means the network only needs to cover 70%–80% of her problems. In our experience, there are diminishing returns after that point.

Now, motivation. As we review Ruby's vignette considering motivation, we notice some potentially relevant information. Her statement that she "hasn't figured out who [she is]" when describing the challenge of balancing her own desires with those of her parents stands out. Her treatment goal of figuring out a "life direction" also fits this theme. Using ACT terms, we would say Ruby is unclear about her values. This lack of clarity appears to be related to how she views herself and might be inhibiting helpful social behaviors. Given the relevance of [unclear values] to Ruby's treatment goals, we will add it to the Motivation row and make it our 11th node.

Moment of Reflection

How are you doing so far? You should have chosen at least a handful of nodes to build a network with. Consider which nodes we had in common and which ones we didn't. You might have picked up on the Motivation dimension immediately, which we had initially overlooked, or chosen to include an Attention node to reflect Ruby's inability to focus and excessive worrying. You might have used different language to describe similar variables. None of that means one of us is right and one of us is wrong—it simply means we have different perspectives on the same person, as humans with different experiences are wont to do. As we progress through this chapter, continue being intentional about how you're making your choices.

Compare our reasons for including (vs. excluding) and grouping certain variables to your own. Perhaps you conceptualized the overlap among variables differently—that's to be expected. For instance, we chose to group multiple variables into a [history of rejection] node, and you might have wanted to imbue your conceptualization with more nuance. Similarly, even though [fear of abandonment] is a partly affective node, we subsumed it under a cognitive node, [core belief: "everyone will leave me"], as we felt that the affective aspect of [fear of abandonment] was adequately captured by the broad [anxiety] node.

There's no "right" way to do this—the only way we'll know if we selected "good" nodes is to see how Ruby responds to treatment. However, there are "wrong" ways to go about identifying nodes. If none of your selected nodes relate to Ruby's treatment goals, you're missing key variables. If none of your nodes reflect Ruby's cultural background and salient identities (e.g., pressure from parents to get married, internalized racism), you're also missing something. See if there's anything you want to change about your selected nodes. Once you're ready with your list, let's begin building a network.

Network Building

Let's begin by getting our nodes organized (step 5: convert variables to visual nodes). Whether you're using pencil and paper or software (e.g., draw.io; available at https://github.com/jgraph/drawio) to build your network, draw each of your variables with either rounded (contextual) or square (malleable) corners and label them with their corresponding EEMM dimension(s) or level(s). Optionally, you can adjust the size of the nodes based on perceived severity (we did this in Chapter 5 but have not done it here to streamline Ruby's network building). Our selected nodes are presented in Figure 8.1.

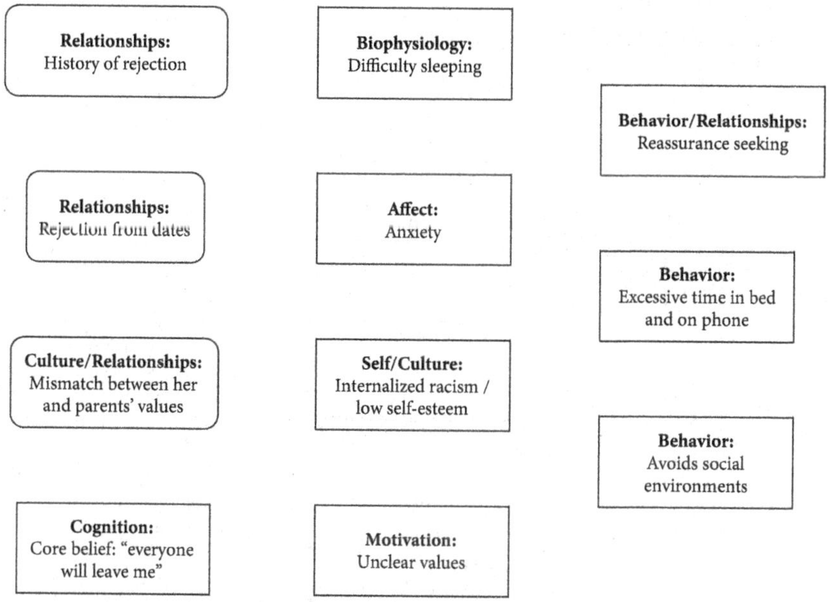

Figure 8.1 Visualizing Ruby's nodes (step 5 of network building).

Now it's time to add arrows (step 6: connect the nodes). Do this one node at a time. Consider each variable and connect it to other nodes where there is some evidence of, or rationale for, a relationship. If you're using pencil and paper, start with light lines as you will likely erase and edit as you flesh out your network. If using software, don't hesitate to move nodes around or adjust arrows to increase legibility. Don't worry about the size of arrowheads at this point (that'll come later in step 8). Just get the relationships down without thinking too much about the magnitude of the association.

1. **[anxiety]:** We chose to start with [anxiety] because it seems central to many of Ruby's concerns (see Figure 8.2). You could surely make a case to start with any of the other nodes. It doesn't matter much; we will review them all. From our perspective, there are clear paths to

[reassurance seeking] and avoidance behavior: [avoids social environments] and [excessive time in bed and on phone]. More speculatively, we hypothesized that [anxiety] would likely affect her sleeping as well as self-esteem and added these arrows. These seem like reasonable assumptions that we will hold lightly as they may be modified as we collect more data. Note that we are only drawing one-way arrows away from [anxiety] at this point. We find it easier to think about what each node is contributing to, one at a time, rather than trying to consider all possible relationships at once.

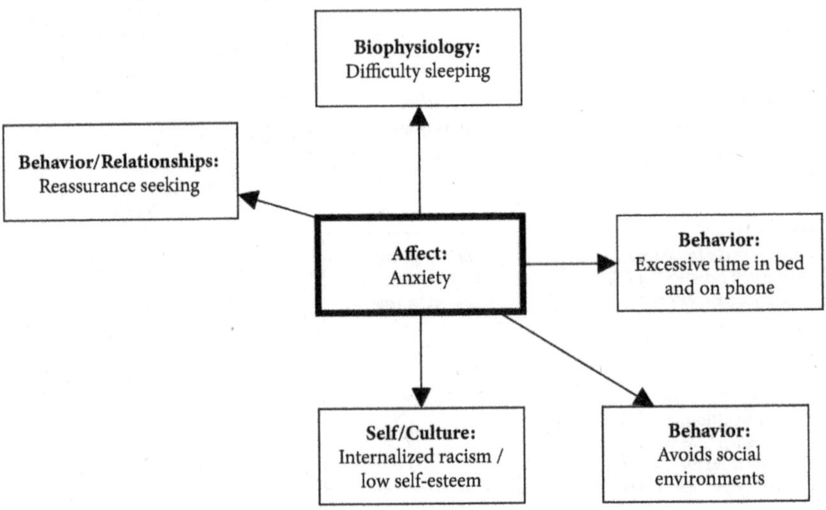

Figure 8.2 Adding arrows from [anxiety] (step 6 of network building).

2. **[reassurance seeking]:** Next, we move to one of the nodes we have added. We chose [reassurance seeking] and noted two negative or inhibitory relationships. We add open arrowheads to denote this type of relationship (see Figure 8.3). These indicate that [reassurance seeking] leads to a reduction in [anxiety] and the strength of the [core belief: "everyone will leave me"]. We're hypothesizing that these effects occur in the short term, so we used dashed arrows to represent immediate effects. We also draw an arrow to (rejection from dates), assuming that her reassurance seeking is contributing to this problem. Although rounded boxes typically don't have arrows going into them, we added an arrow here to show how Ruby's behavior may influence outcomes,

even if they are not *directly* changeable by Ruby. For example, she could eliminate reassurance seeking and still be rejected by her dates.

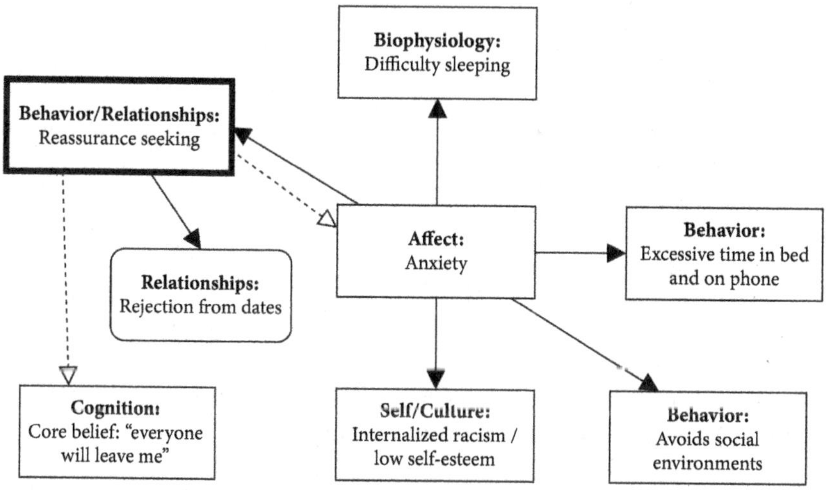

Figure 8.3 Adding arrows from [reassurance seeking] (step 6 of network building).

3. **[core belief: "everyone will leave me"], (rejection from dates):** These arrows were fairly straightforward additions (see Figure 8.4). Ruby reported that [rejection from dates] was contributing to [anxiety], the [core belief: "everyone will leave me"], feelings of low self-worth, and likely internalized racism too. Moreover, her core belief that everyone will leave her is clearly causing [anxiety] and leading to [reassurance seeking].
4. **[difficulty sleeping], [excessive time in bed and on the phone], [avoids social environments]:** Ruby said that [difficulty sleeping] is causing [anxiety]. Without a thorough assessment of her sleep behavior, we tentatively hypothesized that spending excessive time in bed trying to sleep and using her phone in bed are causing more sleep problems. We add open dashed arrows from her avoidance behaviors to [anxiety] to reflect negative reinforcement of these behaviors through immediate decreases in anxiety (see Figure 8.5). Observe that the network becomes messier with the dashed arrows, which is why we suggest using them sparingly and only if key to your case conceptualization. In Ruby's case, we wanted to emphasize the consequence (i.e., short-term relief) maintaining several undesired behaviors, especially

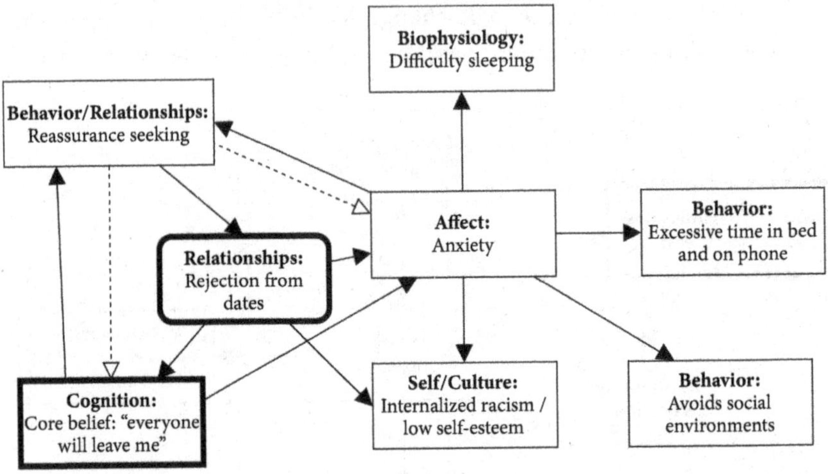

Figure 8.4 Adding arrows from [core belief: "everyone will leave me"] and (rejection from dates) (step 6 of network building).

given her ostensible limited insight into these relationships. However, a different therapist could easily replace them with solid excitatory arrows to map their long-term effects on anxiety instead, given an alternative clinical rationale. Finally, time in bed on phone and avoidance of social events appear to be interrelated, as the more time she spends in bed at home, the less time she spends out with her friends. Thus, we add a double-sided arrow between [excessive time in bed and on phone] and [avoids social environments].

5. **[internalized racism/low self-esteem]:** We hypothesized that the internalized racism and low self-esteem that make up a portion of Ruby's self-concept are contributing to [anxiety], [core belief: "everyone will leave me"], and [avoids social environments]. Moreover, it seems that the way she views herself impacts what she believes she is capable of and clouds her ability to explicate what is important to her; that is, her self-concept feeds [unclear values]. Arrows are therefore drawn to each of these four nodes (see Figure 8.6).
6. **[unclear values], (mismatch between her and parents' values), and (history of rejection):** Finally, we consider Ruby's motivations and add two contextual nodes to the network to flesh out her story (see Figure 8.7). There's a clear link between Ruby's long history of rejection, being bullied, and lack of support to her core belief that everyone

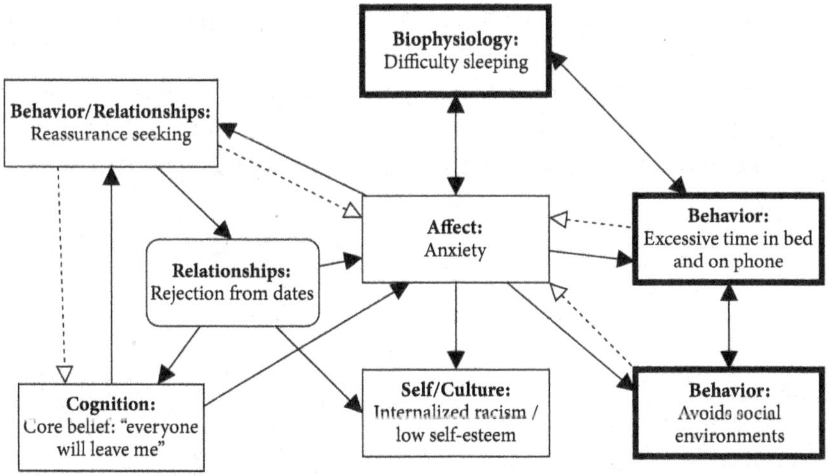

Figure 8.5 Adding arrows from [difficulty sleeping], [excessive time in bed and on the phone], and [avoids social environments] (step 6 of network building).

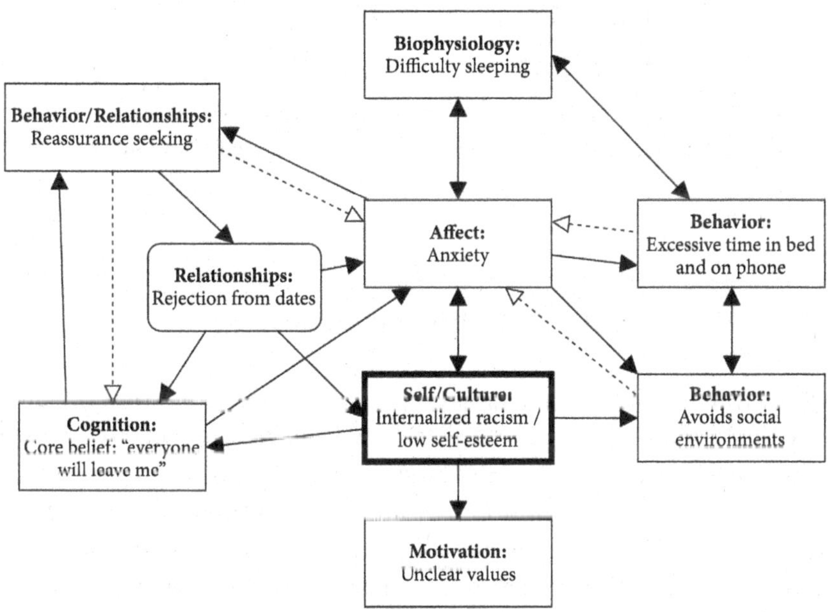

Figure 8.6 Adding arrows from [internalized racism/low self-esteem] (step 6 of network building).

will leave her. Further, we hypothesized that the divergence between her values and those of her parents reinforces this core belief and makes it difficult for her to know her own values. Not having a clear purpose may then further contribute to low self-worth and avoidance of goal-directed activity, which would be social interactions in Ruby's case.

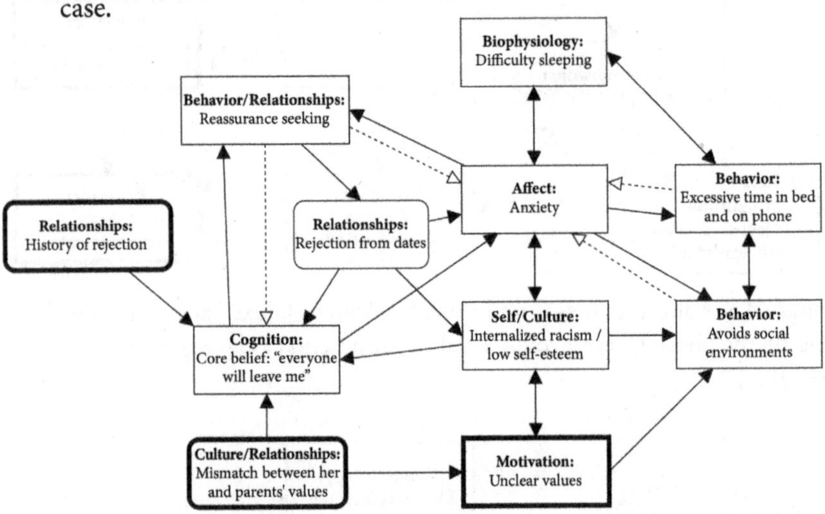

Figure 8.7 Adding arrows from [unclear values], (mismatch between her and parents' values), and (history of rejection) (step 6 of network building).

Network Review and Adjustment

OK, let's review what we have so far (step 7: check for missing arrows). Have we missed anything? Are there any right-angled rectangles without arrows going into them? Does our network capture the core of Ruby's problems? We think we could use this network to walk Ruby through our conceptualization of her concerns. Thus, we chose not to add or edit any arrows at this point, of course recognizing that the network is simply a hypothesis and bound to be revised. Review your own network and see if you'd like to make edits before moving on to step 8.

Now that we have all the nodes and arrows in place, we can fine-tune the arrowheads (step 8: adjust arrowhead size). Generally, we prefer to use three arrowhead sizes (small, medium, and large)—or even just two (small, large)—to show the magnitude of influence of one node on another. Feel free to use a different number of sizes; however, be careful not to lose sight of the objective of your network: to succinctly depict Ruby's presenting concerns so as to support treatment planning.

Networks are highly flexible tools that should serve us and our clients. That flexibility allows for a range of network building approaches and techniques. We imagine people could use color, shapes, annotations, and so on to enhance their networks. Feel free to play around with what works best for you. However, if you're just beginning, the notations we've presented are a good place to start. What is useful will depend on your clients' situation and needs at the time.

We chose these arrowhead sizes after a single intake session, so we don't have complete information, and the sizes may change as we learn more. Large arrowheads were used for relationships that were most obvious and impactful. For example, [core belief: "everyone will leave me"] is clearly causing significant [anxiety] and the main reason for [reassurance seeking]. We hypothesized that [anxiety] has a large impact on [avoids social environments], [excessive time in bed and on phone], and [reassurance seeking]. Moreover, [anxiety] seems to be meaningfully, but less strongly, influencing [internalized racism/low self-esteem] and [difficulty sleeping]. Ruby's completed network is presented in Figure 8.8.

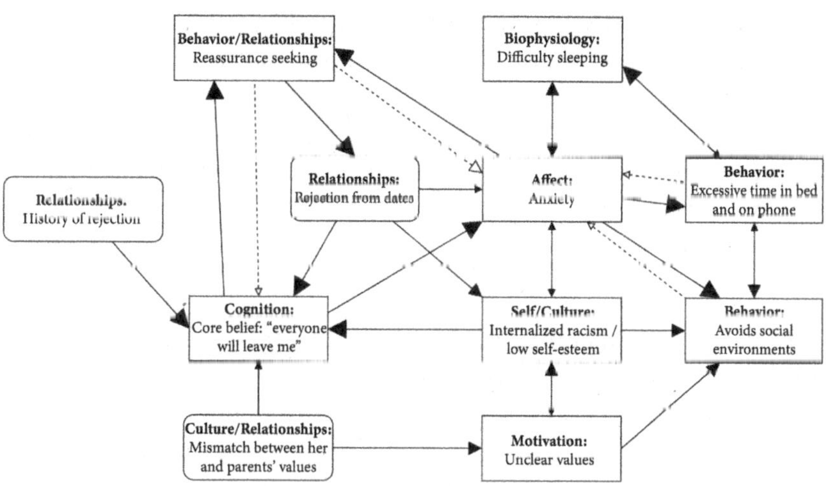

Figure 8.8 Ruby's completed network.

Further modifications could be made to Ruby's network. For example, additional nodes and arrows could be added to create a higher-resolution image of Ruby and her problems. However, more complicated networks often become cumbersome and less useful. In fact, we sometimes intentionally work in the other direction to create super simplified versions of our networks. We find that this can be helpful if your network feels overwhelming to you or your clients. We've created a simplified version of Ruby's network so you can compare it with the original network. Creating this network involved three steps:

1. **Combine nodes:** We combined the [excessive time in bed and on phone] and [avoids social environments] nodes. While there is some nuance that gets lost with this decision, these two nodes overlap a lot in terms of their function of avoidance.
2. **Remove nodes:** We removed two contextual nodes, (history of rejection) and (mismatch between her and her parents' values). Again, we lose some resolution by doing this. These nodes serve as important contextual, etiological markers that should be factored into treatment planning regardless of whether they are in the network. At the same time, removing them can simplify the picture and help us more easily see the current factors maintaining Ruby's problems.
3. **Simplify arrowheads:** We removed the smallest arrowheads and now just have two sizes: medium and large (see Figure 8.9). Like the other steps, this move has pros and cons. Drawing only moderate and strong relationships reduces clutter and can make important relationships stand out. This comes at the cost of losing more subtle relationships among nodes. For example, we are now missing an antecedent node for [unclear values].

We stress that neither the original network nor this simplified one is the "truth." Neither tells the full story of Ruby. Neither captures the unyielding undulations of human life. The question is not which is truer, but which is more *useful*? We'll be using the original, more complicated network as it better serves the needs of this chapter. In this case, it's the more useful network.

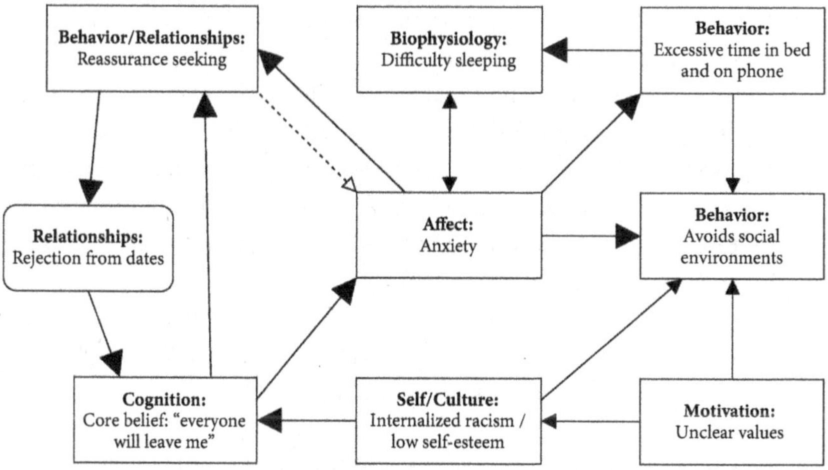

Figure 8.9 Ruby's simplified network.

Pre-Treatment Considerations

It's time to put our network to use. Where do we begin? What do we target? Before we make any decisions, let's consider the four main criteria for selecting treatment targets from Chapter 6:

1. Centrality in the network or to outcomes
2. Cultural responsiveness
3. Malleability in response to treatment
4. Relevance to clients

Centrality in the Network or to Outcomes

- **Out arrows:** The [anxiety] and [internalized racism/low self-esteem] nodes have the most "out" arrows at five and four, respectively. In terms of arrowhead weight, [anxiety] seems to have a stronger impact on the other nodes.
- **Meaningful outcomes:** [avoiding social environments] has removed a significant source of support and purposeful activity from Ruby's life. She reported that [difficulty sleeping] has had an outsized effect on how she feels and functions as well. Finally, we might consider [reassurance seeking] as it appears to have affected her ability to maintain supportive relationships that are important to her.

- **Long-term benefits:** Targeting the [avoids social environments] and [reassurance seeking] nodes could strengthen Ruby's support system and engagement in meaningful activities. These are likely to have a lasting impact on her functioning and well-being, given that loneliness is a consistent undercurrent in her presenting problem. We might also consider [internalized racism/low self-esteem] and [unclear values], as improving these nodes might build a foundation to more adaptive living in the long term.

Cultural Responsiveness

- **Values:** Ruby grew up in a traditional household. Her family and the mosque she attends generally hold a collectivistic worldview. However, outside these contexts, her social, school, and work environments have been largely individualistic. When exploring Ruby's values, it will be important to consider whether and to what extent she has integrated these worldviews and how they impact what gives her meaning and purpose.
- **Contextual factors:** These include a history of rejection, bullying, lack of support, invalidation, being a first-generation college student, being Indian American in predominantly white spaces, and family and societal pressure to marry. These influence the nodes we target, kernels we choose, or ways we involve Ruby in treatment. For instance, any kernel targeting [internalized racism/low self-esteem] must take Ruby's context into account and recognize the painful roots from which her sense of self has developed, rather than vaguely encourage her to "be more self-compassionate." If working on [unclear values], we should be mindful of the complicated relationship Ruby has with her parents and refrain from dismissing their values too readily. Relatedly, given societal pressure to be partnered, we might explore with Ruby whether she truly finds romantic companionship fulfilling or simply believes she "should" be in a relationship.
- **Therapist identities:** This will be dependent on the therapist working with Ruby. Whoever they are, there will be biases, power differentials, and misunderstandings in the room when working together, though the extent of these will vary. For example, a white male married therapist who was raised in an individualistic, Christian environment may be prone to inadvertently downplaying or even

overlooking the impact racism, sexism, Islamophobia, bullying, and/or pressures to assimilate have had on Ruby. Whereas someone with more shared identities may be able to—but not always—better appreciate the relentless burden of trying to belong and feeling like you're failing that drives Ruby's suffering. Regardless of therapist identities, humility and care should be taken to ensure that we are treating Ruby the person, not Ruby the "client with generalized anxiety disorder."

Malleability in Response to Treatment

- **Potential "quick" fixes:** The [difficulty sleeping] node has the potential to be relatively easy to target using evidence-based sleep hygiene techniques like those found in CBT for insomnia protocols. Depending on Ruby's buy-in, she may be willing to target the [reassurance seeking] and [avoids social environment] nodes. If done well, these could have an immediate impact on her network and functioning. Also, because of her goals, [unclear values] might be an area she is eager to work on that could have a sizeable and sustainable impact.
- **Potential "stubborn" nodes:** Due to their pervasiveness and longstanding nature, [internalized racism/low self-esteem] and [core belief: "everyone will leave me"] may be less malleable in the short term. Similarly, the [anxiety] node is influenced by many other nodes and may require multiple treatment strategies before meaningful progress is made.
- **Treatment setting:** Ruby plans to engage in weekly sessions in a private practice setting and has stated that she will work on the problem "for as long as it takes." Assuming treatment goes well, we can assume we'll have ample time to address Ruby's concerns. Timescale would be an important consideration if we were in a more rigid or time-limited treatment setting.

Relevance to Clients

- **Client goals:** The nodes, [unclear values] and [anxiety] clearly map onto Ruby's stated treatment goals.

- **Insight:** Ruby appears to have relatively good insight into her problems. However, she may not fully grasp the extent of her reassurance seeking and avoidance and their impact on her anxiety and general functioning.

Treatment Planning

Walking through the above criteria clarifies areas that should be emphasized when treatment planning. There are many evidence-based treatment options. In fact, we imagine you could create a dozen or more treatment plans emphasizing different combinations of nodes and kernels that would feasibly address Ruby's concerns, demonstrating the flexibility of a process-based approach.

To highlight this versatility, we present two treatment plans that each take a different approach to Ruby's problems. For the following examples, imagine two versions of Ruby. Both have the same history and set of current symptoms and problems; however, the events of their lives and how they respond to each plan vary.

A Tale of Two Rubys

Ruby 1

In this scenario, when we present our conceptualization and network to Ruby, she quickly recognizes the role avoidance plays in maintaining her network. While timid, she displays an eagerness to confront her fears and "get back to normal." We decide on these initial nodes to target:

- [anxiety]
- [difficulty sleeping]
- [reassurance seeking] and [avoids social environments]

Anxiety is clearly a central node and, although potentially "stubborn," could make a significant impact to Ruby's network if disrupted. Because anxiety is likely to be difficult to change if targeted on its own (given its multiple antecedents), we will also target Ruby's poor sleep and help her to meaningfully engage in social activities without reassurance seeking. Improving sleep has the potential to quickly improve Ruby's psychological well-being and may foster the energy required to address social avoidance and anxiety.

Ruby 2

In an alternate scenario, Ruby becomes tearful when viewing her network, stating, "I feel torn and broken. I don't know who I'm supposed to be." She strongly agrees that previous rejections and parental conflict have shaped her view of herself and her core belief that everyone will leave her. Despite a desire to examine these processes, she is hesitant and afraid. We decide on these initial nodes to target:

- [internalized racism/low self-esteem]
- [unclear values]
- [core belief: "everyone will leave me"]

Like anxiety, Ruby's internalized racism and low self-esteem are pervasive and central to the network. They too though are unlikely to change quickly, and Ruby is unsure whether she is ready to explore these topics. Yet, she is most intrigued by this part of the network and recognizes that her view of herself is a major obstacle to living more freely. We make a plan to support these efforts by targeting her unclear values to increase motivation as well as her core belief that everyone will leave her to loosen its hold over her.

Kernel Considerations

Now that we have a plan—or two in this case—let's get specific. We know which nodes we want to target. The question is, how to best target them? Before selecting any kernel, we'll consider the criteria for kernel selection in Chapter 6 (also in Appendix G). Although selecting treatment kernels is not an exact science, given it's impossible to have perfect information for decision making, reviewing these criteria can guide our decisions in ways that keep our kernels personalized and grounded in science:

1. Relevance to target node
2. Evidence base
3. Cultural responsiveness
4. Relevance to clients
5. Ability to deliver kernel competently

Note that the considerations we make in this section lean on our own theoretical orientations and preferences and are far from comprehensive. A full review of the evidence base for treating the targeted problems could fill a book by itself. The point here is the principles underlying decision making, not which kernels we've chosen.

Relevance to Target Node

- **EEMM:** When selecting kernels, it's helpful to consider which dimensions and levels are entailed in your treatment targets. For instance, targeting [anxiety] may call for an affective and/or biophysiological kernel, whereas [internalized racism/low self-esteem] may warrant a self and/or culturally informed kernel. Similarly, many of Ruby's nodes are related to relationships, including with her family, friends, and romantic partners. Therefore, we need to consider kernels that help her apply skills in various interpersonal settings.
- **Principles of change and context:** We also need to clarify if we are targeting variation, selection, retention, context-matching, or some combination of these areas. We're usually interested in all these areas to some degree, but are there any that stand out? For Ruby, we want to begin with kernels that encourage variation in responding, especially in domains where her behavioral repertoire is limited. We see a lack of variation in her response to anxiety and insight into her values. We'll eventually want her to be skilled in adaptively selecting responses in appropriate contexts as well. For example, we've identified at least five social contexts that are potentially relevant to Ruby's problems: work, mosque, peers, romantic relationships, and parents. Ruby has adapted and learned to differentially respond in each of these contexts, such as by hiding her more progressive views when she's around her parents but sharing them with her friends. As she learns new skills, context-matching will be important as skills in one environment may not be as helpful in another, and she'll need to reliably choose behaviors that are effective in a given environment. But to streamline treatment and avoid overwhelming Ruby, we'll focus on variation to start.

Evidence Base

- **Nomothetic (group-level):** Given the identified targets, we need to review what the empirical literature says about effective treatments for them. When it comes to anxiety, there is a great deal of evidence that supports the use of exposures (Bandelow et al., 2015). This would be relevant to [reassurance seeking] and [avoids social environments]. Moreover, Ruby's anxiety tends to manifest physiologically (e.g., racing heart, dizziness). Interoceptive exposure is an evidence-based treatment kernel that would specifically target these bodily sensations and the fear associated with them (Pompoli et al., 2018).

As previously stated, regular sleep problems have been shown to be alleviated by interventions that advocate for sleep hygiene like those found in CBT for insomnia protocols (Alimoradi et al., 2022). Moreover, these principles have shown effectiveness even with people who have co-occurring mental health problems (Hertenstein et al., 2022).

To date, most of the literature on internalized racism pertains to Black Americans (David et al., 2019). Evidence for interventions that specifically target internalized racism is sparse. Given the available evidence, we might try narrative (e.g., rewriting one's story), mindfulness, or self-compassion approaches (Chopra, 2021).

Values interventions from ACT would be a clear fit for values clarification (Levin et al., 2012). Motivational interviewing techniques are another evidence-based option shown to be an effective adjunct to CBT when treating anxiety (Marker & Norton, 2018).

To promote cognitive flexibility with regard to Ruby's core belief that everyone will leave her, cognitive restructuring (Ezawa & Hollon, 2023) and cognitive defusion techniques (Larsson et al., 2016) may be helpful.

- **Idiographic (individual-level):** Because we haven't had much interaction with Ruby, we'll lean more heavily on the nomothetic evidence for now. As we progress in treatment, we'll use what we learn about Ruby to refine our clinical decision making around appropriate treatment kernels. For instance, we might start with a narrative therapy kernel and ask Ruby to rewrite her life story, situating her problems in a more helpful context (e.g., external). If we notice Ruby struggling to come up with words and instead expressing strong interest to redraw her life narrative, we could then pivot to that. Over the course of treatment, we'll update our hypotheses about how kernels will affect particular nodes and the network overall, adjusting our approach as indicated by the data.

Cultural Responsiveness

- **Ruby's identities:** Foremost, selecting culturally responsive kernels requires us to understand and respect Ruby's identities. We do so by being mindful of how the content and delivery of kernels align with Ruby's worldview. For instance, as we consider kernels for [unclear values], we must appreciate how Ruby conceptualizes values and refrain from imposing our expectations for how she should orient her life. This could look like adding common collectivistic values (e.g., group harmony, community, interdependence) in a values card sort exercise as possible options Ruby can choose from. Similarly, if considering mindfulness or meditation-based treatment kernels, we need to be educated in its implementation with South Asian Americans and consider that Ruby might have a different perception or even reservations about westernized, secular forms of mindfulness found in many empirically supported treatment protocols (Masuda & Qinaʻau, 2022).

- **Contextual factors:** Another aspect of cultural responsiveness is to recognize the cultural contexts in which Ruby's behaviors and problems have been shaped. For instance, we want to be cognizant of Ruby's predominantly white New England environment and the racism, sexism, and ageism present in dating, explicitly acknowledging these realities in treatment. Overemphasizing intrapersonal factors like low self-worth may make us yet another contributor to Ruby's history of invalidation.

Relevance to Clients

- **Consider Ruby as an individual:** When selecting kernels, we may either ask Ruby broadly what kinds of approaches she thinks would be helpful or selectively propose kernels that align with her worldview and/or leverage existing strengths. For instance, we know that Ruby cares about her friendships and that they have generally been a positive influence on her well-being. As such, we may plan for social exposures that capitalize on these resources to target anxiety and avoidance, rather than inwardly focused interoceptive exercises.
- **Check in with Ruby:** Regardless of which kernels are suggested, it would be helpful to ask Ruby about final kernel choices and ensure that she understands the rationale and nature of each kernel. For instance, mindfulness has many connotations and sometimes has a secular (or religious) valence that might contradict our clients' beliefs. To avoid misunderstanding about what we mean by mindfulness, we might explain to Ruby that our version of mindfulness refers to

being fully present in and connecting with every moment and can be practiced anywhere—at work, at home, or when praying. Understanding why Ruby prefers a different kernel would also aid treatment planning. Is it about avoidance, cultural mismatch, or something else?

Ability to Deliver Kernel Effectively

- **Training:** This is a great time to reflect on your abilities as a therapist. Do you have the training required to use these kernels? Might you benefit from reading a book or treatment manual? Do you have access to the supervision or consultation needed to help you navigate this case? For the sake of this example, we will assume that we have the requisite training, support, and skills needed to competently deliver our selected treatment kernels.

Kernel Selection

Based on these criteria, we've chosen three kernels for each Ruby. These are simply the starting point of therapy. While it's good practice to have some idea of your long-term treatment plan, the kernels should be written in pencil, not ink. It's more likely than not that as treatment progresses, new kernels will be introduced, different nodes will be targeted, nodes and relationships will be added to the network, etc. Ultimately, PBT should be sensitive to your clients' needs and not beholden to any prescribed protocol. Plans can and will shift from session to session and even within sessions themselves. The constant is that you are focused on your clients' goals, which themselves may even change over time.

Ruby 1

- [anxiety]: Social exposures
- [difficulty sleeping]: Sleep hygiene
- [reassurance seeking] and [social avoidance]: Social exposures without reassurance seeking

Ruby 2

- [internalized racism/low self-esteem]: Self-compassion

- [unclear values]: Values exploration
- [core belief: "everyone will leave me"]: Cognitive restructuring

Assessment Planning

Ruby's treatment goals will guide our assessment decision making. She stated three treatment goals. First, "get my life back together." This is the most broad and undefined of her goals. When asked about what she meant by this, Ruby said that she would like to engage more in activities she used to enjoy, specifically exercising and socializing. Second, "figure out a life direction." This is captured in the [unclear values] node. Third, "stop feeling so scared and anxious all the time." This refers to [anxiety] and [core belief: "everyone will leave me"]. With these goals in mind, we chose the following assessment tools for each Ruby.

Ruby 1

- **Personal relevance:** A daily tracker with checkboxes for "exercised" and "socialized" was used to monitor daily engagement in these behaviors. At the start of treatment, the minimum requirements to earn a checkmark were defined as "walk around the block" and "talk to another person, besides your parents, face-to-face."
- **PBAT:** We gave Ruby the PBAT and worked with her to identify the items most germane to her goals. The following items were measured on a weekly basis:
  - "I was able to change my behavior, when changing helped my life." (sleep hygiene behaviors)
  - "I found personally important ways to challenge myself." (social exposures)
  - "I acted in ways that helped my physical health." (exercise)
  - "I felt stuck and unable to change my ineffective behavior." (avoidance)
  - "I did things to connect with people who are important to me." (social connection)
  - "I chose to do things that were personally important to me." (social exposures, exercise)
- **Anxiety:** A general measure of anxiety could be useful to monitor overall changes every other session. Specifically, we would be interested in

a measure that captures physiological symptoms as well as cognitive ones. We chose the Depression Anxiety and Stress Scale (Henry & Crawford, 2005) that has subscales intended to measure these different components of anxiety that are relevant to Ruby.

- **Sleep:** Sleep was initially tracked by Ruby writing down how many hours of sleep she got when she woke up in the morning. She reported that tracking hours of sleep daily led to feeling stressed at night, negatively affecting her sleep even further. Thus, we changed the measure to tracking specific sleep hygiene behaviors with a simple "yes/no" answer and rating her sleep quality from one to five each morning.
- **Reassurance seeking:** Once Ruby began going on dates again, we tracked her reassurance seeking by identifying specific phrases she used and keeping a count of how many times she used these phrases during each date or social event. New phrases were added as Ruby gained insight into other ways she was seeking reassurance from others.

Ruby 2

- **Personal relevance:** The same daily tracker as described for Ruby 1 was used.
- **PBAT:** Ruby 2's weekly PBAT items, also determined collaboratively, were as follows:
    - "I acted in ways that helped my physical health." (exercise)
    - "I felt stuck and unable to change my ineffective behavior." (avoidance)
    - "I did things to connect with people who are important to me." (social connection and values)
    - "I chose to do things that were personally important to me." (valued action, exercise)
    - "I paid attention to important things in my daily life." (values)
    - "My thinking got in the way of things that were important to me" (core belief that everyone will leave her)
    - "I did things only because I was complying with what others wanted me to do." (valued action)
- **Anxiety:** While not directly targeted at the beginning stages of this plan, improvements in anxiety were an expected byproduct of network

disruption. Specifically, we would expect anxiety symptoms to decrease as we successfully alter maintaining nodes such as [core belief: "everyone will leave me"] and [internalized racism/low self-esteem]. Thus, we assessed anxiety at the start of treatment to have a baseline to compare later scores to, using the DASS on a monthly basis (less regular than Ruby 1's plan because it's a secondary target and change may occur more gradually).

- **Self-compassion:** We used the Self Compassion Scale (Neff, 2003) on a monthly basis, given that we would not expect significant change in how Ruby sees herself within a short period of time. Although this is another standardized measure, we found that its subscales and some of its individual items were especially pertinent to Ruby's concerns. For example, Ruby reported high scores on items related to feelings of isolation and self-judgment.
- **Values:** While several measures of values and valued engagement exist, we relied on the PBAT items above to track values. Ruby stated that these items sufficiently captured her primary concerns in this area. Moreover, not adding another measure had the benefit of minimizing assessment burden.

Updating Ruby's Network

We'll now jump forward in time and see how the Rubys have fared. There are countless possibilities for how treatment could have gone. We illustrate two possible scenarios. As treatment progresses, an effective PBT therapist doesn't lose sight of the principles they used to develop their case conceptualization and treatment plan. Hence, we'll use those same principles to update our networks for both versions of Ruby's treatment.

Ruby 1

Ruby's eagerness to dive headfirst into exposures and behavior change paid off. With practice and some trial and error, sleep hygiene techniques were successfully implemented. She made a firm rule to stay out of bed unless she was going to sleep, resulting in far less time spent on her phone in bed. With the extra time, Ruby got back into her exercise routine, first with short walks around the block and eventually jogging long distances like she used to. Increasing physical activity made a large impact on her sleep difficulties (note the new open arrowhead from [exercise] to [difficulty sleeping] in Figure 8.10). She now reports generally sleeping well and waking up rested.

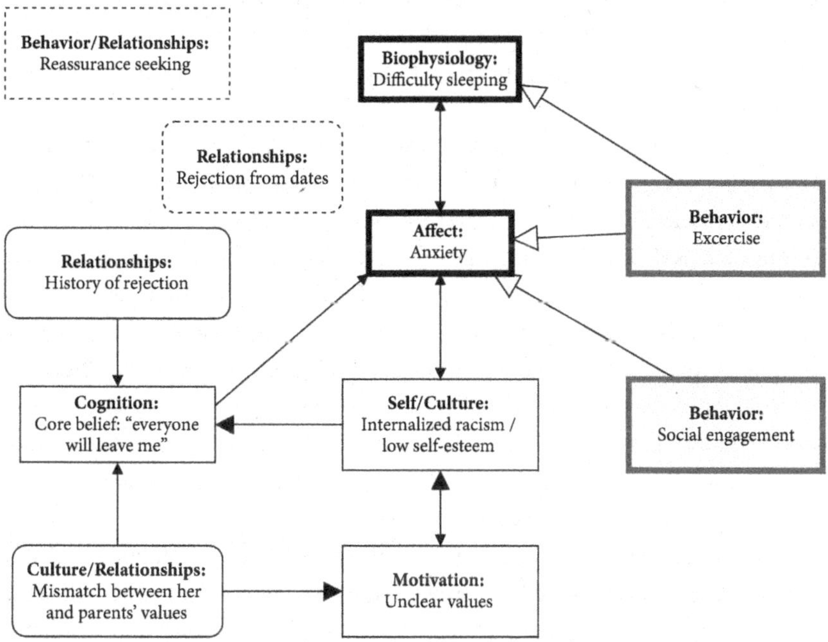

Figure 8.10 Ruby 1's network after starting treatment.

Through social exposures, she increased engagement with friends and coworkers and eventually dating. As she felt less anxious and reduced her reassurance seeking, she reported having quality dates, and even several follow-up dates, with multiple people. Lastly, the changes to her [reassurance seeking], [rejection from dates], and [anxiety] have had a downstream effect of reducing the intensity of her core belief that everyone will leave her.

Let's pause here and examine how her network has changed. Nodes that were directly targeted are drawn with bold lines. Notice the two grey nodes [exercise] and [social engagement], which have replaced [excessive time in bed and on phone] and [avoids social environments], respectively. The open arrows going from [exercise] and [social engagement] are solid because these effects hold over time (e.g., exercise generally improves sleep) rather than are temporary (e.g., exercise only improves sleep for a few minutes).

The nodes [difficulty sleeping], [anxiety], and [core belief: "everyone will leave me"] have also been reduced in size to denote improvement in but not elimination of these concerns. In addition, arrowhead sizes have been adjusted to reflect weakened impact of certain nodes, including (history of rejection) and [core belief: "everyone will leave me"]. Finally, we added dashed outlines to [reassurance seeking] and (rejection from dates) as they have largely been eliminated from Ruby's repertoire (see Figure 8.10).

Sadly, that is not the end of Ruby's story. The climbs to resolve problems are rarely paved in gold; they are windy and confusing, teeming with unexpected obstacles. In Ruby's case, despite her progress, she couldn't shake the feeling of dissatisfaction with her life. Even as anxiety decreased and she had more free time for herself, she expressed that she often "felt empty" and didn't know what to do. During sessions, Ruby used a great deal of "should" language, often reflecting on what her parents want from her. For example, when we asked how she felt about her progress with dating, she would answer from the perspective of her parents, describing their aloof reactions to her dating choices and disappointment that she was not yet married, unlike her two younger brothers.

We now have a stronger appreciation of the extent to which her history of rejection has contributed to not only the core belief that everyone will leave her but internalized racism and low self-esteem. Given this new information, we updated Ruby's network, adding the nodes ["I should" language] and [dissatisfaction/"feel empty"], accompanying hypothesized arrows, as well as an arrow from (history of rejection) to [internalized racism/low self-esteem] (bolded in Figure 8.11 for emphasis).

With the additions, Ruby's network is looking a bit overwrought with nodes and arrows less pertinent to her current concerns or no longer significantly impacting her functioning, such as (rejection from dates) and [difficulty sleeping]. We can simplify the network by removing these nodes. Doing so leaves us with Figure 8.12. From here, we would reconsider our conceptualization of Ruby's current problems and goals, identify nodes to target, and decide which kernels to use to target those nodes. Like before, there are many "right" possibilities. Values and work on self-confidence seem highly relevant and could meaningfully disrupt her network. Furthermore, considering Ruby's core belief that everyone will leave her and "I should" language, we could target cognitive flexibility.

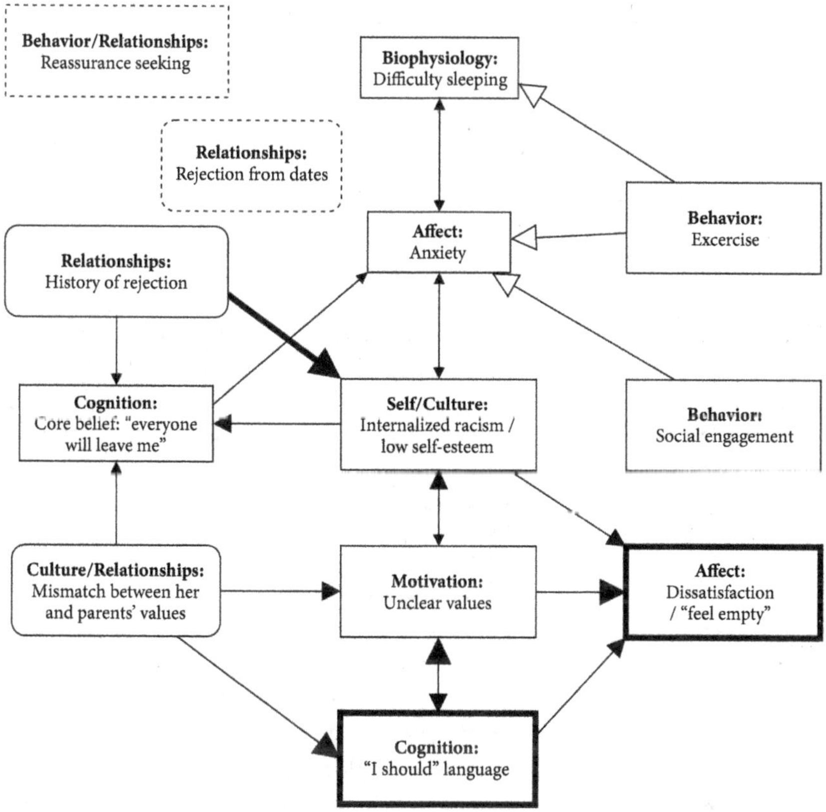

Figure 8.11 Ruby 1's updated network.

Ruby 2

Early sessions with Ruby 2 focused on values clarification. Despite our best efforts, no progress was made in this area. Conversations around meaning and purpose triggered intense feelings of shame, and Ruby became reluctant to discuss topics related to her sense of self. Over the next few weeks, Ruby's feelings of apathy grew, and she reported having consistently low mood. This in turn increased the time she spent in bed on her phone as well as excessive napping throughout the day that exacerbated her low mood. As these new symptoms surfaced, Ruby's anxiety became less central to her network.

On the encouraging side, Ruby responded to cognitive restructuring techniques targeting her core belief that everyone will leave her, leading to some improvement. However, it became clear that she held another entrenched

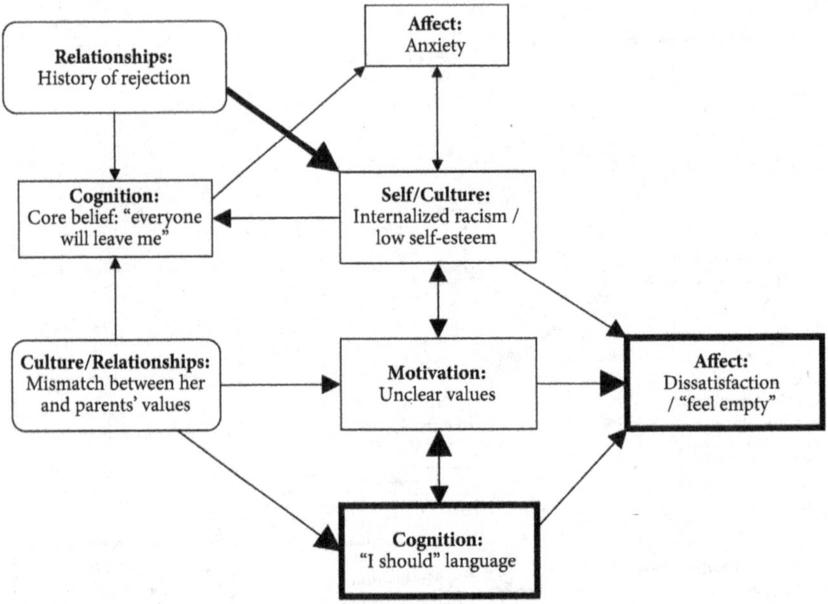

Figure 8.12 Ruby 1's updated network, simplified.

core belief that she will "never be enough" stemming from her social and family history. As these core beliefs were explored through Socratic dialogue, Ruby recognized that the pressure to date came solely from her parents and not her own desires. As such, she decided to take a break from dating apps to engage in other hobbies. As [shame] and [low mood] became more central to her struggles and Ruby shifted away from dating, the parts of her network linked to relationship stress were no longer the focus of treatment.

If we stop to examine her network at this point, we will see significant changes, as certain nodes have dropped off and new nodes have been added (see Figure 8.13). Nodes that were directly targeted are drawn with bold lines. We added dashed outlines to [reassurance seeking], (rejection from dates), and [anxiety], because they're not actively contributing to our conceptualization of Ruby's problems, at least for the time being.

Notice that the [unclear values/apathy] and [excessive sleeping] nodes (highlighted in grey in Figure 8.13) have been updated to denote her new feelings of apathy and change in sleep behavior. The [core belief: "everyone will leave me"] node has been reduced in size to reflect improvement in that area. Finally, three nodes have been added to describe her new symptoms: [low mood], [core belief: "I'll never be enough"], and [shame].

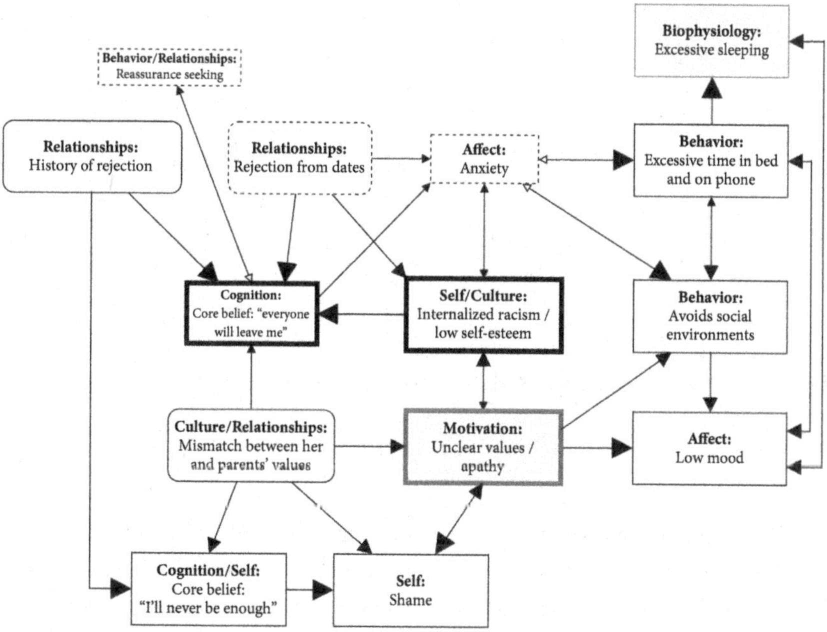

Figure 8.13 Ruby 2's network after starting treatment.

The complexity of this revised network is now obfuscating our conceptualization and treatment planning, so before moving on, let's clean it up. First, we'll remove [reassurance seeking], [rejection from dates], and [anxiety], which are no longer informing treatment planning. They may be important again in the future, but for the time being, they're needlessly complicating the picture. We then combine [excessive sleeping] and [excessive time in bed and on phone] as they serve a similar function: avoidance of painful emotions.

With the updated network in Figure 8.14, we can reconsider our conceptualization and treatment plan. In this case, Ruby has become severely unmotivated. The values clarification kernels did not connect with her and instead brought up apathy and shame. Moving away from exploring Ruby's deeper life purpose, we select more straightforward kernels of goal setting and weighing pros and cons of choices to target motivation. Additionally, a behavioral activation kernel is selected to target [low mood].

Ruby connects with the more concrete approach to increase motivation and improves her ability to set goals related to social engagement, leading to her volunteering at a local grassroots organization. She has a glimmer

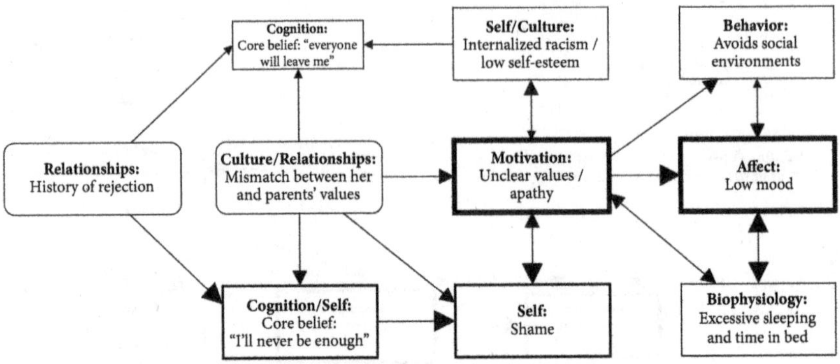

Figure 8.14 Ruby 2's network after starting treatment, simplified.

of insight in a later session, recognizing that she might find joy in investing in her community, stating "I care about my community." These changes (highlighted in grey in Figure 8.15) have a positive effect on feelings of shame, internalized racism, and low self-esteem as well as motivation and goal-directed behavior. As Ruby continues to progress in these areas, the plan is to continue to leverage her success with cognitive restructuring to target her core beliefs and incorporate a self-compassion kernel to target negative self-concept and shame.

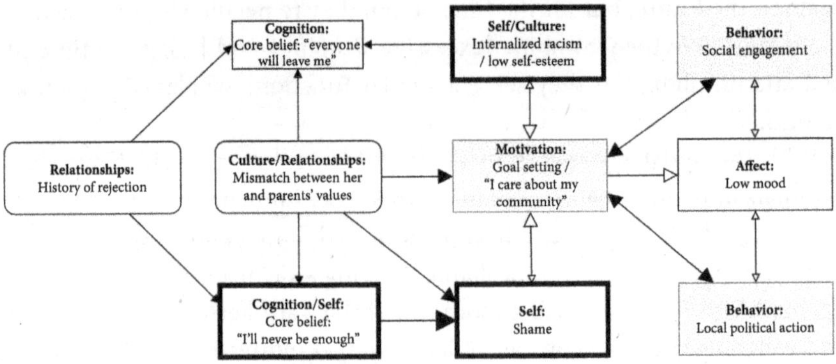

Figure 8.15 Ruby 2's updated network with new adaptive responding.

Ending Treatment

Our ultimate goal is to help clients make changes such that their networks become adaptive and self-sustaining. Below, we show stable adaptive networks for both versions of Ruby.

Ruby 1

With further work and exploration, Ruby gained insight into her sense of self and associated automatic thoughts and behaviors that were keeping her from living the life she wanted. As she became more cognitively flexible, her self-efficacy grew as well. In turn, this loosened up her rigid thinking patterns about who she "should" be, allowing her to explore her values more fully. One session, she realized that she wasn't actually interested in being in a relationship at this time. She continued socializing, but not for the purpose of finding a partner. Rather, she recognized that she found purpose in giving back to her community, by becoming more politically active and joining a grassroots movement.

Looking at Ruby's network in Figure 8.16 now, you can see that [cognitive flexibility] skills have helped Ruby to more effectively respond to her core belief that everyone will leave her. Still, this is a long-standing thought, seeded by a rich cultural and social history and unlikely to simply vanish, so it remains in her network. [Cognitive flexibility] also supports [self-efficacy] which in turn inhibits the effects of [internalized racism/low self-esteem]. The work on values has replaced [unclear values] with [valued action] that serves [self-efficacy] and [social engagement/local political action]. Ruby's sleep has improved considerably as she has resumed her exercise routine and maintained good sleep hygiene; however, it is still a factor. Her sleep is somewhat poor, especially when she's stressed or anxious.

Of course, we'll have been monitoring our assessment data throughout treatment and adjusting plans as needed. Besides the objective data, we want to hear from Ruby herself. As treatment is wrapping up, we find it helpful to present an updated network like the one in Figure 8.16 to our clients. This can open the door to discussion of unknown concerns your clients may have about ending therapy. It also has the benefit of highlighting potentially fragile nodes or relationships in the network that relate to retaining adaptive responding. Overall, Ruby's network appears to be stable and healthy. Ruby has met her goals and has the skills she needs to keep her network going.

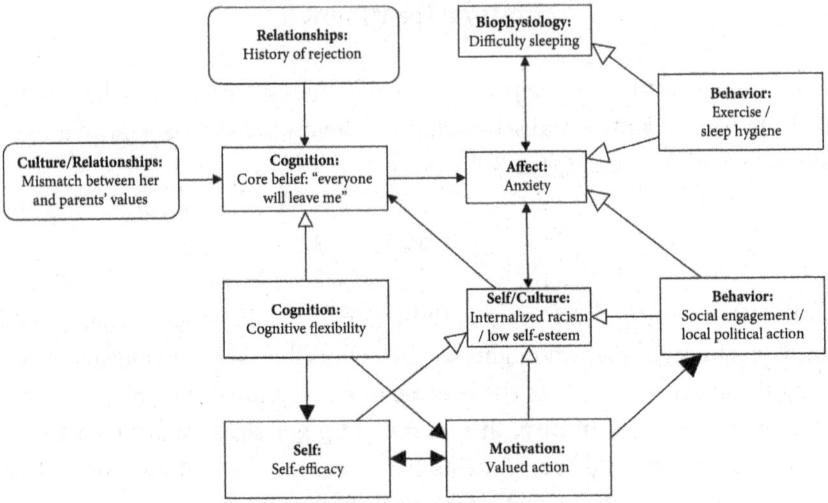

Figure 8.16 Ruby 1's network at the end of treatment.

Ruby 2

Ruby continued to thrive using skills from the goal setting and behavioral activation kernels. As her mood and motivation improved, she experimented with potential valued actions such as participating in local politics. Next, although still somewhat reluctant, she became willing to explore feelings of shame, internalized racism, and low self-esteem. She strongly connected with self-compassion and learned to practice treating herself kindly and to recognize her struggles as less a personal failing and more a part of the human condition. Finally, she continued to build her cognitive restructuring skills, learning to develop believable alternative thoughts more in line with her goals.

Her final network in Figure 8.17 includes multiple nodes and connections that foster adaptive functioning. [Cognitive flexibility] supports [self-worth/self-compassion] as she no longer over-identifies with self-critical thoughts, enabling her to set goals aligned with her values, such as [social engagement] and [local political action]. Ruby recognizes that she, like all humans, will have times when painful thoughts and low mood return. She also knows that she has the skills to navigate those struggles effectively.

Ruby's lack of current anxiety symptoms is notable and worth considering as we look to wrap up therapy. We compare her anxiety scores to those at the

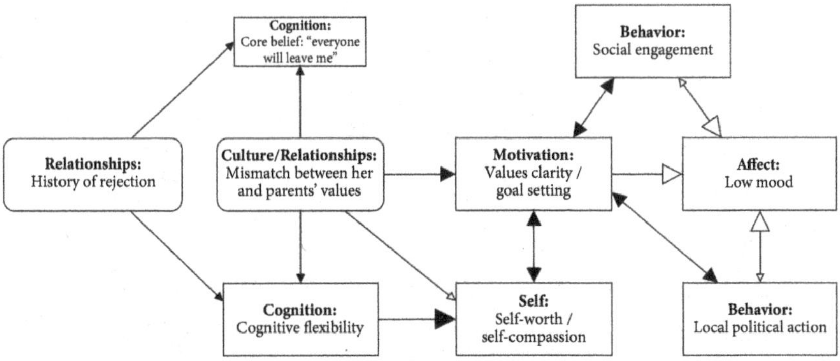

Figure 8.17 Ruby 2's network at the end of treatment.

start of treatment and see a significant reduction that has been maintained over several weeks, similar to the pattern observed for other symptoms. As her mood has improved, so too has her sleep; however, she may still benefit from sleep hygiene to prevent future problems. Currently, Ruby is pleased with her progress and says that she has no significant concerns. We agree that her network is stable and adaptive and that she's ready to graduate from therapy.

Chapter Summary

- The intake form in Appendix C specifies information to get from clients that would be helpful for a PBT case conceptualization. All dimensions and levels of the EEMM should be considered, even if not ultimately included in your network.
- Node selection and network construction is an art that takes practice. Stick to the steps we've outlined if you're new to this approach. Once you have a few networks under your belt, try tailoring the approach as you like to better serve the needs of yourself and your clients.
- Expect your network to change and evolve over the course of treatment. Update and reconceptualize your clients' problems and goals as you learn more about them.

9

Next Steps

So, what's next? We've covered PBT principles and how to apply them, building a network, using your network to inform treatment planning, and adjusting treatment based on client progress and feedback. Now, how do you put these concepts into practice? In this chapter, we recommend steps to further develop your PBT skills and begin integrating PBT into your clinical practice. These are merely options for you to consider and should be treated as a starting point on your PBT odyssey—not mandatory checkpoints. You may even already be doing some of them.

Before we go further, we want to emphasize that perfection is not the objective. Incrementally applying PBT principles and skills goes a long way toward building a *sustainable* process-based practice. For instance, being mindful of one aspect of your clients' context (e.g., gender identity, disability) is likely going to be more helpful than ignoring all aspects of context, even if you don't consider every single facet. Like our clients, we need to vary our responses, select the ones that work, and keep doing them to instigate sustainable change.

Apply Principles to a Current Client

Consider how the five PBT principles can be applied to your current clients. To start, pick one client from your caseload, maybe the one you are most familiar with off the top of your head. With this client in mind, ask yourself the following questions about their case conceptualization:

1. **Am I thinking in terms of processes (Process)?** Reflect on what you've been targeting in your work with this client. Is your treatment target defined topographically (e.g., restrictive eating, low mood) or functionally (e.g., avoidance of body-related shame, attachment to negative view of self)? Do you have a solid understanding of how your client's strengths, problems, and context are interrelated

A Process-Based Approach to Psychotherapy. Clarissa W. Ong and Eric B. Lee, Oxford University Press.
 DOI: 10.1093/oso/9780197696378.003.0009

(e.g., you would expect eating behaviors to change if your client was more self-compassionate)?

2. **Am I considering all EEMM dimensions and levels (EEMM)?** Therapists usually have a bias with respect to which dimensions and levels they focus on. As behaviorists, we tend to emphasize overt behaviors, whereas a more cognitively oriented therapist may emphasize cognition. Review the EEMM checklist and see if there's a dimension or level you missed in your case conceptualization. For example, a client struggling with concentration difficulties may benefit from better sleep hygiene (Biology/Physiology) rather than—or in addition to—mindfulness techniques (Attention).
3. **Do I know how my client is stuck (EEMM)?** If you're at an impasse with this client, reflect on how they are stuck. Do they need to vary their responses, learn to identify what is working, or solidify skills they've already acquired? How effectively is your client matching their responses to environmental demands?
4. **Am I tailoring treatment based on client variables (Personalization)?** Sometimes, we get so lost in the procedures of "evidence-based treatment" that we forget to respond to the human sitting before us. This may look like delivering rote exercises plucked from the internet or administering standardized clinical questionnaires without first checking whether they fit your clients' experiences. Tailoring treatment means you've adjusted treatment in ways that respect and appreciate your clients' full humanity, including their identities, history, and worldview.
5. **Is treatment aligned with my client's goals (Workability)?** It can be easy to fall into a pattern of problem solving and reducing symptoms—in a way disconnected from treatment goals—especially if a client tends to use therapy sessions to vent about their "problem of the week." Of course, resolving problems and reducing distressing symptoms are helpful, but putting out fires is not the same as completing fire safety training. PBT is intentional, which means it's about going toward something: your clients' goals.
6. **Am I using data to guide decision making (Empiricism)?** Part of PBT is being empirically minded, remembering that data comes in many forms (e.g., self-report, clinician-observed). Data don't have to come from psychometrically validated measures to be useful. Consider these questions for your clients: What outcomes are you tracking and

why did you select those outcomes? How have you integrated those data into treatment planning? For instance, if you're tracking time spent practicing the piano and the number has not changed in the past month, do some troubleshooting. Perhaps the target node is misguided and you need a new target, or the kernel needs to be modified. Either way, something needs to change.

How many questions did you answer "yes" to? If you answered "yes" to all of them, wonderful. Ask yourself the same questions for another client. If you answered "no" to at least one of the questions, reflect on what you can do differently in your subsequent sessions. For instance, if you can't describe how your client's problems are related to each other, take some time to draw an approximate network for them—or even better, talk to your client about it. If you haven't been assessing your client's response to treatment, consider what variable would be helpful to track and how you would track it. It may not be an outcome per se. It could be a skill your client has been practicing or even the amount of time spent practicing between sessions.

At this point, we suggest selecting *one* thing to change for *one* client, even if you said "no" to all the questions above. That's because it can feel overwhelming to incorporate these process-based ways of thinking all at once. In fact, setting the expectation that you need to implement everything immediately might lead you to constantly notice where you fall short—at least, that's how we feel sometimes. Ten percent is less than 100%, but it sure is more than 0%.

Prepare for Trial and Error

Let's be clear: you're going to mess up delivering PBT. After all, being a therapist is tough. On top of learning evidence-based interventions and being present with clients, PBT asks you to consistently attend to process and function, weigh intra- and extra-individual variables, monitor incoming data, as well as continually adjust treatment to meet your clients' ever-shifting needs. This is especially onerous if you're a therapist with a full caseload of clients who's thankful to have even a few minutes to regroup between back-to-back therapy sessions. Yes, the ideal scenario is that we show up 100% with all our clients, having prepped and reviewed treatment goals before each session; that we have time to learn new evidence-based treatments; that we have space to reflect on how to adjust treatment for every client. If we lived in this ideal world, PBT would be a lot easier to implement.

But since we don't, relieve yourself of the pressure to do everything right. The more realistic approach is to use PBT in a targeted way based on your clients' needs and adjust as you learn more about PBT. For example, if you work in a community setting where clients face various systemic barriers beyond psychological concerns, you might find that developing networks with multiple context variables improves your case conceptualization and reminds you to address environmental factors in intervention planning (e.g., connecting your clients to social services). Over time, you might even cut out networks altogether and focus on directly identifying contextual barriers to streamline case conceptualization—whatever works for you and your clients.

Similarly, your work setting may not be set up to automate regular data collection and you may not have the bandwidth to track unique idiographic variables across your 50 clients. But bearing in mind the Empiricism Principle, you could instead open or end each session with a global question that gives you information about whether treatment is helping your clients. It could be "rate your well-being on a scale of 1 to 10 over the past week" or "rate your level of confidence in reaching your goals." As you get feedback from your clients, you can alter how you measure treatment response, to better suit their needs. Either way, the principle of using client responses to inform treatment still applies. Through trial and error, you'll gradually figure out the most effective and sustainable way to integrate PBT into your current workflow. But it'll take time, as most good things do.

Practice Creating a Network

Pick a client and create a network case conceptualization for them (see Chapter 5 for steps). If that feels intimidating, create a network for yourself. Focus on a problem you're struggling with or behavior you're trying to change. We have found this exercise to be enlightening in terms of learning more about ourselves and what it's like for our clients to build a network for themselves.

The point of this exercise is to practice fleshing out the relationships among variables and visualizing a person's psychological ecosystem. It doesn't need to be elaborate or even accurate. Think of network building like learning a new language. (In fact, in some ways, it is a new language for communicating case conceptualizations.) Your grammar isn't going to be solid in the beginning, and you'll only get fluent with more practice. For now, do your best with what you know. Start with three to five nodes. Then continue building on them. This practice will help you transition from diagnosis-driven case formulation to network-based thinking.

If you're up for a challenge, select a client you've been feeling stuck with or a client whose problems meet criteria for multiple diagnoses. Set aside 30 minutes or so and follow the steps in Chapter 5. If you notice resistance to taking this step, try reframing the exercise as part of the learning process and give yourself credit for taking the harder valued path toward growth and greater competency as a therapist.

Use Evidence-Based Kernels Intentionally

You might already be using evidence-based kernels, but are you using them *intentionally*? In other words, are you delivering kernels to target a specific node per your case conceptualization and treatment plan and do you know why you selected those specific kernels? For example, if you've been teaching DBT skills to a client with a diagnosis of borderline personality disorder, clarify which process each DBT kernel is intended to affect (e.g., TIPP skill for difficulty tolerating intense emotions, DEAR MAN for overly permissive interpersonal boundaries). Intentionality means you're delivering kernels with precision, like painting over a small scratch on your wall vs. painting over the entire wall. When you know what process you're targeting, you're also more able to adapt your approach depending on how your clients respond. For instance, rather than ensuring that your client knows how to use DEAR MAN in general, you might emphasize the Assert part of the skill for a client who has difficulty stating their needs.

Because evidence-based kernels usually come from evidence-based protocols, treatment manuals are a helpful source of kernels. If you're treating someone with problematic hair pulling you could select kernels from an acceptance-enhanced behavior therapy manual, such as stimulus control or habit reversal training, depending on what you've identified as the target node. Similarly, you could focus on teaching organization skills rather than going through a full CBT manual for attention deficit hyperactivity disorder when working with someone who struggles with inattentive symptoms.

Bring in Other Therapeutic Approaches

Under the aegis of the EEMM, you may find it easier to experiment with a wider range of therapeutic orientations without losing sight of the theoretical backbone of treatment. In particular, the principles of change in the EEMM can be helpful for clarifying the objective of methods drawn from different approaches. For example, if you have a client who struggles with their self-concept, you might want to increase *variation* in how your client views themselves. Once you've clarified this aim, you can then identify techniques from a range of theories to support variation in the Self dimension, including the empty chair technique from Gestalt therapy and parts mapping from internal family systems.

The pool of clinical methods available to you depends on your training and competence. However, the way in which you would integrate techniques from divergent orientations is the same: they are tools to be used to achieve a particular therapeutic purpose linked to your clients' goals. Just like you might use a knife, grater, garlic press, or food processor to mince garlic, a clinician can use methods from ACT, CBT, DBT, art therapy, psychodynamic therapy, emotion-focused therapy, or schema therapy to induce behavioral change. The key is to know what you are using a specific technique *for*, vis-à-vis your clients' case conceptualization and treatment plan.

Make an Assessment Plan

With a full caseload and its corresponding administrative responsibilities, it can be difficult to remember to engage in routine outcome monitoring, especially if your clinic or professional setting is not set up to do this automatically. Yet, part of determining if treatment is having its intended effect requires appropriate assessment of target variables. For example, if your treatment target is increased social interaction, it's insufficient to only track your client's mood because it may be unrelated to the target and doesn't tell you whether they have practiced social skills.

As an initial step, introduce an assessment plan with a client. The plan can be as simple or detailed as is helpful. If you're not already tracking personally relevant variables (e.g., linked to treatment goals), start there. Ask your client what they want to see changes in and how both of you can measure changes in those variables. For instance, if your client wants to be more self-accepting, both of you can brainstorm ways to operationalize "self-acceptance," such that it's trackable. Self-acceptance could be defined as time spent on self-care activities, frequency of stating individual needs to others, or time spent experiencing emotions without fighting them. Alternatively, check out the PBAT, which is designed to map on to the EEMM and has been linked to clinically relevant outcomes, including distress and well-being (Ciarrochi et al., 2022).

If you're still feeling stuck, use the EEMM as a checklist. Have you overlooked any dimensions or levels? Perhaps you've been so heavily focused on intraindividual psychological skills that you haven't been tracking how your client's physical health behaviors or social environment may be contributing to their struggles. If it becomes clear that other aspects of your client's context are relevant to their goals, tracking those variables may become part of your new assessment plan.

That said, keep your assessment plan manageable. It's much more useful to do *some* assessment than to attempt to develop the perfect assessment plan and procrastinate indefinitely because making the perfect plan feels daunting. As we said earlier, 10% is less than 100%, but it's still more than 0%. In fact, we encourage you and your clients to pick just one process or outcome to track regularly and to do so consistently before adding more items to your assessment plan.

Look up PBT Resources

This book was written as a starting point for therapists interested in PBT. It's the equivalent of a book on chess for beginners, which means you won't be a PBT expert after reading this book. However, we hope that you will have established the foundation you need to be an expert. After all, even chess grandmasters Judit Polgár and Garry Kasparov had to start somewhere.

Below, we provide a list of resources to get you started. We selected resources more likely to withstand the test of time, so they tend to include theoretical readings or active organizations. Empirical studies yet to be replicated do not appear here. As with everything else in this book, take what's helpful and leave what's not. The resources you choose will depend on your needs and bandwidth as a therapist. Maybe reading dense theoretical exposition is not what you need to better manage patients in crisis—that's OK. Stick to the Workability Principle: do whatever will serve your clients' goals and well-being.

- Become a member of the Association for Contextual Behavioral Science (ACBS). Contextual behavioral principles jive well with PBT, and ACBS has a special interest group for PBT. We have found the ACBS listservs—where members post questions and discuss topics of interest—to be fertile ground for learning. Dues are values-based (still true as of June 2025), so people pay what they think their membership is worth
    - The PBT special interest group maintains a webpage that lists PBT resources: https://contextualscience.org/processbased_therapy_sig_resources (you need to be an ACBS member to access it). The page includes articles, talks, books, and assessment tools related to PBT.
- Read books on PBT. So far, *Learning PBT* by Stefan Hofmann, Steven Hayes, and David Lorscheid, and this one are the only clinician-oriented books we know of. For a theoretical overview of PBT from a CBT perspective, we recommend *Process-Based Cognitive Behavioral Therapy*, edited by Steven Hayes and Stefan Hofmann.
- Read manuals containing treatment kernels. There are many evidence-based treatment protocols you can draw from, such as those in the *Treatments That Work* series from Oxford University Press. You can read those as you encounter specific presentations. We also suggest reading manuals organized by kernels, so you get a better sense of this way of thinking about treatment. Certain therapies are easier to kernelize than others (e.g., CBT vs. psychodynamic therapy), so this list is biased toward the former.
    - *Doing CBT: A Comprehensive Guide to Working with Behaviors, Thoughts, and Emotions* by David Tolin
    - *General Principles and Empirically Supported Techniques of Cognitive Behavior Therapy* edited by William O'Donohue and Jane Fisher
    - *Unified Protocol for Transdiagnostic Treatment of Emotional Disorders: Workbook (Treatments That Work)* by David Barlow, Shannon Sauer-Zavala, Todd Farchione, Heather Murray Latin, Kirsten Ellard, Jacqueline Bullis, Kate Bentley, Hannah Boettcher, and Clair Cassiello-Robbins
    - *DBT Skills Training Manual* by Marsha Linehan
    - *Learning ACT: An Acceptance and Commitment Therapy Skills Training Manual for Therapists* by Jason Luoma, Steven Hayes, and Robyn Walser

  - *ACT Made Simple: An Easy-to-Read Primer on Acceptance and Commitment Therapy* by Russ Harris
  - *Brief Dynamic Therapy* by Hanna Levenson (Note: This is the least kernel-y book on the list, but it contains "intervention strategies" for time-limited psychodynamic therapy.)
- Learn more about functional case conceptualization. In *Behavioral Assessment and Case Formulation*, Stephen Haynes, William O'Brien, and Joseph Kaholokula explain how to use behavioral assessment and functional analysis to develop case conceptualizations that inform treatment planning and further assessment. It takes a non-PBT—albeit PBT-consistent—perspective on functional case formulation, so you'll see a different version of how to approach case conceptualization using process-based principles.
- Whenever you're ready to dig into the technical aspects of PBT, we suggest starting with the following journal articles:
  - Hofmann, S. G., & Hayes, S. C. (2019). The future of intervention science: Process-based therapy. *Clinical Psychological Science, 7*(1), 37–50. https://doi.org/10.1177/2167702618772296
  - Hayes, S. C., Hofmann, S. G., Stanton, C. E., Carpenter, J. K., Sanford, B. T., Curtiss, J. E., & Ciarrochi, J. (2019). The role of the individual in the coming era of process-based therapy. *Behaviour Research and Therapy, 117*, 40–53. https://doi.org/10.1016/j.brat.2018.10.005
  - Hayes, S. C., Hofmann, S. G., & Ciarrochi, J. (2020). A process-based approach to psychological diagnosis and treatment: The conceptual and treatment utility of an extended evolutionary meta model. *Clinical Psychology Review, 82*, 101908. https://doi.org/10.1016/j.cpr.2020.101908
  - Hofmann, S. G., Curtiss, J. E., & Hayes, S. C. (2020). Beyond linear mediation: Toward a dynamic network approach to study treatment processes. *Clinical Psychology Review, 76*, 101824. https://doi.org/10.1016/j.cpr.2020.101824

Make a Behavioral Plan

Just as we ask our clients to vary their responses, select ones that work for them, and keep doing those, we as therapists need to do the same in the spirit of learning. The suggestions above call for variation, and you will need to determine which behaviors make you a more effective therapist for your clients. To ensure you continue doing what is useful, a behavioral plan may come in handy.

Start small. The goal is to develop sustainable habits, like flossing daily, rather than to radically change your clinical practice, like getting braces. What behavioral changes are you willing to commit to over the next month? Think in terms of SMART goals. For example:

- Select a client and make a mini network (3–5 variables) for that person.
- Deliver a kernel intentionally to three clients.
- Identify an outcome to track for one client and ask them about it every session.
- Read an article on PBT or an evidence-based treatment.

We can only start from where we are, so meet yourself where you're at. Be honest about what changes you can realistically make and retain. Notice if you're overly concerned about doing PBT "right" or rigidly following this book. Delivering therapy is about doing the best for our clients and establishing a human-to-human connection with people who are suffering, not to never make mistakes or be an unimpeachable expert. So focus on the former. Try things that are likely to help you help your clients and go from there. After all, it's about the process, not the outcome.

Chapter Summary

- To continue developing your PBT skills, practice applying some of the principles and ideas described in this book to your current clients. See what changes occur and adjust your approach accordingly.
- Expect to make missteps; they're part of learning.
- Use the resources listed at the end of this chapter to expand your knowledge.
- Learning PBT is a lifelong process, so focus on making *sustainable* changes—no matter how small.

References

Alimoradi, Z., Jafari, E., Broström, A., Ohayon, M. M., Lin, C.-Y., Griffiths, M. D., Blom, K., Jernelöv, S., Kaldo, V., & Pakpour, A. H. (2022). Effects of cognitive behavioral therapy for insomnia (CBT-I) on quality of life: A systematic review and meta-analysis. *Sleep Medicine Reviews, 64*, 101646.

Allsopp, K., Read, J., Corcoran, R., & Kinderman, P. (2019). Heterogeneity in psychiatric diagnostic classification. *Psychiatry Research, 279*, 15–22. https://doi.org/10.1016/j.psychres.2019.07.005

American Psychological Association. (2017). *Ethical Principles of Psychologists and Code of Conduct.* https://www.apa.org/ethics/code

Bailey, M. (2021). *Misogynoir Transformed: Black Women's Digital Resistance.* NYU Press.

Bandelow, B., Reitt, M., Röver, C., Michaelis, S., Görlich, Y., & Wedekind, D. (2015). Efficacy of treatments for anxiety disorders: A meta-analysis. *International Clinical Psychopharmacology, 30*(4), 183–192.

Bhattacharya, S., Goicoechea, C., Heshmati, S., Carpenter, J. K., & Hofmann, S. G. (2022). Efficacy of cognitive behavioral therapy for anxiety-related disorders: A meta-analysis of recent literature. *Current Psychiatry Reports.* https://doi.org/10.1007/s11920-022-01402-8

Borgogna, N. C., Owen, T., & Aita, S. L. (2023). The absurdity of the latent disease model in mental health: 10,130,814 ways to have a DSM-5-TR psychological disorder. *Journal of Mental Health*, 1–9. https://doi.org/10.1080/09638237.2023.2278107

Bronfenbrenner, U. (1977). Toward an experimental ecology of human development. *American Psychologist, 32*(7), Article 7. https://doi.org/10.1037/0003-066X.32.7.513

Burton, A., Burgess, C., Dean, S., Koutsopoulou, G. Z., & Hugh-Jones, S. (2017). How effective are mindfulness-based interventions for reducing stress among healthcare professionals? A systematic review and meta-analysis. *Stress and Health, 33*(1), 3–13. https://doi.org/10.1002/smi.2673

Carter, C. R. (2022). Gaslighting: ALS, anti-Blackness, and medicine. *Feminist Anthropology, 3*(2), 235–245. https://doi.org/10.1002/fea2.12107

Chopra, S. B. (2021). Healing from internalized racism for Asian Americans. *Professional Psychology: Research and Practice, 52*(5), 503.

Ciarrochi, J., Sahdra, B., Hofmann, S. G., & Hayes, S. C. (2022). Developing an item pool to assess processes of change in psychological interventions: The Process-Based Assessment Tool (PBAT). *Journal of Contextual Behavioral Science, 23*, 200–213. https://doi.org/10.1016/j.jcbs.2022.02.001

Ciharova, M., Furukawa, T. A., Efthimiou, O., Karyotaki, E., Miguel, C., Noma, H., Cipriani, A., Riper, H., & Cuijpers, P. (2021). Cognitive restructuring, behavioral activation and cognitive-behavioral therapy in the treatment of adult depression: A network meta-analysis. *Journal of Consulting and Clinical Psychology, 89*(6), 563–574. https://doi.org/10.1037/ccp0000654

Cristea, I. A., Stefan, S., Karyotaki, E., David, D., Hollon, S. D., & Cuijpers, P. (2017). The effects of cognitive behavioral therapy are not systematically falling: A revision of Johnsen and Friborg (2015). *Psychological Bulletin, 143*(3), 326–340. https://doi.org/10.1037/bul0000062

Cuijpers, P., Sijbrandij, M., Koole, S., Huibers, M., Berking, M., & Andersson, G. (2014). Psychological treatment of generalized anxiety disorder: A meta-analysis. *Clinical Psychology Review, 34*(2), 130–140. https://doi.org/10.1016/j.cpr.2014.01.002

Cuijpers, P., van Straten, A., & Warmerdam, L. (2007). Behavioral activation treatments of depression: A meta-analysis. *Clinical Psychology Review, 27*(3), 318–326. https://doi.org/10.1016/j.cpr.2006.11.001

David, E. R., Schroeder, T. M., & Fernandez, J. (2019). Internalized racism: A systematic review of the psychological literature on racism's most insidious consequence. *Journal of Social Issues, 75*(4), 1057–1086.

de Abreu Costa, M., D'Alò de Oliveira, G. S., Tatton-Ramos, T., Manfro, G. G., & Salum, G. A. (2019). Anxiety and stress-related disorders and mindfulness-based interventions: A systematic review and multilevel meta-analysis and meta-regression of multiple outcomes. *Mindfulness, 10*(6), 996–1005. https://doi.org/10.1007/s12671-018-1058-1

Ezawa, I. D., & Hollon, S. D. (2023). Cognitive restructuring and psychotherapy outcome: A meta-analytic review. *Psychotherapy, 60*(3), 396–406. https://doi.org/10.1037/pst0000474

Ferrari, M., Hunt, C., Harrysunker, A., Abbott, M. J., Beath, A. P., & Einstein, D. A. (2019). Self-compassion interventions and psychosocial outcomes: A meta-analysis of RCTs. *Mindfulness, 10*(8), 1455–1473. https://doi.org/10.1007/s12671-019-01134-6

Gates, K. M., & Molenaar, P. C. M. (2012). Group search algorithm recovers effective connectivity maps for individuals in homogeneous and heterogeneous samples. *NeuroImage, 63*(1), Article 1. https://doi.org/10.1016/j.neuroimage.2012.06.026

Grau, P. P., Kusch, M. M., Williams, M. T., Loyo, K. T., Zhang, X., Warner, R. C., & Wetterneck, C. T. (2022). A review of the inclusion of ethnoracial groups in empirically supported posttraumatic stress disorder treatment research. *Psychological Trauma: Theory, Research, Practice, and Policy, 14*(1), 55–65. https://doi.org/10.1037/tra0001108

Hayes, S. C., Ciarrochi, J., Hofmann, S. G., Chin, F., & Sahdra, B. (2022). Evolving an idionomic approach to processes of change: Towards a unified personalized science of human improvement. *Behaviour Research and Therapy, 156*, 104155. https://doi.org/10.1016/j.brat.2022.104155

Hayes, S. C., & Hofmann, S. G. (2017). The third wave of cognitive behavioral therapy and the rise of process-based care. *World Psychiatry, 16*(3), 245–246. https://doi.org/10.1002/wps.20442

Hayes, S. C., Hofmann, S. G., Stanton, C. E., Carpenter, J. K., Sanford, B. T., Curtiss, J. E., & Ciarrochi, J. (2019). The role of the individual in the coming era of process-based therapy. *Behaviour Research and Therapy*, *117*, 40–53. https://doi.org/10.1016/j.brat.2018.10.005

Henry, J. D., & Crawford, J. R. (2005). The short-form version of the Depression Anxiety Stress Scales (DASS-21): Construct validity and normative data in a large non-clinical sample. *British Journal of Clinical Psychology*, *44*(Pt 2), 227–239. https://doi.org/10.1348/014466505X29657

Hertenstein, E., Trinca, E., Wunderlin, M., Schneider, C. L., Züst, M. A., Fehér, K. D., Su, T., Straten, A. V., Berger, T., & Baglioni, C. (2022). Cognitive behavioral therapy for insomnia in patients with mental disorders and comorbid insomnia: A systematic review and meta-analysis. *Sleep Medicine Reviews*, *62*, 101597. https://doi.org/10.1016/j.smrv.2022.101597

Hofmann, S. G., Asnaani, A., Vonk, I. J. J., Sawyer, A. T., & Fang, A. (2012). The efficacy of cognitive behavioral therapy: A review of meta-analyses. *Cognitive Therapy and Research*, *36*(5), Article 5. https://doi.org/10.1007/s10608-012-9476-1

Hofmann, S. G., Hayes, S. C., & Lorscheid, D. N. (2021). *Learning process-based therapy: A skills training manual for targeting the core processes of psychological change in clinical practice*. Context Press.

Kliem, S., Kröger, C., & Kosfelder, J. (2010). Dialectical behavior therapy for borderline personality disorder: A meta-analysis using mixed-effects modeling. *Journal of Consulting and Clinical Psychology*, *78*(6), Article 6. https://doi.org/10.1037/a0021015

Larsson, A., Hooper, N., Osborne, L. A., Bennett, P., & McHugh, L. (2016). Using brief cognitive restructuring and cognitive defusion techniques to cope with negative thoughts. *Behavior Modification*, *40*(3), 452–482. https://doi.org/10.1177/0145445515621488

Levin, M. E., Hildebrandt, M. J., Lillis, J., & Hayes, S. C. (2012). The impact of treatment components suggested by the psychological flexibility model: A meta-analysis of laboratory-based component studies. *Behavior Therapy*, *43*(4), 741–756. https://doi.org/10.1016/j.beth.2012.05.003

Marker, I., & Norton, P. J. (2018). The efficacy of incorporating motivational interviewing to cognitive behavior therapy for anxiety disorders: A review and meta-analysis. *Clinical Psychology Review*, *62*, 1–10.

Masuda, A., & Qina'au, J. (2022). Application of secular mindfulness to Asian Americans in the US: Cultural considerations. In C. M. Fleming, V. Y. Womack, & J. Proulx (Eds.), *Beyond white mindfulness: Critical perspectives on racism, well-being and liberation* (pp. 64–82). Routledge. https://doi.org/10.4324/9781003090922-5

Mendoza, D. B., Williams, M. T., Chapman, L. K., & Powers, M. (2012). Minority inclusion in randomized clinical trials of panic disorder. *Journal of Anxiety Disorders*, *26*(5), 574–582. https://doi.org/10.1016/j.janxdis.2012.02.011

Molenaar, P. C. M. (2004). A manifesto on psychology as idiographic science: Bringing the person back into scientific psychology, this time forever. *Measurement: Interdisciplinary Research and Perspectives*, *2*(4), 201–218. https://doi.org/10.1207/s15366359mea0204_1

Neff, K. D. (2003). The development and validation of a scale to measure self-compassion. *Self and Identity*, *2*(3), 223–250. https://doi.org/10.1080/15298860390209035

Ong, C. W., Hayes, S. C., & Hofmann, S. G. (2022). A process-based approach to cognitive behavioral therapy: A theory-based case illustration. *Frontiers in Psychology, 13*. https://doi.org/10.3389/fpsyg.2022.1002849

Park, S.-C., Kim, J.-M., Jun, T.-Y., Lee, M.-S., Kim, J.-B., Yim, H.-W., & Park, Y. C. (2017). How many different symptom combinations fulfil the diagnostic criteria for major depressive disorder? Results from the CRESCEND study. *Nordic Journal of Psychiatry, 71*(3), 217–222. https://doi.org/10.1080/08039488.2016.1265584

Payne, J. S. (2022). *Out of the fire: Healing Black trauma caused by systemic racism using acceptance and commitment therapy*. New Harbinger Publications.

Pompoli, A., Furukawa, T. A., Efthimiou, O., Imai, H., Tajika, A., & Salanti, G. (2018). Dismantling cognitive-behaviour therapy for panic disorder: A systematic review and component network meta-analysis. *Psychological Medicine, 48*(12), 1945–1953.

Rangarajan, S. (2018, June 25). Here's the clearest picture of Silicon Valley's diversity yet: It's bad. But some companies are doing less bad. *Reveal*. https://revealnews.org/article/heres-the-clearest-picture-of-silicon-valleys-diversity-yet/

Reid, J. E., Laws, K. R., Drummond, L., Vismara, M., Grancini, B., Mpavaenda, D., & Fineberg, N. A. (2021). Cognitive behavioural therapy with exposure and response prevention in the treatment of obsessive-compulsive disorder: A systematic review and meta-analysis of randomised controlled trials. *Comprehensive Psychiatry, 106*, 152223. https://doi.org/10.1016/j.comppsych.2021.152223

Tsai, M., Fleming, A. P., Cruz, R. A., Hitch, J. E., & Kohlenberg, R. J. (2015). *Functional analytic psychotherapy: Using awareness, courage, love, and behaviorism to promote change*. The Guilford Press.

Twohig, M. P., Hayes, S. C., Plumb, J. C., Pruitt, L. D., Collins, A. B., Hazlett-Stevens, H, & Woidneck, M. R. (2010). A randomized clinical trial of acceptance and commitment therapy versus progressive relaxation training for obsessive-compulsive disorder. *Journal of Consulting and Clinical Psychology, 78*, 705. https://doi.org/10.1016/j.ypsy.2011.04.009

Veehof, M. M., Trompetter, H. R., Bohlmeijer, E. T., & Schreurs, K. M. G. (2016). Acceptance- and mindfulness-based interventions for the treatment of chronic pain: A meta-analysis. *Cognitive Behavioral Therapy, 45*(1), Article 1. https://doi.org/10.1080/16506073.2015.1098724

Virgili, M. (2015). Mindfulness-based interventions reduce psychological distress in working adults: A meta-analysis of intervention studies. *Mindfulness, 6*(2), 326–337. https://doi.org/10.1007/s12671-013-0264-0

Watson-Singleton, N. N., Black, A. R., & Spivey, B. N. (2019). Recommendations for a culturally-responsive mindfulness-based intervention for African Americans. *Complementary Therapies in Clinical Practice, 34*, 132–138. https://doi.org/10.1016/j.ctcp.2018.11.013

Wilkerson, I. (2020). *Caste: The Origins of Our Discontents*. Random House.

Williams, M. T., Powers, M., Yun, Y.-G., & Foa, E. (2010). Minority participation in randomized controlled trials for obsessive-compulsive disorder. *Journal of Anxiety Disorders, 24*(2), 171–177. https://doi.org/10.1016/j.janxdis.2009.11.004

Wilson, A. C., Mackintosh, K., Power, K., & Chan, S. W. Y. (2019). Effectiveness of self-compassion related therapies: A systematic review and meta-analysis. *Mindfulness, 10*(6), 979–995. https://doi.org/10.1007/s12671-018-1037-6

Wolitzky-Taylor, K. B., Horowitz, J. D., Powers, M. B., & Telch, M. J. (2008). Psychological approaches in the treatment of specific phobias: A meta-analysis. *Clinical Psychology Review, 28*(6), 1021–1037. https://doi.org/10.1016/j.cpr.2008.02.007

Zimmerman, M., Ellison, W., Young, D., Chelminski, I., & Dalrymple, K. (2015). How many different ways do patients meet the diagnostic criteria for major depressive disorder? *Comprehensive Psychiatry, 56*, 29–34. https://doi.org/10.1016/j.comppsych.2014.09.007

Appendices

Appendix A

PBT Competency Checklist

This checklist reflects the necessary but insufficient ingredients for PBT. That is, to be doing PBT, you'll need to at least be following these guidelines, but the expansiveness of PBT allows you to do much more and still work within a process-based framework. We recommend using this checklist to see if you are "on track" and as a means of self-reflection.

- Used network-based thinking (i.e., functional analysis) for case conceptualization? (Process)
- Considered the six EEMM dimensions: *Affect/Emotion*, *Cognition*, *Self*, *Attention*, *Motivation*, and *Overt Behavior*? (EEMM)
- Considered the three (four if counting Relationships and Culture separately) levels of analysis: *Psychological*, *Biology/Physiology*, and *Relationships/Culture*? (EEMM)
- Considered relevance of principles of change and context-matching to clients' presentation? (EEMM)
- Developed treatment plan based on case conceptualization and clients' goals? (Personalization/Workability)
- Adjusted treatment based on clients' response to treatment? (Personalization/Workability)
- Used evidence-based kernels matched to clients? (Personalization/Empiricism)
- Used idiographic methods to track progress over time? (Personalization/Empiricism)
- Generated hypotheses and tested them using data collected from clients? (Empiricism)

Appendix B

Intake Questions for Clients

This list is organized by the five types of information we would like to get from our clients by the end of the intake interview. It is not exhaustive and designed to be more of a launchpad in case you don't know where to start. Note that [behavior/response] below is used as a placeholder for the range of responses you could be asking your clients about, from overt behaviors (e.g., smoking cigarettes) to unobservable responses like feeling an emotion (e.g., sad, angry) and thinking (e.g., "everyone hates me").

Relationships Among Symptoms (Process)

- What usually comes before/after [behavior/response]?
- For many people, [e.g., low mood, anxiety] is associated with [e.g., low motivation, avoidance]. Does that match your experience?
- What makes it difficult for you to try [new behavior/response]?
- What are examples of situations where [behavior/response] occurs?
- What usually leads to [behavior/response]?
- What makes you more or less likely to do [behavior/response]?
- How do different aspects of the problem relate to each other?
- What do you hope will happen when you do [behavior/response]?
- What happens after you do [behavior/response]?
- How does [behavior/response] help you to cope?
- How do your current patterns benefit you, even if in the short term?
- Why might it be difficult for you to develop habits more aligned with your goals?
- What factors are keeping you stuck where you are?
- What do you do that keeps you from reaching your goals?

EEMM Checklist (EEMM)

- Are there any [dimension/level] variables that we haven't discussed?
- Which area of functioning (referring to EEMM dimensions and levels) do you struggle the most in?
- Are there any current or recent stressors that have been bothering you?
- What does your typical routine look like in terms of diet, sleep, and physical activity?
- How would you describe your relationships with others?

Client Variables (Personalization)

- What do you want to work on?
- How would you define the problem you're struggling with?
- What identities are important to you? How do they influence your experiences?
- What does having this problem mean to you?
- What does struggling with this problem mean about you?
- Why do you think you're stuck?
- What do you do to handle the problem?
- What has been helpful for you?

- What are your strengths?
- Whom do you rely on for support?
- What resources do you have access to? What resources would you like to have access to?
- What are your expectations for therapy?
- What kinds of messaging about mental health did you receive growing up? What's your perspective on mental health now?
- What factors affect your struggle? For example, what makes your struggle more challenging/easier to handle?

Treatment Goals (Workability)

- If you were "better," what would you be doing differently?
- What does "getting better" look like for you?
- What [behavior/response] would you like to be different?
- What [behavior/response] do you want to change?
- What needs to change for you to get unstuck?
- What change would most meaningfully impact your life?

Concrete Examples (Empiricism)

- If I was following you with a video camera, what would I see when you feel/think/do ______________________?
- What sensations show up in your body when you feel ______________?
- Can you give me examples of times when you feel/think/do ____________?
- How would your [friend/partner/child/parent] describe your actions when you feel/think/do ______________________?
- What specific thoughts do you have when you're thinking/ruminating/worrying about ______________________?
- Walk me through what a [typical/"bad"/"good"] day looks like for you, from the time you wake up to the time you go to bed. Give details, as if I were making a documentary about you.

Appendix C

Intake Interview Template

This intake interview template is designed to guide your intake assessments, such that they will achieve the following goals

1. Identify how aspects of your client's problem **relate** to each other (Process)
2. Consider all the **EEMM** dimensions and levels (EEMM)
3. Identify variables **unique to your client** that influence their current presentation (Personalization)
4. Identify concrete **treatment goals** to guide treatment planning (Workability)
5. Identify specific, objective **examples** to better understand your client's problems (Empiricism)

After your intake session, you will use these data to build a network. For now, focus on gathering as much relevant data as possible. See Chapter 8 for an example of a completed form.

Presenting Problem (EEMM/Empiricism)

Ask about each EEMM dimension and level as well as context.

EEMM Dimension/Level	**Client's Description**	**Specific Examples (What Does This Look Like?)**
Affect/Emotion *What your client feels or how they respond to their feelings*		
Cognition *What your client thinks or how they respond to their thoughts*		
Attention *What your client pays attention to or their ability to shift attention*		
Self *Your client's sense of self, how they see themselves, or how they treat themselves*		

Continued

Continued

EEMM Dimension/Level	Client's Description	Specific Examples (What Does This Look Like?)
Motivation *Your client's reasons for acting—or lack of them*		
Overt Behavior *Your client's observable behaviors and accomplishments—or failure to engage in them*		
Context *External events that influence your client, including learning history, housing situation, and current stressors*		
Biology/Physiology *Related to physical functioning and routine (e.g., diet, sleep, physical activity, medication, substance use)*		
Relationships *Past and current interpersonal factors, including family expectations and social support*		
Culture* *Related to societal norms and events that affect your client, including discriminatory practices and changes in national policies*		

* Your client's identities could also fall under here, but we ask about it in the *Client Variables* section to streamline the interview.

Relationships Among Problems (Process)

Once you have identified your client's primary struggles (aim for 3–5), list them in the *Target Problem/Symptom* column (leftmost below). Then, ask about antecedents and consequences related to each one.

Target Problem/Symptom	**Antecedent**	**Consequence**
Select discrete and specific problems (e.g., avoidance of social interactions rather than avoidance)	Variables that tend to come before or contribute to the problem	Variables that tend to come after or are caused by the problem

Client Variables (Personalization)

Consider how factors unique to your client influence their experience of their struggles.

Areas	Client's Description	Relationship to Problem
Client Identities *Includes intersecting demographic identities (e.g., gay Black man) and identities meaningful to your client (e.g., parent, worrier, smart)*		
Strengths *Includes current coping strategies, skills, resources, and prior attempts to solve the problem*		
Interpretation/Understanding of Problem *How your client conceptualizes their struggle and its causes*		
Treatment Expectations *What your client thinks therapy is and what it can achieve*		
Reason for Seeking Treatment Now *Why your client is seeking treatment at this point—what changed for them?*		

Treatment Goals (Workability)

Identify 2–5 concrete treatment goals that meet SMART criteria:

- Specific
- Measurable
- Achievable
- Relevant
- Timebound

What is the specific goal?	How will it be measured?	Is it attainable?	Why is this goal important to the client?	What is the timeline for completion?

Appendix D

Network Questions for Client

The following line of questioning shows one way to practice network building with your clients based on the principles of network building outlined in Chapter 5. The questions you prefer may vary depending on your therapeutic style, so use the following as a starting point. The crux is to create a network representing your client that will facilitate effective treatment.

1. What do you see as your biggest problems and/or strengths? **Action: List them on a whiteboard (or other visual space).**
2. Which problems do you think go together? By "go together," I mean that they tend to be part of the same pattern or serve a similar function in your life. **Action: Group functionally related nodes.**
   a. What label would you use to describe this group of problems?
3. From this list of problems and/or strengths, which ones are the most relevant to your current struggles? Pick 5–10 things. (Note: We strongly recommend keeping to no more than 10 nodes.) **Action: Circle the 5–10 most relevant nodes and transfer them to another area of the whiteboard.**
4. Are we missing anything from [EEMM dimensions and levels not included among current variables]? Would adding something from this dimension/level help us understand your struggles better? **Action: If a new node is identified, add it to the shorter list. If the list becomes longer than 10, return to step 3 and ask your client to identify the most relevant nodes again.**
5. Let's draw a box around each item on your list. We'll use rectangular boxes for things that are changeable, like your current actions, and rounded boxes (or ovals) for things that cannot be changed, like a past event. **Action: Convert list of problems to an array of nodes.**
6. Now I want us to look at how these problems and strengths are related to each other, but we'll go one by one to stay organized. Let's start with [node 1]. What variables does [node 1] contribute to? **Action: Draw arrows going from [node 1] to other related nodes.** How about [node 2]? **Action: Continue for each node on the whiteboard.**
7. Usually, every problem has at least one arrow going into it, because if there weren't any variables maintaining it, it would naturally disappear, just as a flame would eventually extinguish without a constant flow of oxygen.
   a. It looks like all your boxes have arrows going into them, so we can move to the final step.
   b. It looks like [node] doesn't have any arrows going into it. From the items in your network so far, what do you think could be contributing to [node]? **Action: Add missing arrows.**
8. Which of these relationships seem stronger to you? That is, X has a bigger impact on Y compared to its impact on other variables. **Action: Increase the size of identified arrowheads.**

For an even simpler list, especially once you are well-versed in network building, refer to the following questions. They are designed to be simplified questions that capture the essence—but not nuance—of each step. We have found them helpful for ourselves as therapists as well, to ensure we don't miss any steps.

1. Which elements are central to the problem?
2. Which variables can be grouped together?
3. Which 5–10 variables are most important?
4. Are we missing any relevant variables?
5. [Draw the nodes.]
6. How is everything related?
7. [Add first round of arrows.]
8. Are we missing any arrows?
9. Which relationships are stronger?

Appendix E

Network Drawing Templates

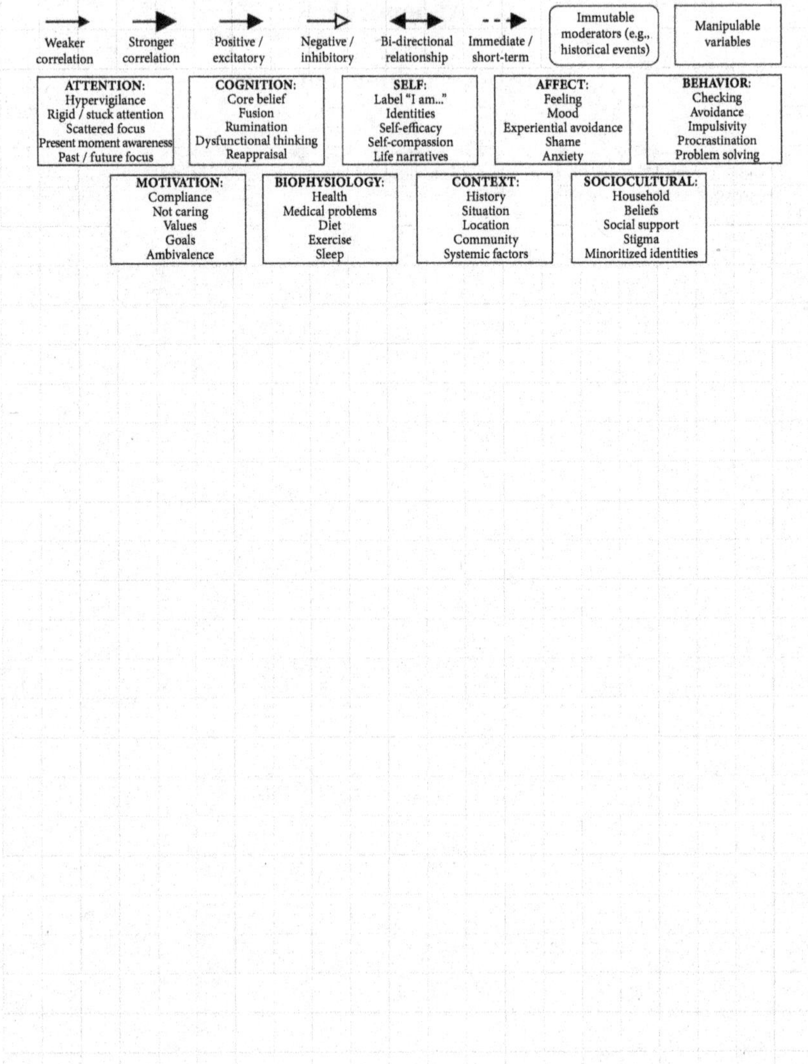
Weaker correlation
Stronger correlation
Positive / excitatory
Negative / inhibitory
Bi-directional relationship
Immediate / short-term
Immutable moderators (e.g., historical events)
Manipulable variables
ATTENTION:
Hypervigilance
Rigid / stuck attention
Scattered focus
Present moment awareness
Past / future focus
COGNITION:
Core belief
Fusion
Rumination
Dysfunctional thinking
Reappraisal
SELF:
Label "I am..."
Identities
Self-efficacy
Self-compassion
Life narratives
AFFECT:
Feeling
Mood
Experiential avoidance
Shame
Anxiety
BEHAVIOR:
Checking
Avoidance
Impulsivity
Procrastination
Problem solving
MOTIVATION:
Compliance
Not caring
Values
Goals
Ambivalence
BIOPHYSIOLOGY:
Health
Medical problems
Diet
Exercise
Sleep
CONTEXT:
History
Situation
Location
Community
Systemic factors
SOCIOCULTURAL:
Household
Beliefs
Social support
Stigma
Minoritized identities

Appendix F

PBT Treatment Plan

Treatment Goals	Client Strengths & Resources
1.	•
2.	•
3.	•

Plan

Target Nodes (Dimension/Level)	Kernel (Dimension/Level)	Desired Effect of Kernel	Measurable Outcome (Unit)	Consistent with Goals? (Goal #)

Example Treatment Plan for Hermine (see Chapter 6)

Treatment Goals	**Client Strengths & Resources**
1. Learn more effective ways to cope with work stress	• Maintains mindfulness practice
2. Re-engage in hobbies	• Motivated to engage in therapy
3. Reduce marijuana use	• Strong social support network

Plan

Target Nodes (Dimension/ Level)	Kernel (Dimension/ Level)	Desired Effect of Kernel	Measurable Outcome (Unit)	Consistent with Goals? (Goal #)
Stress over work performance (Affect)	Self-compassion meditation (Affect/Self)	More flexibility with respect to work performance expectations	Subjective units of distress when expectations are not met (1–10 scale)	Yes (Goal 1)
Avoids hobbies shared with ex (Behavior)	Pleasant activity scheduling (Behavior)	Increase time spent on hobbies	Time spent on hobbies per week (hours)	Yes (Goal 2)
Excessive marijuana use (Behavior/ Biophysiology)		Increase time spent on hobbies and decrease marijuana use	Time spent on hobbies per week (hours) Amount of marijuana used per week (mg)	Yes (Goals 2 & 3)

Appendix G

Decision Trees for Node and Kernel Selection

To select a node to target or kernel to deliver, use the following decision trees to guide your choices. The first decision tree helps to determine which node is appropriate to target, whereas the second one helps to determine which kernel to use. The rationale behind each decision criterion is described in Chapter 6. Similar to other aspects of PBT, you can make this exercise as collaborative as is helpful to your clients. For example, you could go through the decision tree and select a node, then present it to your clients, or you could show your clients the decision tree and walk through it together.

Node Selection

- **Centrality:** Identify a node that is central to your client's network and/or personally meaningful outcomes. This node should make a meaningful difference to your client's life if changed.
- **Cultural responsiveness:** Is trying to change this central node consistent with culturally responsive practice? Consider what the node means to your client in their cultural context. For example, you may choose not to target a node that is deemed maladaptive from the majoritized perspective if it's culturally important to your client.
- **Malleability:** Is this node changeable given current treatment parameters? Parameters refer to variables that make up the context of treatment (or meta-treatment variables), including treatment setting, clinician—or clinician's supervisor—competence, client insight, client environment, and client strengths and resources. If not, can treatment parameters be changed?
- **Relevance to clients:** Does your client believe changing this node would be helpful or are they invested in working on the node? Ultimately, we work for our clients, so it's crucial to ascertain that your clients are bought into the rationale for treatment.

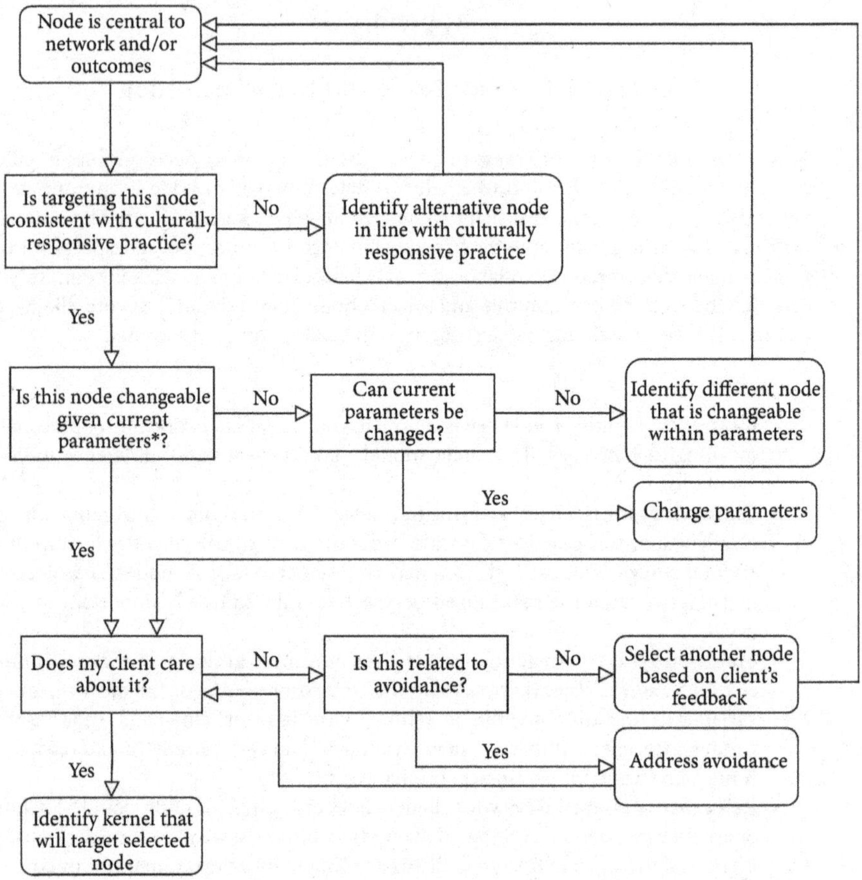

Note. Parameters here refer to variables that make up the context of treatment (or *meta*-treatment variables), including treatment setting, clinician—or clinician's supervisor—competence, client insight, client environment, and client strengths and resources.

Kernel Selection

- **Relevance to target node**: Will the kernel change the target node or the strength of the arrows linked to it? Checking that the kernel and target node share EEMM dimensions is one way to verify this criterion.
- **Evidence base**: Is there evidence supporting the efficacy of the kernel for this particular node? Such evidence can be from either the empirical literature or idiographic work with your clients.
- **Cultural responsiveness**: Do the kernel and your plan for delivering it acknowledge and respect your client's cultural identities? For example, choosing a cognitive restructuring kernel for thoughts related to microaggressions may come across as invalidating, even though it's an "evidence-based" kernel for unhelpful thinking.
- **Relevance to clients**: Does your client believe that the kernel will be helpful? In addition to agreeing on the problem, you and your client also need to agree on how to go about changing it (which could still be influenced by their cultural background).

- **Clinical skill**: Do you have the skills needed to deliver the kernel competently? Even if you don't, you may have access to a supervisor who does. Consider what you can realistically learn within the timeframe of treatment.

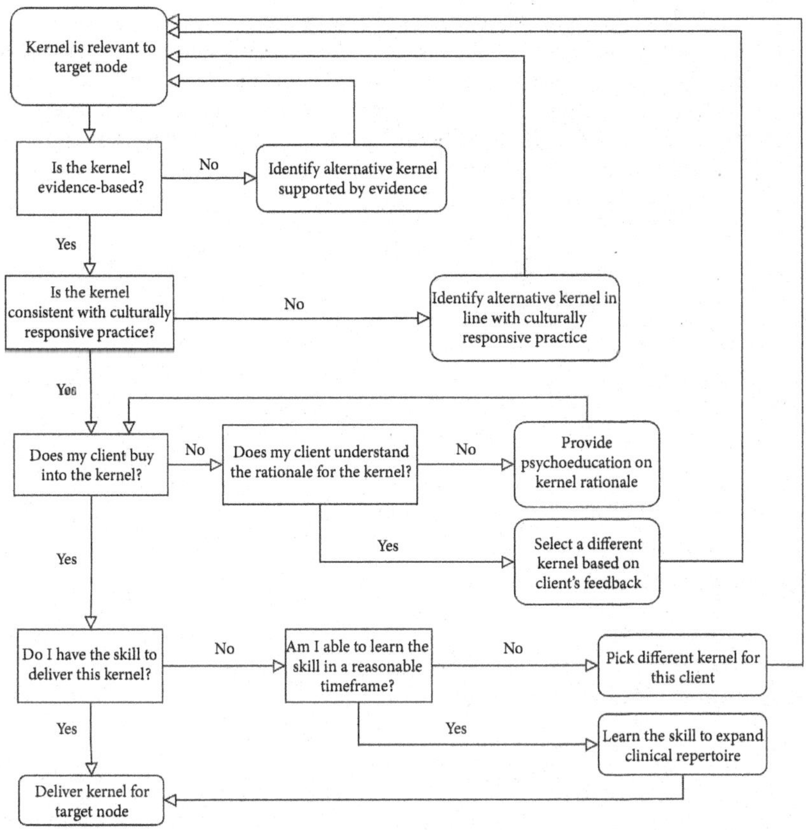

Appendix H

Example Kernels Organized by EEMM Dimension

In the table below, we provide examples of kernels from evidence-based treatments and how they map on to EEMM dimensions and levels. Although we selected the most "obvious" dimensions related to each kernel, kernels can link to multiple EEMM dimensions and levels depending on how they are delivered. For instance, DEAR MAN in the context of asserting one's rights in a discriminatory setting can be construed as a culturally relevant kernel. Similarly, cognitive reappraisal applied to core beliefs about the self and one's narrative can become a self-oriented kernel.

Kernel	Affect /Emotion	Cognition	Attention	Self	Motivation	Overt Behavior	Biology /Physiology	Relationships	Culture
Awareness training (HRT)			X						
Cognitive defusion visualization (e.g., leaves on a stream; ACT)		X	X						
Cognitive reappraisal (CBT/CPT)		X							
Competing response training (HRT)	X					X			
DEAR MAN (DBT)						X		X	
Emotion processing (IPT)	X								
Exploring ambivalence (MI)					X				
Guided meditation (ACT/DBT/MBSR/etc.)			X						
Imaginal exposures (CBT/ERP/PET)	X								
Interoceptive exposures (CBT)	X						X		
Opposite action (DBT)	X					X			
Pleasant activity scheduling (BA/CBT)	X				X	X			

Power analysis (feminist therapy)		X		X					X
Self-as-context (ACT)				X					
Self-compassionate letter writing (CFT)				X					
Self-disclosure (feminist therapy)	X							X	X
Self-monitoring/reflection (CBT)		X		X		X			
Sleep hygiene strategies (CBT-I)						X	X		
Social support enhancement (IPT)								X	
Stimulus control (CBT/AEBT)			X		X	X			
TIPP (DBT)	X								
Two-chair enactment (EFT)	X			X				X	
Values clarification (ACT/MI)					X				

Note. ACT = acceptance and commitment therapy; AEBT = acceptance-enhanced behavior therapy; BA = behavioral activation; CBT = cognitive behavioral therapy; CBT-I = cognitive behavioral therapy for insomnia; CFT = compassion-focused therapy; CPT = cognitive processing therapy; DBT = dialectical behavior therapy; EFT = emotion-focused therapy; ERP = exposure and response prevention; HRT = habit reversal training; IPT = interpersonal psychotherapy; MBSR = mindfulness-based stress reduction; MI = motivational interviewing; PET = prolonged exposure therapy.

Appendix I

PBT Progress Note

Progress Note Template

Client: ______________ **Session #:** ______ **Date:** ________________

Subjective		
Objective	**Target Node(s)**	
	Kernel(s)	
	Rationale	
Assessment	**Client Response**	
	Dimension(s)	
	Level(s)	
	Area(s) of Change	
Homework		
Plan		

Progress Note Guidelines

Client: _______________ **Session #:** _______ **Date:** ________________

Subjective		• Describe specific concerns, symptoms, phrases, beliefs, affect, strengths, resources, etc. *unique* to your client, rather than diagnosis-specific symptoms (Personalization). • Consider contextual factors (EEMM).
Objective	**Target Node(s)**	• Identify which node(s) you are targeting in your client's network (Process).
	Kernel(s)	• State what kernel(s) or intervention method(s) you used in session (Process/Workability). • Consider adaptations to your approach based on cultural variables or client identities (Personalization).
	Rationale	• Why did you choose that kernel for that node for your client? (Personalization/Workability)
Assessment	**Client Response**	• Include any relevant assessment data (e.g., standardized measures, idiographic items, behavioral observations), noting any changes in your client's presentation (Empiricism/Personalization). • Describe how your client responded to the kernel delivered (Empiricism/Workability). • Record any disproven hypotheses (Empiricism).
	Dimension(s)	• Identify target dimension(s): *Self, Cognition, Affect/Emotion, Attention, Motivation,* and *Behavior* (EEMM). This could be in session or in your treatment plan more broadly.
	Level(s)	• Identify target level(s): *Psychological, Biology/Physiology, Relationships,* and *Culture* (EEMM). This could be in session or in your treatment plan more broadly.
	Area(s) of Change	• Identify target area of change: variation, selection, retention, and context-matching (EEMM). This could be in session or in your treatment plan more broadly.

Goals	• List short- and long-term goals (Workability).
Homework	• Describe between-session practice linked to goals (Workability).
Plan	• Describe plan for future sessions linked to goals (Workability). • Posit any new hypotheses (Empiricism).

Example 1 (Clarissa's Version)

Client: Nadiya Session #: 3 Date: 04/08/2024

Subjective		Since being demoted due to company downsizing, Nadiya has been engaging in excessive worry behavior to prepare for and prevent future catastrophes. The worrying has negatively affected her concentration and performance at work.
Objective	**Target Node(s)**	Worry about job security.
	Kernel(s)	Cognitive restructuring worksheet.
	Rationale	Cognitive restructuring was used for self-critical thoughts with some success several sessions ago.
Assessment	**Client Response**	Nadiya reported an increase in time spent seeking reassurance from her partner (from 30 min/day to 1 hour/day). She seemed more distracted and tangential in session than usual. She was able to come up with alternative thoughts for catastrophizing thoughts (believability > 90%) and expressed confidence in her ability to complete worksheets independently. Current hypothesis: Practicing self-compassion meditation will decrease power of self-critical thoughts, as evidenced by more direct communication with partner (from previous session). Hypothesis was not tested; Nadiya did not practice self-compassion meditation due to focusing on worry related to recent demotion.
	Dimension(s)	Cognitive
	Level(s)	Psychological
	Area(s) of Change	*Context-matching* to teach Nadiya to generalize restructuring skill to other kinds of thoughts and *retention* of skill through more practice.

Goals	Short-term goals: Learn skills to cope with worry about job security. Long-term (overall treatment) goals: Increase self-care activity, use more direct/assertive communication with partner, re-engage in hobbies.
Homework	Complete cognitive restructuring worksheet 1x/day.
Plan	Next session: Assess if cognitive restructuring was helpful for managing worry. New hypothesis: Completing cognitive restructuring worksheets will decrease time spent worrying and reassurance seeking within 4 weeks.

Example 2 (Eric's Version)

Client: Nadiya Session #: 3 Date: 04/08/2024

Subjective		Past conceptualization: Since being demoted due to company downsizing, Nadiya engages in excessive worry behavior in an attempt to prepare for and prevent future catastrophic scenarios which have negatively affected her concentration and performance at work and home. New to conceptualization: She is the only woman in upper management at her company. Described feeling "overlooked" and "put down" by her coworkers. Stated that she feels like she is "not good enough." Has struggled with this thought since she was young. Grew up as the person with the lowest socioeconomic status in her school and felt out of place.
Objective	**Target Node(s)**	Cognition (worry). Consider shifting to Self (self-concept), dependent on results.
	Kernel(s)	Worry psychoeducation. Functional analysis using worry-tracking worksheet. Specified worry time each day.
	Rationale	It appears that her history of being overlooked due to socioeconomic and patriarchal factors has negatively affected her self-concept. This contributes an attentional bias to future problems and excessive worry. These are causing feelings of anxiety and irritability which negatively impact her engagement at work as well as her value of spending quality time with her kids.

Assessment	**Client Response**	Anxiety measure (GAD-7) remains high (16; 17 at session 1). PBAT Items (scores for sessions 1, 2, 3, etc.): • My thinking got in the way of things that were important to me (90, 85, 85) • I struggled to connect with the moments in my day-to-day life (80, 80, 75) • I did things to connect with people who are important to me (40, 50, 50) • New this session: I did things only because I was complying with what others wanted me to do (-, -, 80) Nadiya tracked worry behavior throughout week. Consistent pattern of fears and worry prior to work meetings and social events. She responded well to worry functional analysis. Appears to be gaining insight ("my worry doesn't actually solve anything, does it?"). Hypothesis: "not good enough" self-concept is exacerbating fears of social catastrophe.
	Dimension(s)/ Level(s)	Relevant dimensions/levels: Cognition (worry), Affect ("on edge"), Attention (future focus "catastrophe"), Motivation (values: "doing quality work" and "being a good mom"). Added this session: Self ("not good enough" self-concept), Context (only woman at job).
	Area(s) of Change	Nadiya lacks variation in responding to future fears and is stuck in a narrow view of self and her potential.
Goals		Stated long-term goals: Cope with anxiety more effectively; improve work performance; spend more quality time with kids. Current short-term goals: Gain understanding of fears and worry behavior using tracking worksheet; confine worry behavior to specified worry times.
Homework		1. Use tracking worksheet 1x/day. 2. Use worry time between 5:30–6:00 p.m., daily.
Plan		Need to discuss potential goals related to self concept. Consider self-as context kernels in future. Need to explore potential lack of variation in dealing with unfair work conditions. Future work will involve selection and retention of new skills appropriate to different contexts (work, home).

Index

Note: Tables, figures, and boxes are indicated by an italic *t*, *f*, and *b* following the page number

For the benefit of digital users, indexed terms that span two pages (e.g., 52–53) may, on occasion, appear on only one of those pages.